FACILITATING
CHILDREN'S DEVELOPMENT

FACILITATING CHILDREN'S DEVELOPMENT

A Systematic Guide for Open Learning

Volume I
Infant and Toddler Learning Episodes

by
John H. Meier, Ph.D.
Director, Children's Village, USA
Beaumont, California

and

Paula J. Malone, Ph.D.
Director, Child Development Center
Alfred I. duPont Institute
Wilmington, Delaware

University Park Press

Baltimore

UNIVERSITY PARK PRESS
International Publishers in Science, Medicine, and Education
233 East Redwood Street
Baltimore, Maryland 21202

Copyright © 1979 by University Park Press
Composed by University Park Press, Typesetting Division
Manufactured in the United States of America by
Kingsport Press.

Library of Congress Cataloging in Publication Data
Meier, John, 1935–
Infant and toddler learning episodes.
(His Facilitating children's development; v. 1)

1. Education, Preschool — Handbooks, manuals, etc. 2. Creative activities and seat work — Handbooks, manuals, etc. 3. Perceptual-motor
learning — Handbooks, manuals, etc. 4. Open plan schools — Handbooks, manuals, etc.
I. Malone, Paula J., joint author. II. Title.
LB1140.2.M43   vol. 1   372.21s [372.21] 78-21872
ISBN 0-8391-1261-0

CONTENTS

Acknowledgments xiii

INTRODUCTION   The System for Open Learning   1

How to Use the Learning Episodes Effectively   6

Suggestions for SOL Episodes during Daily

Infant/Toddler Routines   7

Principles for Using SOL Episodes   8

Facilitating Parent Learning   9

Evaluation   9

Principles of Behavior Change   9

SENSORY/RECEPTIVE EPISODES   21

Unit I   1 / HEARING   23

    Episode A   / Attending to Noise   23

    Episode B   / See a Voice: 180°   24

    Episode C   / See a Sound: 180°   25

    Episode D   / Stop Activity on Command   26

    Episode E   / Parallel Talking   27

    Episode F   / Learn Names of Objects   28

    Episode G   / Object Discrimination Given Two

                 Stimuli   29

    Episode H   / Searches for Named Object Within Sight . .   31

    Episode I   / Picture Book: Point and Name   32

Unit T   1 / HEARING   33

    Episode A   / Naming Properties and Objects   33

    Episode B   / Rhythm Games: Imitation or Circle

                 Activities   34

    Episode C   / Action Words along with Actions   35

    Episode D   / Understanding Wh-Questions   36

    Episode E   / Understanding the Concept of One   37

    Episode F   / Direction Following   38

Unit I   2 / SEEING   39

    Episode A   / Geometric Patterns   39

    Episode B   / Eyes Focus on Objects, Begin to

                 Track   41

    Episode C   / Eye Following Objects: Up and Down,

                 Side to Side, On Stomach and Back   42

    Episode D   / Tracking a Flashlight   43

    Episode E   / Visual Tracking Tube   44

    Episode F   / Two Eyes   45

    Episode G   / Looking Back and Forth   46

    Episode H   / Attention to Hands   47

Unit T 2 / SEEING 49

    Episode A / Follow the Flashlight 49
    Episode B / The Shell Game 50

Unit I 3 / TOUCHING 51

    Episode A / Touch Pressure Stimuli for
                    Tactile Awareness 51
    Episode B / Feeling Objects for Comparison:
                    Texture, Weight, Temperature, etc. 53
    Episode C / Bean-Filled Box 54
    Episode D / Using Both Hands to Feel Textures 55
    Episode E / Creepy-Feely......................... 56

Unit I 4 / SENSORY INTEGRATION 57
    Episode A / Exploring with Mouth.................. 57
    Episode B / Finding an Object with Eyes and Ears
                    in a Complete Circle 58
    Episode C / Touch and Name Body Parts 59
    Episode D / "This Little Pig": Hands and Feet 60
    Episode E / Swinging............................. 61
    Episode F / Thermal Awareness 62
    Episode G / Localization of Touch 63

COGNITIVE/AFFECTIVE EPISODES 65

Unit I 5 / PROCESS — SPATIAL RELATIONSHIPS 67

    Episode A / Knocking a Toy Off a Surface, Taking
                    Turns Putting It Back 67
    Episode B / Anticipating Movement of Objects 69
    Episode C / Mirror Play: Facilitator, Learner,
                    Toy 70
    Episode D / Put and Take Different Objects from
                    Different Containers 71

Unit T 5 / PROCESS — SPATIAL RELATIONSHIPS 73

    Episode A / Dump and Fill 73
    Episode B / Water Play: Pouring, Object
                    Properties 74
    Episode C / Block Building 75
    Episode D / Form Board Play 76

Unit I 6 / PROCESS — OBJECT PERMANENCE 77

    Episode A / Disappear/Reappear 77
    Episode B / Hide and Seek: Getting Partly Hidden
                    Object 78
    Episode C / Barrier Game: Object in View 80
    Episode D / Hide and Seek: Finds Object that
                    Has Disappeared 81

Unit T 6 / PROCESS — OBJECT PERMANENCE 83

    Episode A / Find Object under Box 83
    Episode B / Unwrap a Toy 84

         Episode C / Searching Game: Alternating Two,
                      Then Three, Covers 85
         Episode D / Searching Games: Two, Then Three,
                      Times Hidden 86
         Episode E / Find Toy Moved from One Hiding Place
                      to Another 87

Unit I 7 / PROCESS — CAUSE AND EFFECT 89

         Episode A / Repeat an Interesting Act 89
         Episode B / Different Toys, Different Ploys 91
         Episode C / Playing with One Toy in a Variety
                      of Ways 92
         Episode D / Getting Toy by Pulling Cloth 93
         Episode E / Pull the String to Get the Toy:
                      Horizontally, Vertically 94
         Episode F / Wind Up an Action Toy 95

Unit T 7 / PROCESS — CAUSE AND EFFECT 97

         Episode A / Peg Pound 97
         Episode B / Using Stick to Drag in Toy 98

Unit T 8 / COGNITIVE CONTENT — CLASSIFICATION, SERIATION,
GENERALIZATION 99

         Episode A / Learner Opens Jar to Take and Put 99
         Episode B / One- or Two-Piece Puzzles 101
         Episode C / Stacking Rings 102
         Episode D / Attribute Blocks 103
         Episode E / Correctly Choosing the String with
                      Toy Attached 104

Unit I 9 / SELF-IMAGE 105

         Episode A / Pat-a-Cake: Hands and Feet 105
         Episode B / Naming and Touching Body Parts 106

Unit T 9 / SELF-IMAGE 107

         Episode A / Body Parts: Function 107
         Episode B / Mirror Play with Pictures of Learner
                      and Facilitator 108
         Episode C / "Mary Wore Her Red Dress" 109
         Episode D / "Where, Oh, Where Is Dear Mario?" 112
         Episode E / "Bunny Blackears" 114
         Episode F / Make-A-Face Game 117

Unit T 10 / CREATIVITY: ART ACTIVITIES 121

         Episode A / Modeling Media (Play Dough) 122
         Episode B / Sculpture Media (Wire and Box) 124
         Episode C / Pasting Collages 126
         Episode D / Painting Activities (Tempera and Soap) 129
         Episode E / Chalk and Crayon Activities 131

Unit T 11 / EMOTIONAL DEVELOPMENT: FEAR (Fear of the Dark) . . . 133

         Episode A / "Bedtime for Frances" 133

Episode B / Story Completion 136
Episode C / "Cat at Night" 138

Unit T 12 / ROLE PLAYING 141

Episode A / Role Play 141

Unit T 13 / EMOTIONAL DEVELOPMENT: FAMILY IDENTITY 145

Episode A / "Home" Visits 145
Episode B / Making Family Books 148
Episode C / Family Lotto 150

MOTOR/EXPRESSIVE/SOCIAL EPISODES 155

Unit I 14 / GROSS MOTOR 157

Episode A / Arm and Leg Flex and Stretch 157
Episode B / Roughhousing 159
Episode C / Tick-Tock............................160
Episode D / Weight Shifting on Elbows 161
Episode E / Scooter Board Play 162
Episode F / Roll Over in a Blanket 163
Episode G / Pull to a Sit 164
Episode H / Getting to a Sit 166
Episode I / Postural Shifting for Beginning
             Sitting Balance......................167
Episode J / Sitting with Straighter Back 168
Episode K / See-Saw: Push and Pull 169
Episode L / Balancing Rock and Roll 170
Episode M / Thrust to Floor 172
Episode N / Creeping Up on All Fours..............173
Episode O / Going over Obstacles to Get a Toy 175
Episode P / Crawling Up and Down Steps for Toy
             or Reward 177
Episode Q / Ball Rolling and Chasing.................178
Episode R / Bouncing on Feet......................179
Episode S / Cruising................................181
Episode T / Pull Ups..............................182
Episode U / Pulling Up to Stand on Knees 183
Episode V / Weightshifting in Standing for
             Balance...............................185
Episode W / Stoop and Pick Up 187

Unit T 14 / GROSS MOTOR 189

Episode A / Pushing a Learner in a Cart 189
Episode B / Playing Ball: Throwing and Kicking 190
Episode C / Tug of War............................192
Episode D / Walking Game 193
Episode E / Stepping On, In, and Over 194
Episode F / Walking Up Steps to Get Reward 196

Unit I 15 / FINE MOTOR................................197

Episode A / Holding Toys, Listening.................197
Episode B / Reaching for a Dangling Object 199

Episode C / Paper Play...........................200
Episode D / Reaching Up High 201
Episode E / Hand One, Two, Three Objects in a Row ...202
Episode F / Clapping Two Objects Together.........203
Episode G / Poking Bubbles and Spaces.............204
Episode H / Scribbling...........................205
Episode I / Picking Up Small Objects..............206
Episode J / Reaching with Palm Up.................207

Unit T 15 / FINE MOTOR............................209

Episode A / Placing Pegs.........................209
Episode B / Winding Up Action Toys...............210
Episode C / Stringing Beads......................211
Episode D / Clothes Wash and Wring...............212
Episode E / Stacking Hands.......................213
Episode F / Rolling Ball into Box................214
Episode G / Precision Placement..................215

Unit I 16 / LANGUAGE.............................217

Episode A / Imitation of Speech Sounds...........217
Episode B / Place of Articulation................219
Episode C / Imitating Gestures: "So Big," etc. 221
Episode D / Point and/or Name Pictures in a Book 222

Unit T 16 / LANGUAGE.............................223

Episode A / First Words..........................223
Episode B / Tape Record Sounds, Play Back.........224
Episode C / Telephone Talk.......................225
Episode D / Run, Spot, Run.......................226
Episode E / Flannel Board: Place and Label
              Shapes and Pictures..................227
Episode F / Scrapbook............................228
Episode G / Two-Word Varieties...................229
Episode H / "Mine," "Your what?"..................230
Episode I / Three Words Together.................231
Episode J / "Same As" 232

Unit I 17 / SOCIALIZATION AND IMITATION 233

Episode A / Faces................................233
Episode B / Visual Tracking, Human Face: Up and
              Down, On Stomach and Back............234
Episode C / Mirror Play: Facilitator and Learner 235
Episode D / Reach and Touch Faces................236
Episode E / Peek-a-Boo with Facilitator's Face 237
Episode F / Ball Play: Rolling Back and Forth.........238

Unit T 17 / SOCIALIZATION AND IMITATION 239

Episode A / Stop Activity for Change of Activity 239
Episode B / Doll Play and Imitation...............240
Episode C / Activity Songs.......................241
Episode D / "Follow the Leader": Label Activities 242
Episode E / "Boat" Rocking and Singing............243
Episode F / Marching and Following...............244
Episode G / Cooperative Scribble.................245

Unit I 18 / SELF-HELP 247

    Episode A / Finger Feeding 247
    Episode B / Cup Holding 249

Unit T 18 / SELF-HELP 251

    Episode A / Clothing Skills 251
    Episode B / Taking Turns Sharing Clothes............252
    Episode C / Good Grooming Merry-Go-Round.........253

Unit T 19 / SOCIAL COOPERATION — COOKING..................255

    Episode A / Instant Pudding and Icing 255
    Episode B / Green Salad 259
    Episode C / Applesauce............................262
    Episode D / People Cookies 265
    Episode E / Ice Cream Making 268

Unit T 20 / CULTURAL SHARING — COOKING...................271

    Episode A / Soul Cooking 271
    Episode B / Chinese Cooking 274
    Episode C / Chicano (Mexican) Food 276
    Episode D / Native American Cooking 278

Unit T 21 / CULTURAL SHARING — FESTIVALS..................281

    Episode A / Let's Have a Party.....................281
    Episode B / Hanukkah or Chanukah 284
    Episode C / Christmas in Mexico 288
    Episode D / Christmas in America 291

Unit I 22 / READINESS.....................................295

    Episode A / Position to Facilitate Head Control 295
    Episode B / Positioning on Stomach for a Learner
        Who Tends to Stay Stiffly Bent 297
    Episode C / Positioning on Back for a Learner
        Who Tends to Stay Stiffly Bent 299
    Episode D / Positioning on Side for a Learner
        Who Tends to Stay Stiffly Bent 300
    Episode E / Towel Rubdown in Preparation for
        Touching 301
    Episode F / Environmental Cues 302
    Episode G / No More Yuks! 303
    Episode H / Frontal Jaw Control for Feeding.........304
    Episode I / Therapeutic Spoon Feeding for
        Development of Oral-Motor and
        Prespeech Skills.......................306
    Episode J / Chewing to Develop Oral-Motor
        and Prespeech Skills 307
    Episode K / Relaxing a Fist 308
    Episode L / Arm Stretch for Reaching 309
    Episode M / Keeping Both Arms Forward with Wrap
        to Help with Grasping 310
    Episode N / Passive Pressure on Shoulder Joints to
        Help Learner Reach Out 311
    Episode O / Relaxation and Reaching over Ball........312

Episode P / Lifting a Learner Who Tends to Be
              Stiff in Order to Relax the Learner 314
Episode Q / Carrying a Learner Who Tends to Be
              Stiff in Order to Relax the Learner 315
Episode R / Trunk Rotation for Relaxation and
              Facilitation of Movement 316
Episode S / Deep Pressure for Preparing the
              Learner to Sit, Crawl, or Stand............317
Episode T / Trunk Rotation for Rolling and
              Reaching..............................319
Episode U / Stretching Tight Hamstrings in
              Preparation for Standing 321
Episode V / Bending Over with Support to Help
              with Standing 322
Episode W / Active Stretch to Heel Cords
              for Standing 323
Episode X / Balance Activities to Increase
              Trunk Rotation in Preparation for
              Erect Postures 324
Episode Y / Standing Balance Activities to
              Increase Trunk Rotation for Standing 325
Episode Z / Regularization of Bowel Movements 326
Episode AA / Therapeutic Toothbrushing and
              Mouth Cleaning 327

Unit T 22 / READINESS.......................................329

Episode A / Touching Textures Artistically 329
Episode B / Straightening an Outward Pointing
              Foot While Cruising or Walking 330
Episode C / Play in Stimulus-Free Environment 331
Episode D / Play in Environment with
              Some Distractions 332

ACKNOWLEDGMENTS

The original sources for all direct quotations and many of the learning episodes in Volume I of *Facilitating Children's Development: A Systematic Guide for Open Learning* are identified in the usual literary form within the respective episodes. Nevertheless, there are several sources that warrant special attention. Most of the Infant and Toddler Learning Episodes were developed by the junior author. Her colleagues, Julia G. Amos, B.A., Beverly H. Kaplan, M.A., CCC-Speech, Sharon T. Meyer, R.P.T., and Nancy Thomas, O.T.R., at the Alfred I. duPont Institute's Child Development Center, made many valuable contributions. Additional episodes for Volume I were developed by the staff of the pediatric program of the Delaware Curative Workshop, especially, Martha Klauck, O.T.R., Peter Miyashiro, R.P.T., Margaret Moore, M.O.T., O.T.R., Janet Nutter, M.A., and Celeste Ryan, B.S. Thanks, too, are extended to Christine Hunko for typing and retyping most of the manuscript for Volume I.

Some of the episodes in Volume I for developmentally more advanced toddlers were produced through a grant (1967–1969) from Title XI of the National Defense Education Act to explore Remote Microtraining of Early Childhood Educators under the direction of the senior author. Other episodes for more advanced toddlers in Volume I were produced through grants (1969–1973) from the Early Childhood Branch of the Bureau of Education Personnel Development, also under the direction of the senior author. The many people who contributed to these particular episodes have been gratefully acknowledged in earlier publications and in Volume II of this series, which consists of learning episodes for the preschool child.

FACILITATING
CHILDREN'S DEVELOPMENT

INTRODUCTION
The System
for Open Learning

The two volumes of *Facilitating Children's Development: A Systematic Guide for Open Learning* provide a structure for open education by organizing opportunities for learning experiences in a series of carefully tested and sequenced learning episodes. This System for Open Learning (SOL) is Systematic because developmental progress is systematic and an efficient educational model should accommodate this system. It is Open because learning takes place most effectively in an environment that encourages active exploration and discovery. It is Learning rather than teaching, emphasizing the active role of the child in the process of acquiring knowledge and skills. In fact, in these volumes the person guiding the child, usually called a teacher, is called a learning facilitator to emphasize his/her[1] role as a creator and integral part of an open and responsive learning environment.

When applied by these learning facilitators to meet any child's needs, the SOL program constitutes the basis for a comprehensive Individualized Education Program (IEP). This SOL program was designed to promote the learning of all young children, and is quite useful in all sorts of early childhood education efforts, including developmental day care, nursery schools, First Chance, Head Start, and Parent-Child Centers. The program is especially helpful for meeting the special and unique needs of children with developmental disabilities and/or related handicaps. The Education for All Handicapped Children Act of 1975 (Public Law 94-142) now mandates that children with special needs must be provided with an individualized special education program. The System for Open Learning meets the challenge and requirements of this act.

The learning episodes in this guide have been developed over the past decade in a wide variety of facilities serving children with a wide variety of needs. The learning facilitators in many of these programs made valuable contributions in modifying and refining the learning episodes to be practical as well as developmental. Moreover, mastery of the SOL subject matter will more than meet the requirements for learning the basic skills and competencies advocated by the "back to the basics" movement. Therefore, these volumes can be used by anyone — parent, educator, therapist, caregiver, or nurse — who desires to provide effective and efficient learning experiences for infants, tod-

dlers, and young children whose developmental ages range from birth to approximately 6 years. A learning facilitator might note that some of the learning episodes in Volume I are similar in purpose and materials to certain learning episodes in Volume II. However, the actual Procedures for the learning episodes for the older age groups are quite different from those dealing with similar developmental tasks for the younger age group. Also, the performance expectations spelled out in the Entry Behaviors, which indicate readiness for the episode, and the Terminal Behaviors, which indicate achievement of the objectives of the episodes, are quite different as well.

For the user's convenience, each learning episode is identified by a number preceded by a letter: In Volume I the letter "I" designates an "Infant" whose developmental age is from birth to about 18 months; "T" stands for "Toddler" whose developmental age is about 18 months to about 3 years; in Volume II the letter "P" stands for the "Preschooler" whose developmental age is about 3 to 6 years. Each learning episode begins with a description of its Purpose or objective, followed by a description of the Entry Behavior(s), which tells what a child must be able to do *before* beginning the specific learning experience. These are followed by descriptions of the necessary Materials and Procedures, in which behaviors are described to assist the learning facilitator in conducting the episode. The learning episode is concluded by a statement of the Terminal Behavior(s), which describes what a child must be able to do *after* mastering the learning episode. The Terminal Behavior is identical with the performance criterion or objective of the IEP.

The learning episodes have been organized in accordance with an information-processing model, which is shown in Figure 1. Following this model, steps to learning are represented by three major categories: input, the sensory/receptive domain; operations, the cognitive/affective/attitudinal domain; and output, the motor/expressive/social domain. Each of these categories, or domains, represents a significant part of information processing in order to learn, which is actually far more complex than Figure 1 depicts. If you wish to explore the complexity of the developmental and learning process, the diverse characteristics of individual learners, and the events and circumstances that can disrupt the learning process, you may wish to refer to the companion volume to this series, *Interferences with Development* (Malone and Meier, 1979). This book describes the developmental disabilities, outlines the problems that a particular

---

[1]Henceforth, masculine pronouns are used throughout the book for uniformity and simplicity. They are not meant to be preferential or discriminatory.

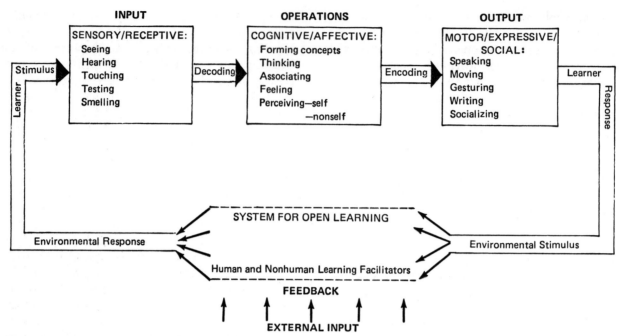

Figure 1. System for Open Learning (SOL) information-processing model.

disability creates for the child, indicates the challenges it presents to the caregiver of that child, and then makes suggestions for meeting the challenge of solving the problems created by the disability. These solutions include specific references to learning episodes in the present Volumes I and II. Other related books include *Developmental and Learning Disabilities* (Meier, 1976), *Developmental Disorders* (Johnston and Magrab, eds., 1976), and *Psychological Management of Pediatric Problems,* Volumes I and II (Magrab, ed., 1978), all published by University Park Press.

The information-processing model depicted in Figure 1 also shows that complete learning must include feedback, shown as the lower portion of the model. Feedback comes from the environment in the form of natural consequences from the learner's actions, as well as the consequences provided by learning facilitators. This is a very dynamic system since a response or reaction from the environment becomes a stimulus to the learner, and a response or action from the learner becomes a stimulus to the environment. Learning occurs through these transactions between an individual learner and his responsive environment consisting of other people and objects.

The dotted lines around the environmental feedback portion of the figure represent the idea that this environment should be open to whatever situation the learner creates and, in turn, that this open environment should provide a wide variety of responses which in turn stimulate the learner and allow him to generalize his learning. In order

to create and maintain openness and the ability to generalize in a learner, it is important to keep the environment as flexible and as responsive as possible. This model, therefore, is not in any way a closed stimulus/response model, but responds to the many possible thoughts or behaviors that the learner may create in reaction to whatever environmental input he receives. The environment then naturally provides feedback to the learner's response, which fosters expansion of knowledge and expression of that knowledge. Thus, the model emphasizes an S-O-R representation of the individual learner, wherein the O stands for the person and the variety of operations the person may perform on information and experiences as they are changed from being stimuli (S), to being understood (O), to becoming responses (R).

In the SOL information-processing model, emphasis is placed upon the fact that a reward or reinforcement for any behavior must be meaningful to the individual learner and be related to the performance itself. The SOL approach supports intrinsic motivation, whenever possible, rather than extrinsic motivation. Being intrinsically motivated means that the learner thinks about the information he receives and solves problems related to it because the information itself is stimulating and the solution of the problem it presents is satisfying to the learner. The learner solves a problem simply for the pleasure of coming up with a solution to the problem. This achievement therefore has its own reward. An example would be a child who solves the problem of matching a round block to a round hole in order to adequately fill the empty space that confronts him and seems incomplete. Sometimes, because of disturbances in the ability to receive this kind of feedback or because of a previous history of environmental unresponsiveness, a learner will need additional extrinsic reinforcement. This reinforcement can be provided by the learning facilitator in order to prompt and support the learning process. Even these external reinforcers, insofar as possible, should be meaningfully related to the performance of the learner. A goal would be to help the child learn for the sake of learning itself. This has been described as a shift from learning for love (or other extrinsic reward) to a love for learning (which is its own intrinsic reward).

Since the feedback to the learner in the information-processing model cues him as to whether his solution to a given problem is correct, the facilitating environment structures the learning process to be self-correcting. In this way, the learner immediately receives corrected feedback from each step he takes in the learning process. In such an ideal responsive environment where the feedback comes naturally, whether it be through experience with objects or transactions with an adult, the immediate and meaningful reinforcement provides self-maintaining motivation that will lead the learner to pursue solutions to problems and generalize them to other relevant situations.

However, the provision of precisely appropriate feedback, especially to delayed and/or disabled learners, often requires an ingenious learning facilitator who is able to match the level of difficulty of the task to the level of ability of the learner. In order to do this, it is important that a needs assessment be made and a profile be kept on each learner. This needs assessment should reveal the learner's ability levels relevant to the Entry and Terminal Behaviors associated with learning episodes designed to meet these needs. Since each learner has his own patterns of levels and needs, the truly response-able learning facilitator must match appropriate learning episodes to these individual needs and should not assume that a level or need in one developmental domain, for example sensory/receptive, reflects the same level or need in another. Similarly, since each learner in a group has his own level of readiness, the learning facilitator must match appropriate learning episodes to individual differences rather than risk leveling out these differences by giving all learners the same episodes at the same time. Above all, the learning facilitator needs to remember that no matter what the nature and severity of his delay or disability, every child has the capacity to learn, provided that his experiences are suitably matched to his interests and abilities.

The learning episodes contained in Volumes I and II are offered to the learning facilitator as suggestions. It is understood that these learning episodes may have to be tailored considerably for some children, especially those with special needs. The flexible nature and wide variety of these learning episodes should enable the learning facilitator to find an appropriate point of entry for each learner's needs and to gradually master the knack of properly matching and adapting learning episodes to meet any learner's unique needs. As the learning facilitator, you are encouraged to be creative and to modify these episodes as you assess and attempt to meet each individual learner's unique needs. It may be necessary to alter and/or to add to the Entry Behavior(s), Materials, and Procedures in order to achieve the stated Terminal Behavior(s). For example, if the learner has a hearing deficit and has a hearing aid, the facilitator must be sure that the device is inserted properly and is working well before proceeding with any episode that requires the complete reception and accurate processing of auditory information which, of course, would include verbal instructions for the episode. In the case of a severely visually handicapped learner, it may be necessary to encourage and stress the manipulation of the materials in order for the learner to understand relationships that normally sighted learners comprehend simply by looking at them. For the learner who has serious problems in controlling motor behavior, special procedures may be necessary to replace activities that require manipulation or ambulation. Suggestions for these and other alterations are found in *Interferences with Development* (Malone and Meier, 1979) and in Volume I under "Readiness," Unit 22.

In cases where the level of difficulty for a given episode is found to be too difficult for a particular learner, it may be necessary to select a less demanding learning episode from those designed for developmentally and chronologically younger learners. Such adaptations, sometimes occurring extemporaneously to accommodate or compensate for a learner's special needs, are what characterize the truly response-able learning facilitator. Since many programs serve learners with one or another type of developmental interference, it is recommended that the learning facilitator write down for ready reference all commonly used modifications for any given learning episode which make it more effective for this program. Space is provided for this exercise in the margins of both volumes.

The primary purpose of *Facilitating Children's Development* (Volumes I and II), and the companion texts, *Interferences with Development* and *Developmental and Learning Disabilities,* is to facilitate optimal learning and development within each learner's individual capabilities and limitations. To the learning facilitator, the learning episodes may resemble recipes in a cookbook. However, the real gourmet cook modifies the basic recipes to suit his own tastes and the tastes of those whom he invites to his table. Therefore, it is recommended that the learning facilitator appropriately season each episode in accordance with his own style and in a manner to make it more appealing and nutritious for each learner/consumer.

HOW TO USE THE LEARNING EPISODES EFFECTIVELY

First, look up the learning episodes by their Unit and Purpose according to the goal you may have for a child. Then choose a learning episode that uses skills the learner has demonstrated he can do, as specified by the Entry Behavior. Do not make it hard for the learner when you are introducing an episode but start instead at a level that guarantees success for him. Then gradually make it a little more complex or more difficult in order to help him learn more.

Gather the materials necessary for the episode. Try to vary the materials and toys used in the learning episodes in order to increase the learner's interest level and to help him to be flexible. In this way you help the learner apply what he learns to other situations.

The Procedure tells you how to do a particular episode. In general, when introducing a new learning episode to the learner, first demonstrate it to him and then let him try it the best way he can. After he tries it, demonstrate the learning episode again if he seems to need another example. Sometimes the learner may need extra encouragement to try a new episode. There are many ways to encourage him to work through each new procedure: 1) direct him by pointing or using other gestures, 2) actually guide his hand if he will allow you to do this, 3) demonstrate over and over again yourself so that he can imitate you, 4) praise his attempts

or perform a favorite activity with him as a reward, even if he is not one hundred percent right, and 5) divide the learning episodes into parts and show him one part at a time. This is the "feedback" part of the information-processing model. A facilitator also can accept at times the learner's own way of using the toys or materials in the learning episode instead of always expecting him to do it the "right way." If you do this, you may have a chance to see how creative the learner is and to notice new skills he may have acquired. For example, if, instead of placing the pegs as in the learning procedure, the learner pushes the peg board around going "vroom, vroom," you can realize that the learner is pretending and you can involve yourself in his imagination. You can help him to pick up "people" on the "bus," go down another "street," turn left, turn right, etc., and so share in his creativity. When you are playing together, allow the learner to make his own mistakes as much as possible, especially if a learning episode is self-correcting, as is the case with the puzzles or stacking toys. Be sure to let him struggle a little bit to puzzle out a problem on his own. Do not be too eager to show him the "right way." He will let you know when it is time to help him or to show him how to do the learning episode again by looking at you. This is a signal to let you know it is time to give more help, to demonstrate the solution, or otherwise to guide him.

Each time you do a learning episode, try to encourage the learner to increase the time that he stays involved and pays attention. However, you should stop a learning episode whenever the learner no longer responds to your encouragement or does not show interest when you vary the learning episode. Other ways of expanding the learner's involvement include adding a new toy or new materials, combining the learning episodes to add variety, or playing them in a series so that when a learner becomes bored with one game you can begin another.

The language used during all learning episodes should be simple and direct. As often as possible the names for toys and objects should be used instead of pronouns such as "it." Actions as well as objects should be named. Examples would be, "Put this round block into the round hole," or "We are crawling under the 'bridge'." However, do not talk so much (directing, naming, describing, etc.) that the learner has no time to stop and think about what you have said. If you give him a chance, he may respond to your language with his own, even if he does not have real words. If he does "talk," show him that you accept and admire his "talking" by repeating and expanding on the sounds he makes or words he uses. If a child is learning single words, and you are showing a picture of a running dog and he says, "Gog," you can say, "Dog. The dog is running."

As much as possible, the interaction between you and the learner should be ended with a learning episode or part of a learning episode that the learner likes and can do easily by himself. In this way he can continue to be involved in a learning episode in an independent manner as he directs his own behavior and continues to learn and practice skills alone.

Although the learning episodes are arranged according to the information-processing model and titled to describe the function that is most involved, each episode also involves and develops other abilities. For example, Unit I 17, Episode F / Ball Play: Rolling Back and Forth (Volume I) is placed in the section called Socialization and Imitation. This episode also involves gross motor skills and develops coordination. Therefore, the episodes are arranged for convenience and direction only, and are not designed to develop one ability alone. For this reason, you can select activities from several categories that may help you to reach a learning goal. Become familiar enough with all of the learning episodes so that the relationships among them become clear and become an almost automatic part of your response repertoire — the hallmark of response-ability in the SOL environment.

SUGGESTIONS FOR SOL EPISODES DURING DAILY INFANT/TODDLER ROUTINES

The learning episodes themselves suggest many household materials and inexpensive toys and supplies for making the episodes easier and less expensive to provide. The following practical suggestions for a daily program have been found to be useful in the management of a SOL program for infants and toddlers. These are a few suggestions for learning episodes during daily routines, which are not included in the more formal procedures contained in the body of this curriculum guide. The creative learning facilitator will think up many other variations as he gives care to the learner throughout the day. These creations should be written down and included in this volume in the margins provided.

Feeding

For optimal physical and emotional development of the infant learner it is necessary for you to hold him close to you in your arms. Bottles should not be propped because no one but you can provide the comfort through sensory stimulation and social interaction that the young learner needs. Unit I 19 describes positions that may facilitate feeding the learner with special needs.

When feeding the older, sitting learner, use food in the following ways for many learning episodes: 1) break off tiny bits of food and place them on the table or tray for the learner to pick up, thereby encouraging a more mature grasp and promoting fine motor development, 2) place food in different areas of the tray or table in front of the learner so that he has to reach out to different places for it to develop eye-hand coordination and space perception, 3) encourage cognitive development by partially or completely hiding pieces of food under a plate, napkin, cup, etc., 4) encourage self-help skills by allowing finger feeding and introducing a spoon for the learner to hold and use as soon as he begins to grasp at your spoon, and 5) make the meal a social occasion by chatting with the learner about the characteristics of his food (smell, taste, etc.), what he is doing, and what the other learners are doing, too.

Provide different textures, and use a spoon and a cup as well as a bottle to help develop oral skills, used later in speech. Self-help skills can also be developed by encouraging the toddler learner to throw away his own uneaten food to help you clean up after a meal. The main point is to make a meal nutritious not only to the body but also to the senses, the mind, and the feelings of the learner.

Dressing

Infants and toddlers with special needs, especially those with tight muscles, may be hard to dress. Unit I 9 provides positions that will be helpful. In general, moving slowly and firmly through the dressing movements is better than moving too fast. When dressing or changing the infant or toddler, provide sensory stimulation by touching various parts of the learner's body with your fingers, with cotton balls, washcloths, textured plastic pot scrubbers, and materials of different textures. For visual perception you can place a mirror, texture board, or a series of frequently changing pictures on the wall next to the changing table; then encourage the learner to look at whatever is displayed and to talk about what he sees. As the learner becomes old enough to cooperate in dressing, you can direct, through manual guidance, the learner's first body adjustment to the changing or dressing procedure to increase self-help skills and independence. Encourage him to pull off his own socks and shoes or to touch his nose, toes, and other parts as you name them, in order to develop body awareness and self-image. Language can be encouraged by talking about what you are doing and what is happening, paying special attention with the older baby to adverbs and prepositions as well as nouns. For example, say, "*through* the sleeves," "*in* the shoe," etc. Learners can also be encouraged to unzip their own coats, unbutton sweaters, etc., and in this way can move toward independence.

Bathing

When bathing the learner, develop his body awareness and self-image by labeling body parts. Encourage the young learner to touch parts of his own body by guiding his hand, and encourage the older learner to "find your nose." For visual coordination even very young learners can be encouraged to follow squeaking toys across or around the edge of the tub. For cognitive development the characteristics of different objects can be shown to the learners and described. For example, give the learner different things that will float, sink, fall apart, absorb or contain water. You can also make air-filled toys disappear and reappear by pushing them under the water and letting them pop up to the surface. For sensory stimulation warm and cool water can be poured into separate bottles and the learner can be helped to feel the difference as you talk about "hot" and "cold." Even the toweling off process can be made developmentally purposeful, as in Unit I 9, rather than engaging in random drying.

All of these suggestions for incorporating learning episodes within routines could be written into formal learning episodes for completion of individualized education programs (IEPs) or achievement of any developmental objectives. Remember, all of the suggestions given above should serve only as examples. Because you understand that everything you do with the learner and everything the learner does in his environment by himself has value and is a learning experience, you can develop your own ways of making routine caregiving activities exciting learning episodes for the learner and creative opportunities for you, the learning facilitator.

PRINCIPLES FOR USING SOL EPISODES

Every learner needs some special time with his own facilitator each day. This special time should be in addition to the time involved in caregiving activities no matter how personal, stimulating, and satisfying those activities are. Even for the most conscientious facilitators it sometimes happens that a day goes by without one learner or another getting this much needed, extra individual attention. For example, there might be one child in your care who was very demanding and troublesome that day and took most of your time and energy. Perhaps there were many visitors or unexpected "emergencies," and your routines were interrupted. Or perhaps you were just busy meeting the moment-to-moment, small but constant demands that arise when you are caring for more than one child. So, it is possible to come to the end of a day and suddenly realize that there seemed to be no time or opportunity for the extra, very special interaction with one of the needy learners. This is especially true in a group care setting where it is sometimes helpful to have some individual activities that will make it easier to take advantage of whatever spare moments there are. Choosing at least one of the learning episodes each day makes it harder to pass over the quieter child for the more demanding one.

At any time throughout the day, if the learner is not occupied in any particular activity, you may choose and try a new appropriate learning episode. Or, at any time, you may enter and expand a learning episode in which the learner is involved already. For this reason, learning facilitators always need to be "good noticers." Carefully observe the learner to match the learning episode to his skills and activity level. Read the listed entry behaviors to determine an appropriate learning episode to use. If you enter a learning episode in which the learner is involved already, you need to notice his skills as well as to judge the pace of play to find an appropriate time to break in that will not intrude upon or interrupt him. If you decide to introduce a learning episode to a learner who is not involved on his own, take the learner to a quiet place apart from the other children so that he can focus complete attention on the learning episode. Or, if the learner is involved in an episode already, while he is still in the crib, for example, you may want to leave him where he is, go over and encourage him to try new ways of doing a learning episode, use other materials, involve other children, etc.

Materials

To make the most of every chance for learning, the particular toys and materials necessary for the learning episodes must be within easy reach and available to the facilitator at all times. This means that the materials must be replaced in an orderly way in a special place set aside for their storage when they are not being used. It also means that you need to have more than one set of certain toys and materials so that you can leave at least some of them out for the learners to use by themselves in spontaneous play in the autotelic (that which is engaged in for its own sake; literally, an end in itself) responsive environment. It is sometimes very useful to have two sets of toys that perform the same function but look different since novelty often will appeal to the learner and help to keep interest high.

FACILITATING PARENT LEARNING

Because of the adaptability of the learning episodes to children with developmental interferences, the episodes are particularly well suited for parent training. The learning facilitator can prescribe learning episodes and demonstrate them to the parent for use in the home. In the parent-training situation, the learning facilitator must pace the prescription of learning episodes according to the parent's ability to insert the learning episodes into the routines of his day. Just as it is important to select the learning episodes according to the learner's skills and activity level, likewise it is important to pace the introduction of the learning episodes to the parent's skills and motivational level. Learning facilitators need to be doubly sensitive in this situation and aware of both the learner's and the parent's needs.

For the training process in general, it is best to first discuss the rationale for the learning episode, pointing out the Purpose and Entry Behavior to the parent. Then, the learning facilitator can show the Material needed and model the Procedure for the parent. The parent should then try the Procedure for suggestions from the facilitator. On the next opportunity for observation, as the parent demonstrates the learning episode to the learning facilitator, the learning facilitator can note the progress of the learner toward the Terminal Behavior. The use of videotape recording and prompt playback is especially effective if the hardware is available. In this way an individualized education program (IEP) can be developed that satisfies the requirement of PL 94-142 (Education for All Handicapped Children Act) and meets the goals of parent-training programs that are focused upon helping parents to become learning facilitators for their developmentally disabled or delayed infants and toddlers.

EVALUATION

Each day the facilitator or parent-facilitator should record the learning episodes performed with the learner. These record sheets should be checked over frequently to see that you have introduced learning episodes that involve all areas of the learner's development, especially for those learners who have special needs. In this way you can also see for yourself just how many new things the infant or toddler has accomplished with your help. Sample record sheets have been included as Figures 2 and 3 if you want to keep a progress record or if you must develop an IEP according to PL 94-142. In the first sample (Figure 2) you simply write down the number of the learning episodes on the left hand column and record the date for each time you and the learner perform this particular episode. In the second sample record (Figure 3), you record the name of the particular learning episode at the top and then check off the learner's reaction to it each day. These record sheets can be reviewed regularly for updating and indicating changes in goals for the learner and thus in the learning episodes themselves. You should select new learning episodes based on the Entry Behavior that is at the next highest developmental level from the Terminal Behavior achieved by the learner.

PRINCIPLES OF BEHAVIOR CHANGE

Most of the learning episodes in the units for infants and toddlers that follow are designed to increase predetermined desirable behaviors. At times, however, a learning facilitator might want to decrease an undesirable behavior. For example, a child may be going through a period when he is showing behavior in a socially and developmentally inappropriate way, perhaps by grabbing toys or hitting other children. Or sometimes a learner may have acquired habits that are detrimental to his further developmental growth because these habits interfere with more adaptive behavior. For example, he may be preoccupied with his own body and exhibit such habits as waving and staring at his fingers, tugging at his hair, etc. In instances of severe behavioral disturbance it is best,

Name _____ Birthdate _____ Age _____

Overall Goals

Planned Learning Episodes

| Sensory/Receptive | | Cognitive/Affective | | Motor/Expressive/Social | |
Learning Episode	Date of Interaction	Learning Episode	Date of Interaction	Learning Episode	Date of Interaction

Figure 2.   Individual record of planned learning episode.

of course, to consult a specialist in behavior management, such as a psychologist. However, before you take this step, as a diagnostic or decision-making tool, you may wish to try your own program for managing behavior problems. Therefore, some general principles to serve as guidelines for learning facilitators who want to try a program in behavior management are included here. This is only a brief introduction; there are a number of excellent books on the market that should be consulted to explain behavioral principles in further depth and to give you more ideas and techniques for implementing behavior change programs.

Simply stated, behavior increases when it is reinforced. Therefore, to increase behavior, as is intended in most of the learning episodes, reinforcement should be provided. Behavior that is not re-

Name _____ Birthdate _____ Age _____

Learning Episode _____

Record the number of times this behavior occurs during a time period for at least three days.

Day	Time Period	How often did it occur?	What came before the behavior?	What followed the behavior?	Rate of occurrence
1					
2					
3					
4					
5					
6					
7					
8					

Figure 3.   Sample chart for recording behavior.

inforced tends to decrease. Therefore, to decrease behavior, as the facilitator might wish to do with behavior that interferes with the learning process, the facilitator should ignore it, follow it with a mild punishment, and/or teach (and reinforce) a competing behavior that is more positive.

Types of reinforcers include social reinforcers, such as pats on the head, smiles, hugs; motor reinforcers, such as swinging the learner around, roughhouse play; tangible reinforcers, such as bits of food or sips of a drink, special treats or toys; and autotelic reinforcers, such as the pleasure in solving a problem or just learning more about something for the sheer joy of understanding or satisfying curiosity. Mild punishments include social reactions, such as frowning at the learner, saying "No," or taking the learner out of a situation that he enjoys and placing the learner in "time-out." "Time-out," short for "time-out from reinforcement," is a special way of ignoring the learner's behavior. It simply means taking the learner out of the situation that is providing reinforcement for the undesirable act, i.e., moving him away from other learners who may have encouraged him to hit by giving in to him, and putting him in a place where it is possible to ignore him for a specified period of time. As a rule of thumb, the mildest punishment that is still effective should be applied. Therefore, if a frown will serve to discourage more of the behavior, then it is unnecessary to take away something that the learner desires. Special techniques outlining procedures that may be used with more serious behavior problems are included in the following books:

Baker, B., Brightman, A., Heifitz, L., and Murphey, D. 1976. *Steps to Independence: A Skills Training Series for Children with Special Needs.* Research Press, Champaign, Ill. (Provides a comprehensive approach to behavior management for handicapped children.)

Kent, L. 1974. *Language Acquisition Program for the Severely Retarded.* Research Press, Champaign, Ill. (Discusses overcorrection; other books from Research Press are helpful and are outlined in its catalog.)

These special techniques include overcorrection, which is especially useful in attempts to extinguish meaningless or repetitive behavior patterns that interfere with more adaptive learning; shaping, which rewards gradual approximation in a step-by-step fashion toward the achievement of a terminal behavior; and fading, which

gradually and systematically removes an extrinsic reinforcer or punishment from a behavior.

Some principles for choosing reinforcers to either increase or decrease behaviors are:

1. Developmental appropriateness. Before working toward the elimination of a behavior, however annoying it may be temporarily, the learning facilitator should give careful thought to its possible developmental significance or appropriateness for the learner's stage of development. For example, children will often throw bits of food off a high chair tray and then watch where the food falls on the floor. When doing this they are often learning about spatial concepts and practicing fine motor acts. Therefore, it is necessary not to erase or extinguish this behavior altogether but to change it into one that is more tolerable for the learning facilitator. On the other hand, a learning facilitator would not attempt to train a behavior beyond the developmental capabilities of the learner. The SOL Entry Behaviors are designed to help in these choices, but sometimes, especially with self-help skills like toilet training, skill acquisition can be prompted too early. (Refer to: Azrin, N., and Fox, R. 1976. *Toilet Training in Less Than a Day.* Pocket Books, New York. This book gives guidelines for toileting readiness as well as the process of training.)

2. Consistency. It is very important, especially when you apply a negative consequence, to be extremely consistent and *always* to either ignore or punish the behavior that you are trying to decrease *every time it occurs*.

3. Immediacy. The sooner you apply the positive or negative consequences after the behavioral event, the more effective they will be. This is especially true for developmentally young learners whose memories may be short.

4. Relevancy. The more relevant the consequence to the behavioral act, the more it will have meaning and the faster the learning will proceed. For example, it is not necessary to use a concrete reinforcer, such as a bit of food, when a smile will suffice to increase a desirable behavior. An intrinsic reinforcer (autotelic one) is preferred over an extrinsic reinforcer (which itself is not meaningfully related to the task nor does it flow directly from the task as an end in itself) when it is effective.

5. Internalization. Always label the new behavior to be learned and/or the consequence of the

behavior to be eliminated so that the learner begins to think and internally direct his own behavior with the correct labels.

6. Substitution. It is always necessary to teach a new behavior to replace one that the learning facilitator is trying to extinguish or change. For example, if the learner is in the habit of grabbing toys or materials from other children, the facilitator would spend some time teaching an alternative behavior to the learner before attempting to erase that behavior. Ways to do this include:

   a. Modeling the desired behavior with another child.
   b. Reinforcing a child who performs the behavior, and pointing out the similar consequences to the learner.
   c. After modeling the behavior, directing the learner to perform the behavior himself and then reinforcing his attempts at imitating the learning facilitator. This "role playing" is successful with toddler and preschool learners who enjoy "pretending to be the teacher."

Based upon these principles, a suggested sequence to be used by a learning facilitator to decrease a targeted behavior, for example, hitting another child, would be as follows:

1. Learner is observed asking another learner for a toy and not hitting. Facilitator approaches learner and says, "I like the way you asked for the toy," and gives the learner a squeeze. (Positive reinforcement, with immediacy, relevancy, consistency, and internalization.)
2. Learner is observed to hit another learner. Frowning, the facilitator says, "No!" (Punishment — immediacy, relevancy.)

3. "You may not hit." (Labeling the behavior to be decreased — internalization.)
4. "Hitting hurts." (Stating the reason for decreasing the behavior — internalization.)
5. "If you hit you may not play with the children." (The consequence of the learner's actions to the learner — internalization.)
6. "Try getting the toy this way, 'Give it to me, please.'" (Modeling getting the toy which precipitated the hitting incident and teaching an alternative — substitution.)
7. Facilitator takes the learner away from the situation, saying, "No! you may not play with the other learners if you hit." (Time-out, with immediacy, relevancy, consistency, internalization.)

To know if your behavioral program is working, it is necessary to keep track of the number of times the behavior occurs to determine if its incidence is increasing or decreasing. There are ways to do this, including simply counting the number of times the targeted behavior occurs over a specific time period, for example, one hour, or noting the number of times the targeted behavior occurs throughout the day. A typical chart for observing and counting behaviors is included as Figure 3 in this introduction.

You can also make these behavioral management procedures part of your own repertoire of learning episodes, which could be included in an Individualized Education Program (IEP). Behavioral learning episodes are not included as a separate unit in this curriculum guide because each would be designed for the specific nature and requirements of the target behavior identified by the facilitator. An example is included on the next page to provide the learning facilitator with a concrete guide for developing his own behavioral learning episodes as needed.

SAMPLE BEHAVIORAL LEARNING EPISODE

UNIT: T 17 / Socialization and Imitation

EPISODE: Learning to Ask

PURPOSE: Learner will reduce toy grabbing and increase the number of times the learner asks for toys.

ENTRY BEHAVIOR: Learner grabs toys from other learners more than is developmentally expected whenever two or more learners are engaged in play. The learner understands one-part directions and engages in imaginative play.

MATERIAL: Toys or activities that require participation by the learner.

PROCEDURE: The facilitator observes and records the number of times the learner grabs toys from other learners during a morning of activities and/or the number of times the learner asks for a toy on the first morning.

The second morning the facilitator will take the learner aside with several favorite toys and a doll. The facilitator will model sharing with the doll, handing the doll a toy and then asking for it back saying, "Give me the *toy*, please," or "Toy, please." The facilitator will encourage the learner to imitate. Then the facilitator may role play with the learner, asking the learner for a toy and then reversing the roles, the learner asking the facilitator for a toy. This "sharing" game may be repeated later with another learner in the game.

The third morning the facilitator will again observe the learner and record the number of times the learner grabs or asks for a toy. Each time the learner asks for a toy, the facilitator will "control" the situation by making sure that the learner gets either the requested toy or one equally as attractive and providing verbal reinforcement, "Good asking. You get the *toy*."

If the number of times the learner grabs lessens and the number of times he asks increases, no punishment may have to be applied. If the number of "asks" does not increase, you may want to apply a punishment procedure as follows: Whenever the learner grabs, the facilitator says, "No! You may not grab the toy. The toy is (*other learner's name*). You ask for it. If you grab you cannot play with the (*name of toy*)." Then the facilitator removes the learner to a quiet, less favorable area of the room.

Later the facilitator repeats the role play or, if an opportunity presents, reinforces the learner for asking. The facilitator consistently applies these rewards and punishments, keeping count of "asking" and "grabbing" behaviors.

The facilitator will gradually decrease the number of rewards given to the learner for "asking" when the criterion of no more than two "grabs" per day has been maintained for 3 days.

TERMINAL BEHAVIOR: Learner usually asks for toys he wants that are in the possession of other learners, grabbing toys no more than two times per day, and needing no more than an occasional reinforcer by the facilitator.

INDIVIDUALIZED EDUCATION PROGRAM

Student's name _____ Birthdate _____ School _____ Student number _____

Parent/Guardian _____ Address _____ Telephone number _____

Current program placement _____ Current exceptional category _____ Date of meeting _____

Signatures of meeting participants

		Concurred with plan	
_____, Committee chairperson	☐	Yes ☐	No
_____, Student's teacher	☐	Yes ☐	No
_____, Parent/Guardian	☐	Yes ☐	No
_____	☐	Yes ☐	No
_____	☐	Yes ☐	No
_____	☐	Yes ☐	No
_____	☐	Yes ☐	No
_____	☐	Yes ☐	No
_____	☐	Yes ☐	No

Recommended program placement _____

Time in regular education program _____ hrs.

Time in special education program _____ hrs.

	Date beginning	Date ending
Services to be provided	_____	_____
	_____	_____
	_____	_____
	_____	_____
	_____	_____

Date of next review _____

Additional comments: _____
_____
_____
_____
_____

Due process hearing requested ☐ Yes ☐ No

Date of request _____

If parent/guardian is not in attendance, check the following as appropriate:

___ Parent/guardian included via telephone call

___ Parent/guardian included via telephone conference call

___ Appropriate copies of correspondence documenting efforts to include parent/guardian attached

___ Copy of log of telephone contacts documenting efforts to include parent/guardian attached

Individual responsible for initiating contacts _____ (Signature)

PROGRAM SUMMARY

Name _____   Case# _____   Eval. date _____
Case manager _____   DOB _____   Age _____

Assessed developmental level	Child's relative strengths	Child's relative weaknesses
1. Receptive language	Primary Learning Style:	
2. Cognitive		
3. Social/Self-help		
4. Fine motor		
5. Gross motor		
6. Expressive language		

RECOMMENDATIONS	Other:
Specific therapeutic educational services needed:	
Justification for educational placement:	
Date program entry:	
Implementation of IEP (Individualized Education Program):	
Projected IEP (Individualized Education Program) evaluation date:	

INDIVIDUALIZED EDUCATION PROGRAM

Name _____ Case# _____ DOB _____ Case manager _____

Parents' names_____ Telephone #_____ Date IEP_____

RECEPTIVE: GOALS AND OBJECTIVES (Key to P.S. "weaknesses") Reviewed:

	LE	Begun	Ended
R-1			
Comments: A.			
B.			
C.			
R-2			
Comments: A.			
B.			
C.			
R-3			
Comments: A.			
B.			
C.			
R-4			
Comments: A.			
B.			
C.			

INDIVIDUALIZED EDUCATION PROGRAM

Name _____ Case# _____ DOB _____ Case manager _____
Parents' names_____ Telephone #_____ Date IEP_____
COGNITIVE: GOALS AND OBJECTIVES (Key to P.S. "weaknesses") Reviewed:

	LE	Begun	Ended
C-1 _____			
Comments: A. _____			
B. _____			
C. _____			
C-2 _____			
Comments: A. _____			
B. _____			
C. _____			
C-3 _____			
Comments: A. _____			
B. _____			
C. _____			
C-4 _____			
Comments: A. _____			
B. _____			
C. _____			

INDIVIDUALIZED EDUCATION PROGRAM

Name _____ Case# _____ DOB _____ Case manager _____
Parents' names_____ Telephone #_____ Date IEP_____
EXPRESSIVE: GOALS AND OBJECTIVES (Key to P.S. "weaknesses")   Reviewed:

	LE	Begun	Ended
E-1			
Comments: A.			
B.			
C.			
E-2			
Comments: A.			
B.			
C.			
E-3			
Comments: A.			
B.			
C.			
E-4			
Comments: A.			
B.			
C.			

RECORD OF LEARNER CONTACTS

Name _____   Case # _____

Date of evaluation _____ (Age: _____)   DOB _____

Case manager _____   Placement _____

Date	Goal	Objective	Procedure/L.E.	Time	Performance	Comments

FACILITATOR/LEARNER LEARNING EPISODE

Learner's name _____ Date _____

Learning Episode (name) _____

	Monday						Tuesday				
	Not at all			Very much			Not at all			Very much	
Pays attention	1	2	3	4	5	Pays attention	1	2	3	4	5
Needs encouragement	1	2	3	4	5	Needs encouragement	1	2	3	4	5
Gets frustrated	1	2	3	4	5	Gets frustrated	1	2	3	4	5
Achieves skill	1	2	3	4	5	Achieves skill	1	2	3	4	5
Continues on own	1	2	3	4	5	Continues on own	1	2	3	4	5

	Wednesday						Thursday				
	Not at all			Very much			Not at all			Very much	
Pays attention	1	2	3	4	5	Pays attention	1	2	3	4	5
Needs encouragement	1	2	3	4	5	Needs encouragement	1	2	3	4	5
Gets frustrated	1	2	3	4	5	Gets frustrated	1	2	3	4	5
Achieves skill	1	2	3	4	5	Achieves skill	1	2	3	4	5
Continues on own	1	2	3	4	5	Continues on own	1	2	3	4	5

	Friday						Saturday				
	Not at all			Very much			Not at all			Very much	
Pays attention	1	2	3	4	5	Pays attention	1	2	3	4	5
Needs encouragement	1	2	3	4	5	Needs encouragement	1	2	3	4	5
Gets frustrated	1	2	3	4	5	Gets frustrated	1	2	3	4	5
Achieves skill	1	2	3	4	5	Achieves skill	1	2	3	4	5
Continues on own	1	2	3	4	5	Continues on own	1	2	3	4	5

	Sunday					Comments
	Not at all			Very much		
Pays attention	1	2	3	4	5	
Needs encouragement	1	2	3	4	5	
Gets frustrated	1	2	3	4	5	
Achieves skill	1	2	3	4	5	
Continues on own	1	2	3	4	5	

SENSORY / RECEPTIVE EPISODES

Unit I 1 / HEARING

The infant learner depends a great deal on the sense of listening to bring information about the world to him. The language and sound environment with which the learning facilitator provides the young infant is crucially important for the development of attention to sound and later the ability to communicate, which includes the development of receptive, associative, and expressive language skills. The learning facilitator should always be conscious of his language input for the learner. Labeling activities and talking to the learner during routines, describing what is happening and what is observed, even before the learner can actually understand words, serve to prepare the learner for communicative skills. For the older learner, introducing picture books in order to label and describe objects, even before the learner can attend to the content of the stories, prepares the learner for later reading skills.

For a learner with a confirmed or suspected hearing deficit, it is especially important to plan the listening environment so that the learner can be provided with a meaningful experience if at all possible. In these instances it is wise to consult a speech pathologist and an audiologist for suggestions to provide the most facilitative learning environment.

UNIT: I 1 / Hearing

EPISODE: A / Attending to Noise

PURPOSE: Learner will demonstrate auditory awareness of the environment.

ENTRY BEHAVIOR: Learner has some hearing.

MATERIAL: Noisemakers (rattles, pots and pans, radio, music box, or a drum).

PROCEDURE: Place the learner in a position that will permit alertness and relaxation, either on his stomach, side, or back (see Unit I 22). Shake or hit the noisemaker, which you are holding outside of the learner's visual field. Make the noise quite loudly for a 5–10-second interval, and then stop for the same amount of time. You can tell when the learner is listening because he will become still and quiet, change the rhythm of his breathing, or change facial expression. After the learner has shown awareness, repeat four to five times. Then vary the sound, using another noisemaker.

TERMINAL BEHAVIOR: Learner shows he is listening to the sound by quieting, changing his breathing rhythm, and/or turning toward the noise the first or second time it is sounded.

UNIT:	**I 1 / Hearing**
EPISODE:	**B / See a Voice: 180°**
PURPOSE:	Learner uses his eyes to find the source of a sound.
ENTRY BEHAVIOR:	Learner has some hearing and can focus his eyes on the speaker when the speaker is within his range of sight. Learner can also turn his head from side to side.
MATERIAL:	Infant seat or other supportive seat to give the learner a semi-upright position.
PROCEDURE:	Place the learner in an appropriate seat or support him so that he is sitting semi-upright and relaxed. Stand behind the learner or to his side so that he cannot see you. Say the learner's name, and talk to him on one side of his head, about level with his ear, while stroking his cheek on the same side or otherwise encouraging him to turn his head toward the sound of your voice. When the learner has turned toward the sound you are making and has found you with his eyes, smile at him and talk to him a few moments more. Then quickly move out of his line of vision, and repeat the game on the other side of his head. Repeat the game, sometimes going to the opposite side, sometimes staying on the same side. When the learner can find you every time you speak at the side of his head near his ear level, you know you can move your face and voice higher or lower so that he has to look up or down as well as side to side.
TERMINAL BEHAVIOR:	Learner turns his head directly toward the voice and focuses rapidly with his eyes on the face of the facilitator.

UNIT ·	**I 1 / Hearing**
EPISODE:	**C / See a Sound: 180°**
PURPOSE:	Learner can locate source of sound with his eyes.
ENTRY BEHAVIOR:	Learner has some hearing and can focus on noisemaking toys or objects within his range of sight. Learner can coordinate turning of his head 180°.
MATERIAL:	Infant seat or other supportive seat to give the learner a semi-upright position; various noisemakers (bells, rattles, music box, etc.).
PROCEDURE:	Place the learner in an infant seat or otherwise support him in a semi-upright position. Have ready several objects, each of which makes a different, pleasant sound. Place yourself behind the learner so that he cannot see you. Shake the noisemaker on one side of the learner's head about 18 inches away at ear level, and encourage him to turn his head in the direction of the sound without using your voice. To do this you can stroke his cheek on the same side as the sound or otherwise guide him with your hand until he turns his head and finds the sound with his eyes. Allow him to look at the object for a while, or handle it if he should reach for it. After a minute take the object out of the learner's sight, and do this game again on the other side of the learner, first with the same object, and then using different objects. After the learner can turn and look at the noises you make at his ear level every time, you can make him look for the noisemaker at higher or lower positions as well as on alternative sides.
TERMINAL BEHAVIOR:	Learner can locate source of the sound directly with his eyes within full range of 180° and at high or low positions.

UNIT:	I 1 / Hearing
EPISODE:	D / Stop Activity on Command
PURPOSE:	Learner follows a command, especially when he is in danger of hurting himself.
ENTRY BEHAVIOR:	Learner does not attend to limiting words such as "No" or "Stop."
MATERIAL:	None.
PROCEDURE:	Although it is generally felt that it is not good for the learners to learn in a negative environment, it is sometimes very important for the learner to listen and comply when told "No" or "Stop." This should be done for the protection of the learner when he may not realize that he is in physical danger. When the learner is reaching for something that might harm him (broken glass, for example), the facilitator may have to say loudly or sternly, "NO!" The "No" or "Stop" should be accompanied by a restraining hand which prevents the learner from performing the activity. The most effective time to use this procedure is just before the learner is about to engage in the activity. The "No" and restraint should be followed by a brief explanation, "No, glass cuts."
TERMINAL BEHAVIOR:	Learner stops his activity when told to do so.

UNIT:	I 1 / Hearing
EPISODE:	E / Parallel Talking
PURPOSE:	Learner builds his understanding or "inner" language.
ENTRY BEHAVIOR:	Learner is able to listen and watches when someone is talking.
MATERIAL:	Things used in routines throughout the day.
PROCEDURE:	When the learner is doing something, the facilitator simply describes what he is doing. During dressing, for example, the facilitator might say, "I'm putting your sock on your foot. Now I'm putting your shoe on." Then the facilitator may say, "Give me your other foot. I'm going to put your sock on," and wait for the learner to lift his foot. The facilitator may then say, "Get your shoe." Then he may say, "Good, you got the shoe. Give the shoe to me."
	Many routines can be described in this way throughout the day. The facilitator may decide to select one aspect of language, the verb *put* for example, and emphasize this throughout the day: "Put your sock on," "Put your shoe on," "Put your cup down," "I'm putting your sock on," "I'm putting your shoe on."
TERMINAL BEHAVIOR:	Learner demonstrates that he understands language by following directions.

UNIT:	I 1 / Hearing
EPISODE:	F / Learn Names of Objects
PURPOSE:	Learner follows short directions and learns the name of objects.
ENTRY BEHAVIOR:	Learner can focus his eyes on an object, hears enough to turn to the source of sound, and watches a person who talks to him.
MATERIAL:	Two or three familiar objects at a time.
PROCEDURE:	When the learner is in an appropriate position with his arms free for movement, start by placing only two familiar objects in front of the learner within his reach or gaze. Tell the learner to get, or look at, one of the objects. For example, the facilitator might say, "Get the _____." "Look at the _____." The facilitator may have to help the learner choose the named object by gesturing, pointing, or using manual guidance to the object. Praise the learner when he chooses the named object, and allow him to play with the object. Once the learner has played with the named object for a moment, pick another object for him to get or look at. Again, guide him to the named object to get it and play with it for a moment. Repeat this game for as many times as the learner will get a toy. Gradually eliminate the gestures and just tell the learner to get, or look at, a familiar object.
TERMINAL BEHAVIOR:	Learner consistently gets or looks at the named object in response to verbal requests only.

UNIT:	**I 1** / **Hearing**
EPISODE:	**G** / **Object Discrimination Given Two Stimuli**
PURPOSE:	Learner develops object discrimination for familiar objects or toys.
ENTRY BEHAVIOR:	Learner is able to look at or give an object when the learning facilitator has pointed it out.
MATERIAL:	Two or three familiar objects (e.g., hat, spoon, soap) or favorite toys at a time.
PROCEDURE:	Placing two objects or toys within sight and reach of the learner, the facilitator says, "Give me (or facilitator's name) the _____," or "Look at the _____." If the learner is unable to discriminate between the two objects, remove one object, introduce the command, "Give me the _____," or guide and then reinforce the learner's successful performance. Using the same object and one other object, reintroduce the discrimination task, using the previously retrieved object. Using the same two objects, switch the positions and again ask the learner to indicate the same object. For example,

"Look at the
"Give me the   A   ."

"Look at the
"Give me the   A   B   ."

"Look at the
"Give me the   B   A   ."

If the learner is able to discriminate Object A, introduce a new object in its place and proceed to ask for Object B. If the learner is unable to discriminate A consistently, change only Object B. Continue this procedure until A is consistently regarded or retrieved and presented. Thus, your presentations may follow the pattern below:

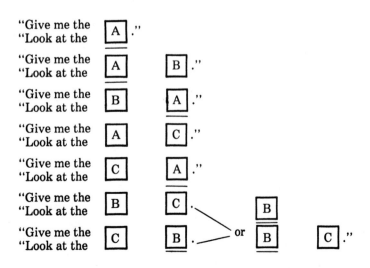

"Give me the
"Look at the   A   ."

"Give me the
"Look at the   A   B   ."

"Give me the
"Look at the   B   A   ."

"Give me the
"Look at the   A   C   ."

"Give me the
"Look at the   C   A   ."

"Give me the
"Look at the   B   C   .   B

"Give me the
"Look at the   C   B   .   or   B   C   ."

"Give me the | D | | B |.
"Look at the   or | D | | A |."
                                    | D |

"Give me the | D | | A |.
"Look at the

"Give me the | A | | D |."
"Look at the

TERMINAL BEHAVIOR: Learner is able to complete an object discrimination task involving two objects by looking at, or handing the facilitator, the indicated item.

UNIT:	**I 1 / Hearing**
EPISODE:	**H / Searches for Named Object Within Sight**
PURPOSE:	Learner learns to follow directions.
ENTRY BEHAVIOR:	Learner can move easily about by rolling, crawling, or walking. Learner can focus eyes on an object at the necessary distance. Learner hears and understands names of objects to be used.
MATERIAL:	Favorite toys or familiar household objects known to the learner by name.
PROCEDURE:	Before putting the learner on the floor, arrange objects that are familiar to the learner around the room. Then name an object and ask the learner to get it for you while directing him by gesturing, pointing, etc. Encourage the learner to "Get the _____," "Bring the _____," and reward him with a hug or smile when he does. Take a moment to play with the learner using the toy he retrieved, and then pick another object for the learner to get. Again, guide him by gesture or by leading him to the toy to get it and to return it to you for a moment of play. Repeat this game for as many times as the learner will retrieve a toy and bring it to you for play.
TERMINAL BEHAVIOR:	Learner can move directly to the named object and return directly to the facilitator in response to verbal requests only.

UNIT:	**I 1 / Hearing**
EPISODE:	**I / Picture Book: Point and Name**
PURPOSE:	Learner learns to recognize pictures of familiar objects, animals, etc.
ENTRY BEHAVIOR:	Learner has understanding of names and objects, animals, etc., in his environment.
MATERIAL:	Simple books with one picture per page, which can be purchased commercially or made by pasting magazine cutouts on plain paper and then stapling the paper together.
PROCEDURE:	Position the learner comfortably on your lap and show him a homemade or other simple book. Do not attempt to "read" the book to the learner yet, but merely point to and name the pictures. If the learner happens to imitate your pointing, praise him and name whatever picture he points to. If the learner only wants to crumple the paper in your book he is telling you that he is not yet interested in looking at the pictures, but instead wants to learn about paper and what he can do with it. Therefore, adapt to the learner's need and save your books by handing him a page of an old magazine or piece of scrap paper for crumpling and tearing.
TERMINAL BEHAVIOR:	Learner attends to pointing and naming activity by looking at the item indicated.

UNIT T 1 / HEARING

UNIT: T 1 / Hearing

EPISODE: A / Naming Properties and Objects

PURPOSE: Learner learns the names of objects and their characteristics.

ENTRY BEHAVIOR: Learner has begun to use single words spontaneously to name familiar things in his environment.

MATERIAL: New types of familiar items and also items ordinarily present in the learner's environment with which the learner does not usually play. Examples would be a piece of metal chain, an ice cube, a new textured ball, etc. (Learning Episode I3B).

PROCEDURE: This game is similar to "Feeling Objects for Comparisons" (Learning Episode I3B), except that the facilitator tries to encourage the learner to use the words he uses to describe the object that he hands to the learner. For example, you would say "ball" and wait for the learner to say "ball" back to you as he takes the ball from your hand. When the learner can repeat a single word to you, you can add words to describe the object and encourage him to repeat. For example, you can say "red ball," "rough ball," etc. Start with familiar items and move to those less familiar and more difficult to say, for example, "chain," "heavy chain."

TERMINAL BEHAVIOR: Learner repeats words used by the facilitator to describe the object.

UNIT:	T 1 / Hearing
EPISODE:	B / Rhythm Games: Imitation or Circle Activities
PURPOSE:	Learner learns to discriminate simple sound patterns.
ENTRY BEHAVIOR:	Learner has demonstrated interest in rhythmic sound patterns by swaying to music, attending to nursery songs or commercials, etc. Learner can coordinate necessary hand movements for imitation of facilitator.
MATERIAL:	Drums and drumsticks, wooden spoons, pots and pans, radio, record and record player.
PROCEDURE:	This is another type of imitation game that you could play with one or more learners. You can clap your hands, drum on the floor, pat, etc., in different patterns and rhythms with or without music ("Slow, slow, slow"; "Fast, fast, fast"; etc.), and encourage the learner to imitate you. Playing music on the radio or records to accompany the clapping, drumming, etc., usually encourages the learner to participate in time with the music. In general, lively music should be on in a learning environment only when it is listened to *actively*. It should not provide a constant background sound, which may only distract the learner or cause him to "tune out" auditory input.
TERMINAL BEHAVIOR:	Learner can accurately imitate rhythms provided by the facilitator or can accurately keep time to the rhythm of the music played.

UNIT:	T 1 / Hearing
EPISODE:	C / Action Words along with Actions
PURPOSE:	Learner learns to describe actions and movements regarding his position in environmental space.
ENTRY BEHAVIOR:	Learner is able to move about his environment, under and over obstacles with ease. Learner has begun to use language to name things and to describe things.
MATERIAL:	Objects for obstacle course, such as cardboard cartons, turned over chairs, tires, large pillows, sturdy low tables, etc.
PROCEDURE:	Set up several things around the room that would require the learner to go around, under, through, etc., them. Have the learner crawl, march, or otherwise follow you as in other follow the leader games, except that with this game you will emphasize saying *what* the learner is doing and *where* he is going by describing his progress. For example, as one, two, or three learners crawl through a carton, you can chant, "Rudolfo is going *through, through, through.* Rudolfo is going *through.*" As the learners go over a tire, "James is going *over,* Rudolfo is going *over,* Sara is going *over,* the tire."
TERMINAL BEHAVIOR:	Learner regularly uses action words to describe his actions in spontaneous speech as well as in imitation of the facilitator's language.

UNIT:	T 1 / Hearing
EPISODE:	**D / Understanding Wh-Questions**
PURPOSE:	Learner will understand early developing question forms, such as *who, what, where,* or *when.*
ENTRY BEHAVIOR:	Learner is able to understand the names of people and objects in his environment.
MATERIAL:	Play materials and objects used in other learning episodes and/or activities during the day, especially those activities that may involve other members of the learning environment and/or various parts of the learning environment.
PROCEDURE:	In the course of his interactions with the learner, the learning facilitator asks the learner such questions as "Who is doing _____?" "What is this?" (demonstrating). This learning episode is most effective when the facilitator concentrates on one question form over a period of time until comprehension by the learner is demonstrated. The learning facilitator may ask, at varying intervals, "*Where* is the juice?" "*Where* is the dish?" "*Where* is the napkin?" etc. Each time the learning facilitator asks the question, he should pause with an expectant expression for a moment as if anticipating the learner's response. If the learner does not respond after a brief pause (3 seconds or so), the learning facilitator can then point to, pick up, or touch the named object of "Where is the _____?" and say, "Here is the _____." Alternative responses would be, "This is Jason" (to "Who is this?") or "That is the *(ball, dog, window, etc.)*" (to "What is this?").
TERMINAL BEHAVIOR:	Learner indicates understanding of Wh-questions by behaving appropriately, i.e., naming the referent of *what* questions, pointing to the location of *where* questions, and naming or pointing to the person of *who* questions.

UNIT:	**T 1 / Hearing**
EPISODE:	**E / Understanding the Concept of One**
PURPOSE:	Learner will demonstrate an understanding of the concept of one.
ENTRY BEHAVIOR:	Learner demonstrates object recognition and can match like objects.
MATERIAL:	Two or three of each of the following: similar toys, utensils, clothing items (e.g., shoes, pants), blocks, clothespins, etc.
PROCEDURE:	

1. The learning facilitator places at least two objects before the learner and prompts the learner to examine them (i.e., touch, manipulate, look). As an illustration using blocks as the objects: As you place each block say, "Here is one block, here is another block...." After all blocks are placed, guide the learner through counting the blocks as you and he touch each one. You might say, "Let's count...1, 2, 3. There are three blocks — 1, 2, 3."
2. After the blocks have been placed, the facilitator proceeds to demonstrate the task of retrieving *one* block from the pile of two or three blocks. The learner's attention is drawn to the *one* block in the facilitator's hand.
3. The learner is then assisted in selecting *one* block in response to the direction, "Give me just one block." If the learner proceeds to give all the blocks, interrupt his response and repeat the model of taking just *one*.
4. Repeat the same procedure using the other sets of materials (e.g., clothespins).
5. During the day, provide opportunities for learning the concept of number by counting buttons on your coat, chairs in the kitchen, windows in the living room, napkins on the table, etc. Try to always associate your counting with meaningful, real objects so that the learner is not merely learning how to rote count but is learning the concept of number, or of what oneness is, what two-ness is, etc. Do this by asking where one window is, asking for one napkin, etc.

TERMINAL BEHAVIOR:	Learner is able to give just *one* object from many when given the directive "Give me one *(object)*."

UNIT:	T 1 / Hearing

EPISODE:	F / Direction Following

PURPOSE: The learner follows a direction involving the command "Give me the _____."

ENTRY BEHAVIOR: Learner attends to communicator by listening and watching.

MATERIAL: Familiar objects (e.g., hat, spoon, soap) or favorite toys.

PROCEDURE: Given one object or toy visible and within reach of the learner, the facilitator says, "Give me (or facilitator's name) the _____." The facilitator prompts a response by pointing to himself and then to the toy/object in association with the command. For example, "Give me (or facilitator's name) (pointing to self) the _____ (pointing to toy/object)." Then the facilitator may say, "Good, you (or child's name) gave me (or facilitator's name) the toy (object)," or "Good, you (or child's name) gave the toy (object) to me (or facilitator's name)." "I (or facilitator's name) have the toy (object)." Gradually fade the cues and prompts. It may be necessary for the facilitator to take the learner's hand and direct it toward the stimulus and then toward himself so as to teach the response of "giving." Repeat this process with numerous items of interest to the learner.

Variation Place three to five objects on a table in front of the learner. Begin by asking for one, then two, and finally three objects. Introduce three objects after the learner is able to retrieve two at a time.

Visual cues (to aid in retrieval of more than *one* object)
For two objects — put out both hands.
For two to three objects — use either boxes or colored paper to indicate the number of objects to be retrieved (i.e., a different color or box per object).

Auditory cues
Pause between each named object.
Vary intonation pattern (pitch) for each object.
Emphasize the position of the object that is consistently missed, e.g., if the second object in a series of three objects is missed, stress that object on presentation ("Give me the ball (cup, shoe)").
Repeat series twice initially, making certain that the learner attends to the presentations and does not begin to respond prematurely.

TERMINAL BEHAVIOR: Learner is able to follow a direction, *giving* one, two, or three objects, as requested.

UNIT I 2 / Seeing

The learner's use of vision to process information from the environment starts right after he is born. Many people used to think that the learner was unable to see adequately until well into early infancy. It is now known that even newborn learners can discriminate the face of a person at a relatively close range. In fact, research shows that the learner seems to be born with an interest in gazing at faces. Therefore, it is important to capitalize on this very important awareness to provide a variety of stimulating environmental and social experiences for the learner right from the beginning.

Many of the visual skills that the learner has are early precursors to later cognitive and intellectual skills. For example, following an object until it goes out of the learner's visual field is a beginning step toward understanding that objects do not cease to exist when they are no longer seen. This is the earliest kind of symbolic behavior that the learner exhibits. As the learner progresses in his development, the visual skills should be further developed because visual discrimination and attention to detail are quite important for later, more complex problem solving, including reading.

For the learner with a confirmed or suspected sensory deficit in the visual area, it will be necessary to experiment to find out what the learner can and cannot see. Of course, a vision specialist such as an ophthalmologist or an optometrist trained in visual problems of children should be consulted. Nevertheless, you may find that you will still have to experiment with different sizes and brightnesses of items and with varying distances of the items from the learner's eyes before you will know which materials can be seen adequately by the learner and which cannot. You can then rely on these materials to encourage visual responses from the learner and adapt all visually oriented learning episodes accordingly.

UNIT:	I 2 / Seeing
EPISODE:	A / Geometric Patterns
PURPOSE:	Learner focuses his eyes and scans a target.
ENTRY BEHAVIOR:	Learner is able to see.
MATERIAL:	Some cards that measure 8½″×11″ and have contrasting geometric shapes, such as a yellow and black bull's-eye, red and white checkerboard, red and yellow stripes. At the end of the year, some greeting card stores discard sample wrapping-paper books which have some appropriate paper for this activity. Otherwise cards can be made with construction paper. Whichever paper is used, gluing the paper on cardboard and covering it with contact paper will help preserve it.
PROCEDURE:	The facilitator can start by placing one card in one place where the learner typically rests. Check to see if the learner turns to gaze at the pattern. If no response is seen, cards may be placed on the sides of the crib, next to the changing table, or on a wall for the learner to see when held. Once the learner begins to focus on a pat-

tern at a particular place, gradual variations should be made by slightly changing the pattern used in that place or adding that pattern to another place.

TERMINAL BEHAVIOR: Learner looks at objects and pictures that are bright and have contrasting geometric shapes.

UNIT:	**I 2** / **Seeing**
EPISODE:	**B** / **Eyes Focus on Objects, Begin to Track**
PURPOSE:	Learner becomes visually aware of the environment and tracks moving object briefly.
ENTRY BEHAVIOR:	Learner is able to see.
MATERIAL:	Mobiles — commercial or homemade — with a variety of colors and shapes and patterns, including a noisemaker, such as a bell.
PROCEDURE:	Place the learner in an appropriate position on his front, back, or side (see Unit I 19, Episodes B, C, D). Hang a mobile within the learner's range of vision, and bounce the objects to create noise. Encourage the learner to look at the mobile, turning his head through manual guidance, bringing the mobile into visual range, etc. Praise him when he has focused on the objects. Then begin to move the mobile to one side slowly while still jingling the mobile. Again, encourage the learner to visually follow the objects, through manual guidance if necessary.
TERMINAL BEHAVIOR:	Learner focuses on the mobile and begins to visually follow movement of the objects.

UNIT:	I 2 / Seeing
EPISODE:	C / Eye Following Objects: Up and Down, Side to Side, On Stomach and Back
PURPOSE:	Learner learns to attend to objects and coordinate eyes in tracking.
ENTRY BEHAVIOR:	Learner can focus his eyes on an object 10 to 18 inches away from his face within his line of sight. Learner can hear.
MATERIAL:	Object that can make a sound and that is interesting for the learner to look at.
PROCEDURE:	Take an object such as a block with a bell in it, a rattle, or other fairly simple but interesting toy. Put the learner on his back and stand behind him so that he cannot see your face. Hold the toy in front of you and about 10 to 13 inches above the learner's face. Shake the toy or other noisemaker until the learner focuses his eyes on it. Watching the learner carefully so that you can see that his eyes follow the object, move the object to the left and then to the right, then up and down, and then in a full circle. First shake the object so that it makes a sound, then move the object silently as long as the learner will still look at it without the sound. After a few complete sequences, turn the learner over on his stomach. Stay behind him and repeat the game as before, dangling the item in front of the learner. Although you may use a toy that is a favorite of the learner for this activity, make sure that you do change the toy from time to time so that the learner will learn to follow many different objects.
TERMINAL BEHAVIOR:	Learner can follow an object *(that is kept noiseless)* with his eyes smoothly, no matter where it is moved in all areas of his visual sphere.

Variation

PURPOSE:	Learner will track an object with his eyes to both sides equally well.
ENTRY BEHAVIOR:	Learner tends to gaze more often or tracks more efficiently to one side.
MATERIAL:	The learning facilitator's face and voice and/or any interesting, developmentally appropriate, brightly colored toy that the learner recognizes and enjoys.
PROCEDURE:	The learning facilitator sits on the side of the learner which is the side that the learner has least efficient tracking. Learning facilitator then proceeds as with Learning Episodes I1A, I1B, or I2C, and I2D, emphasizing tracking through the least efficient side.
TERMINAL BEHAVIOR:	Learner can follow the face or toy, or locate a sound within a 180° horizontal arc in all planes.

UNIT:	I 2 / Seeing
EPISODE:	D / Tracking a Flashlight
PURPOSE:	Learner learns to attend to a light and coordinate eyes in tracking.
ENTRY BEHAVIOR:	Learner is able to discriminate light from dark.
MATERIAL:	A flashlight — either the small pencil variety or a regular flashlight covered with thick, colored cellophane paper. Make sure that the light would not cause you to turn your eyes away if you were to look directly into it.
PROCEDURE:	Position the learner appropriately on his back (see Learning Episode I22C) in a dimly lit room. Hold the flashlight about 12 inches above the learner's eyes, and shine the light down on his face at the midline. Once the learner gazes at the light, slowly move the flashlight from the middle to one side, taking care that the learner diverts his gaze; if necessary, physically turn his face to the midline and start again.
TERMINAL BEHAVIOR:	Learner can follow the light with both eyes smoothly.

UNIT:	I 2 / Seeing
EPISODE:	E / Visual Tracking Tube
PURPOSE:	Learner attends to an object and coordinates eyes in tracking.
ENTRY BEHAVIOR:	Learner is able to see small items at a distance of about 8 to 12 inches.
MATERIAL:	Fill a clean, unbreakable, plastic bottle or tube (about 8″ long) with a sterile, clear liquid. Insert a small (not small enough to be swallowed) brightly colored ball. Seal the bottle tightly.
PROCEDURE:	Place the learner in an appropriate semi-upright position and hold the tube or bottle horizontally in front of his eyes. Tap the bottle, or otherwise encourage the learner to look. When the learner focuses on the ball, tilt the bottle slightly, allowing the ball to roll from one end to another in a slow motion. Watch the learner's gaze to make sure he is following the ball. Tip the bottle back to float the ball in the other direction. When the learner is on his back, the facilitator can hold the bottle above him in a vertical position and reverse the bottle's position when the ball floats down.
TERMINAL BEHAVIOR:	Learner can follow the ball with both eyes smoothly horizontally or vertically.

UNIT:	I 2 / Seeing
EPISODE:	F / Two Eyes
PURPOSE:	Learner will demonstrate eye convergence in tracking.
ENTRY BEHAVIOR:	Learner can focus on an object 12 to 18 inches from his face, but has difficulty keeping both eyes on an object as it is moved toward his face.
MATERIAL:	Food, or an interesting and attractive toy that the learner can easily see.
PROCEDURE:	Place the learner in a supported, upright position that allows him to relax.
	Hold an interesting object at about the level of the learner's nose and at a distance of 12 to 18 inches. Move it slowly toward the learner's nose, making sure that both eyes continue to stay locked onto the object. When the learner reaches the point at which both his eyes are somewhat crossed and equally fixed on the object, or when one eye moves away from the object, begin to move it out again slowly, to a distance of 12 to 18 inches or until the learner's eyes are straight yet still focused on the item. Repeat several times. You can also encourage the tracking during the feeding time by slowly moving the spoonful toward the learner. Of course you would do this only if the learner was not frustrated by the slow pace of the movement.
TERMINAL BEHAVIOR:	Learner can keep both eyes equally on an object as it is moved toward his nose.

UNIT:	I 2 / Seeing
EPISODE:	G / Looking Back and Forth
PURPOSE:	Learner learns to shift his eyes rapidly from one thing to another.
ENTRY BEHAVIOR:	Learner can focus on and follow an object for 180°.
MATERIAL:	Pairs of objects that are interesting to look at and that can make a sound.
PROCEDURE:	Place the learner on his back (see Learning Episode I22C), or supported in a semi-upright position. Hold two very attractive objects of contrasting colors (black and yellow, blue and white, etc.), which also make a noise (like squeeze balls), about 12 inches from the learner's face and about 6 inches apart to begin with. Shake or squeeze one object to make a noise, and after a brief pause shake the other object so that the learner looks from one thing to the other. Then shake or squeeze the first object again so the learner looks back and forth. Gradually stop shaking the object so that the learner looks from one thing to the other without the sound to guide him. When the learner has looked from one object to the other several times, or when he begins to look around the room, replace one of the objects with a new one, and again encourage the learner to look back and forth, perhaps by shaking the objects one at a time. Continue replacing first one and then the other of the objects with a new one. Occasionally allow the learner to handle or play with one of the objects he has looked at should he act like he wants to. Turn the learner over on his stomach (Learning Episode I22B), and repeat the whole interaction by placing the objects just at the limit of the learner's reach, about 18 inches apart. As you did when he was on his back, encourage the learner to reach as well as look back and forth. If he does get either of the toys, allow him to grasp and handle the object for play, and praise his success.
TERMINAL BEHAVIOR:	Learner can look from one object to the other with smooth, rapid eye movements, without the sound cue.

UNIT:	I 2 / Seeing
EPISODE:	H / Attention to Hands
PURPOSE:	Learner builds an awareness of his hands.
ENTRY BEHAVIOR:	Learner is able to see his hands.
MATERIAL:	Wrist cuffs, Band-Aid, water soluble marker, favorite toy, masking tape, and mittens.
PROCEDURE:	The learning facilitator should work with one hand at a time. If there is a hand preference, start with the preferred hand. Vibrate or rub hand with a rough towel first. Then put a wrist cuff on the learner. Encourage learner to look at his hand and/or reach for a toy. Repeat the same activity with the other hand.
	Place a Band-Aid, or paint a face, on the back of the learner's hand. Encourage the learner to look at his hand by tapping it, by manual guidance, or by verbal cueing. Praise the learner for gazing at his hand. Be sure to remove the Band-Aid and painted face from the hand used first before repeating the activity with the other hand.
Variation I	Place a small mitten on one of the learner's hands, leaving it there for a few minutes. When the learner gazes at the mitten praise him. Then remove the mitten and place it on the other hand. You can cut the finger portion of the mitten off so the child's fingers are free to touch things. Move this mitten to the other hand after the learner has gazed at his hand.
Variation II	Place a large rolled up ball of masking tape in the learner's hands. Press the ball into the learner's hands so that it sticks lightly. Urge the learner to look at his hand, and encourage the learner to handle the tape ball.
TERMINAL BEHAVIOR:	Learner becomes aware of his hands and gazes at them or reaches with them purposefully.

Unit T 2 / SEEING

UNIT:	T 2 / Seeing
EPISODE:	A / Follow the Flashlight
PURPOSE:	Learner learns to track smoothly and to coordinate near- and far-point vision. Learner learns names of objects in environment.
ENTRY BEHAVIOR:	Learner can attend to novel stimuli, see, hear, and understand names of familiar objects in his environment, and is not afraid in a dimly lit room.
MATERIAL:	Means to close off direct light in room, such as heavy curtains or shades; flashlight.
PROCEDURE:	The facilitator explains to the learner that he is going to make the room dark and then use a light to find things around the room that the learner can name. The facilitator then turns out the lights and closes the curtains or shades. The facilitator turns on a flashlight and directs the beam along the wall and over the ceiling without shining it on any particular object until he comes close to the item to be "found." The beam of light then stops on that object, such as a lamp, table, or chair, and the facilitator says "The light shines on a _____." When the learner replies correctly, or when the facilitator has supplied the word because the learner has not responded after the pause, he then moves the flashlight slowly up the wall across the ceiling and then shines it on another object to be named, saying, "The light shines on the _____," and waits for the learner to reply.
TERMINAL BEHAVIOR:	Learner follows the flashlight beam smoothly with his eyes and either names the item on which the light beam rests or repeats the name of the item after the facilitator.

UNIT:	**T 2 / Seeing**
EPISODE:	**B / The Shell Game**
PURPOSE:	Learner learns to follow object which he cannot actually see through the use of visual imagery.
ENTRY BEHAVIOR:	Learner has demonstrated object permanence by following objects through the sequences of hiding an object under one cloth and then another without seeing the object in between the cloths. Learner can see and reach, grasp and lift, a small cup or container, or point or gaze at a fixed point.
MATERIAL:	Two containers, such as paper cups or plastic food holders; small attractive toy or bit of food.
PROCEDURE:	Seat yourself and the learner in an appropriate position (using Learning Episode I22M if necessary), face to face at a table or at his high chair. Put two containers, such as paper cups or plastic food holders, upside down on the surface between the two of you. Take something the learner likes, such as a bit of food, and hide it underneath one of the containers. Encourage the learner to pick up, point to, or gaze at, whichever container he thinks is hiding the object. Show the learner how to do it if he does not do it by himself. When the learner can indicate the right container without hesitation, hide the object under a container and then, while the learner is watching, slowly switch the containers around by sliding them over the surface of the table. Then encourage the learner to find the object. This game is self-correcting because if the learner indicates the wrong container he will not get the prize. If he guesses incorrectly, he will usually spontaneously indicate the other container and then can get the prize. Let the learner play with the small toy or eat the bit of food he finds.

As with many other games, you can gradually make this one more difficult by adding more containers, by making the containers identical to each other, or by making the learner wait a moment before he reaches or before you turn the container over so that he must remember under which container you have hidden the prize. You could do the latter by placing a barrier such as a board in front of the two containers after you have shown the learner where you have hidden the food or toy. At first you can wait just a few seconds, but gradually you can increase the time the learner must remember where the prize is without seeing the containers. Always allow the learner to reward himself by eating or playing with the prize when he finds it. |
| **TERMINAL BEHAVIOR:** | Learner follows cup with object in it wherever it is moved and successfully indicates the container to find the reward. *Or* the learner keeps eyes directed to the place where the correct container was placed even with a barrier between himself and the containers. When the barrier is removed he indicates the container immediately. |

Unit I 3 / TOUCHING

The experience of being touched and carried or moved about is an extremely important one from the standpoint of encouraging optimal development of the young child. Many of the tactile and kinesthetic sensory experiences that the child has are necessary precursors to later movement competency. This kind of sensory input provides the young learner with an opportunity to develop an awareness of his own body image. Research also suggests that some movement provides vestibular stimulation to the brain, which is important for total development, including later emotional stability and maturity. This is another very important aspect of the young learner's awareness of the touch of the facilitator. To be held and cuddled when in distress or discomfort definitely provides the young learner with a sense of caring and security. Therefore, touching contributes to the emotional development of the learner.

For learners with sensory deficits in other areas, or with motor handicaps, the sensation of touch becomes even more important as a learning channel. Touch can serve to cue and signal the learner when other senses may not provide this information. Touch is also so basic that it can often create an awareness in those learners who may behave as if they are closed off from other modes of interaction or who may need preparation for the experience of moving. Therefore, the learning facilitator should capitalize on the sense of touch, rather than taking it for granted, when creating a learning environment. An occupational therapist trained in working with young handicapped learners can often be of help in designing learning episodes.

UNIT: I 3 / Touching

EPISODE: A / Touch Pressure Stimuli for Tactile Awareness

PURPOSE: Learner will be able to show awareness of his body parts in response to touch pressure stimuli and become more aware of the feedback from his body moving about the environment.

ENTRY BEHAVIOR: Learner does not respond consistently to touch, nor shows awareness of body contact with objects.

MATERIAL: Soft, thick, terry cloth towel.

PROCEDURE: The facilitator places the learner on the floor or in a chair. The learner takes off his clothes or has them removed, except for shorts or diapers.

The facilitator takes a terry cloth towel and rubs the palm of the learner's right hand, using deep pressure. The learning facilitator spends the same amount of time rubbing the palm as it takes to count from 1 to 10. Then the facilitator moves the cloth to the forearm, working gradually toward the upper arm and shoulders, using slow, deep pressure to rub. The facilitator releases the right arm and rubs the left arm in the same sequence and with deep pressure. For the legs, the facilitator should do the same, starting from feet toward thighs.

When working on each body part, the facilitator should say to the learner, "I am rubbing your _____." The facilitator should encourage the learner to look at the part of the body he is rubbing.

Variation

Before any gross motor activity, the facilitator squeezes learner's palms and the soles of his feet gently but firmly with his hands.

TERMINAL BEHAVIOR:

Learner is able to move about effectively, using his body parts for balancing, and is able to use his hands purposefully in playing.

UNIT:	I 3 / Touching
EPISODE:	B / Feeling Objects for Comparison: Texture, Weight, Temperature, etc.
PURPOSE:	Learner becomes aware of different sensations and uses touching as well as looking for gathering information.
ENTRY BEHAVIOR:	Learner can grasp intentionally and hold an object for several moments. Learner can look at the object he is holding.
MATERIAL:	Pairs of objects which look like each other but which are really different in terms of texture, weight, temperature, etc. For example, a heavy and a light ball that are about the same size; two plastic bottles, one filled with cool water and the other with warm water; a chain made out of plastic, and one made out of metal.
PROCEDURE:	Get together a number of pairs of objects. Hand the learner one of the members of a pair of objects. Encourage the learner to shake, wave, bang, mouth, etc., the objects. Then hand him the other one of the pair, and encourage him to shake, wave, bang, mouth, etc. Tell him about each one of the objects, and praise his exploration of it. You will be preparing the learner for later language learning episodes (I16D and T16A). Then remove that pair, and hand him one member of another pair and repeat.
TERMINAL BEHAVIOR:	Learner anticipates differences between pairs of items by accommodating his grasp or movements to them. For example, he tenses his muscles to receive a heavy chain after a light one, he grasps a soft ball very gently after holding a hard one, etc.

UNIT:	I 3 / Touching
EPISODE:	C / Bean-Filled Box
PURPOSE:	Learner will handle various textures without avoidance or resistance and will begin to develop awareness of differences in textures.
ENTRY BEHAVIOR:	Learner can reach out and grasp or touch.
MATERIAL:	Flat boxes (preferably one with a lid for easier storage), dried beans of various kinds, dried peas, rice, oatmeal, raisins, plastic or metal cups for dumping and filling, spoon, small favorite toy.
PROCEDURE:	The facilitator will place the box partially filled with the items listed above within easy reach of the learner. The facilitator will put his hands in the box, handling the beans, filling the cups and dumping them to demonstrate to the learner what he can do. The facilitator encourages the learner to imitate. The learning facilitator may hide a small toy in the beans and ask the learner to "Find the toy" as a first procedure before dumping and filling (Learning Episodes I5D, T5A).
Variation I	The facilitator may introduce a large spoon with which to fill the cups. The facilitator will show learner how to hold the spoon, scoop up beans, and put them in the cup.
Variation II	
MATERIAL:	High chair or chair and table; smock; Crazy Foam (commercially available) or mixture of soap flakes, a little water, and food coloring, which has been whipped up in a mixer to the consistency of whipped cream.
PROCEDURE:	Place about two tablespoons of Crazy Foam or whipped soap flakes on table surface. From behind the learner, the facilitator will reach over learner and use two hands to play in the soap flakes (i.e., make large circles, dots, lines). The facilitator will gently place both of the learner's hands in soap flakes and encourage movement and exploration with both hands. If the learner resists touching the soap flakes, the facilitator will continue to demonstrate dabbing a little bit of the soap on the back of the learner's hands. As the learner does not withdraw, the facilitator can move around to the palms and then the fingers of the learner.
TERMINAL BEHAVIOR:	Learner will accept and be aware of different kinds of textures, playing in the various materials with pleasure, using both hands.

UNIT:	**I 3 / Touching**
EPISODE:	**D / Using Both Hands to Feel Textures**
PURPOSE:	Learner will consistently use both hands to feel objects and textures.
ENTRY BEHAVIOR:	Learner uses one hand more than the other to feel different objects and textures, but can move both hands.
MATERIAL:	Soft objects in room, e.g., velour towel, fur-like rug, stuffed animal, the family dog or cat, etc.
PROCEDURE:	The learner will be walked or carried around room, and the facilitator will show the learner various soft objects. If the learner is walked, keep arms raised by supporting under forearm. The facilitator will touch each object and say "soft." Support the learner at his shoulders and/or forearms so that he can reach with both hands. Encourage the learner to reach for an object with both hands and to stroke the object. Continue around the room, encouraging the learner to reach for all soft objects with both hands. Position objects at different levels so the learner will experience touching at different heights.
	Learning Episode I3C is also very useful for encouraging the use of both hands.
TERMINAL BEHAVIOR:	Learner will spontaneously reach for and touch, and/or grasp, objects with both hands.

UNIT:	I 3 / Touching
EPISODE:	E / Creepy-Feely
PURPOSE:	Learner will become aware of textures when rolling, crawling, and/or creeping.
ENTRY BEHAVIOR:	Learner demonstrates lack of awareness of different textures when in contact with them or behaves as though he is trying to avoid touching them.
MATERIAL:	Large paper bags cut in half; pieces of rug with different weaves and pile structures; fur or fur-like materials such as raincoat linings; soft bristle mats such as those used for wiping feet, etc.
PROCEDURE:	Using gross motor learning episodes such as I14B, I14D, I14E, I14F, and I14G, the learning facilitator encourages the learner to move over the varying surfaces, which have been placed in his path.
TERMINAL BEHAVIOR:	Learner shows acceptance of movement over different textures by failing to avoid any surfaces, and/or the learner indicates recognition of the change in the surface texture by looking down as he moves over a changing surface.

Unit I 4 / SENSORY INTEGRATION

It is very important from the standpoint of optimal development of the learner that he learn to coordinate and integrate the various senses for full information processing and awareness of the environment's learning potential. Therefore this separate unit for learning episodes that involve more than one sense of the young learner has been developed. Very early in infancy it appears that learners can efficiently attend to only one sensory event at a time. Later they gradually begin to be aware of incoming information from more than one sense and are able to understand information that is more and more complex in a meaningful manner. For the learner with a sensory impairment of one kind or the other, it is essential to emphasize the capability of the remaining senses without neglecting the possibility of providing input for the deficient sense. The learning facilitator can read the entry behaviors of the learning episodes to find which are most beneficial to learners having various sensory deficits. The learning facilitator can also adapt learning episodes to help compensate for any of these deficits.

UNIT:	**I 4 / Sensory Integration**
EPISODE:	**A / Exploring with Mouth**
PURPOSE:	Learner learns how different objects taste and feel. The learner practices speech movements by mouthing objects.
ENTRY BEHAVIOR:	Learner is not overly sensitive in his mouth. The learner avoids exploring toys with his mouth.
MATERIAL:	Several toys or objects that can safely be placed in the learner's mouth.
PROCEDURE:	At a relaxing time during the day, with the learner in a position that allows the learner to be relaxed (Learning Episodes I15B, I15C), the facilitator presents a favorite toy to the learner. The facilitator encourages the learner to reach for the toy himself and explore it by putting parts of it in his mouth to feel the texture. The facilitator simply describes the toy and how it feels or tastes, saying, "You have your rattle in your mouth. Oh, that's smooth," etc. If the learner does not put the object in his mouth by himself, the facilitator may guide his hand to the toy and help him bring the toy to his mouth.
TERMINAL BEHAVIOR:	Learner purposefully explores toys by mouthing them, practicing the mouth movements necessary for speech.

UNIT:	I 4 / Sensory Integration
EPISODE:	B / Finding an Object with Eyes and Ears in a Complete Circle
PURPOSE:	Learner learns how to search for objects in his environment with both his eyes and his ears.
ENTRY BEHAVIOR:	Learner can find noisy objects with his eyes in a field of vision 180° in diameter. Learner can sit, or sit with support, swivel head and trunk, reach out, and grasp or touch. Learner has some hearing.
MATERIAL:	Squeaky toys or noisy objects like bells or rattles.
PROCEDURE:	Sit the learner in the middle of the floor, supported as necessary. Without letting the learner see you, place the squeaky toy behind his back and squeak it, moving your hand away quickly. Encourage the learner to look for the toy. If the learner looks in the wrong direction, put your hand around the learner again and squeak the toy. If the learner cannot find the toy directly behind his back, put it more to the side so he can see it easily as he turns. When the learner finds the toy, praise him and allow him to play with it for a while. See if you can get him to hand it back to you. Get his attention away from the toy in your hand, and place the toy around the other side in back of him when he is not looking, and squeak it again. Repeat the game, but make sure that the learner does not become frustrated by letting him have the toy to play with for a few minutes when he gets it.
TERMINAL BEHAVIOR:	Learner can turn directly toward the sound of an object and reach out without hesitation to pick up, or look at, the object, wherever it is placed around him.

UNIT:	**I 4 / Sensory Integration**
EPISODE:	**C / Touch and Name Body Parts**
PURPOSE:	Learner increases sense of self in relation to others and learns names of body parts.
ENTRY BEHAVIOR:	Learner has some hearing.
MATERIAL:	Items that are gentle to the touch but that have different textures, such as cotton balls, wash cloths, the smooth side of a powder container, a plastic bottle filled with warm water, etc.
PROCEDURE:	When the learner has only a diaper on, or no clothes at all, place him on his back in his crib, on the floor, or any place where you can touch the learner's body easily and he can move freely. Lean over the learner and smile. Start at the learner's head and gently touch his head, cheeks, chin, tummy, shoulders, hands, arms, legs, and feet, saying, "This is your head, this is your cheek, this is your tummy," etc., as you touch the learner.
	Repeat the process in a different sequence by blowing on the learner's arms, legs, neck (but not directly in his face), touching him with a cotton ball or other texture, with warm or cool objects, hard or soft objects, textured or smooth objects, etc. Turn the learner on his stomach, and repeat the procedure by touching or stroking the learner's back and the back of his arms, legs, etc., while speaking as above.
TERMINAL BEHAVIOR:	Learner responds to the voice and touch of the facilitator by changing his activity level and following movements with his eyes, if possible.

UNIT:	**I 4 / Sensory Integration**
EPISODE:	**D / "This Little Pig": Hands and Feet**
PURPOSE:	Learner becomes aware of individual body parts.
ENTRY BEHAVIOR:	Learner has some hearing.
MATERIAL:	None.
PROCEDURE:	This is the traditional game in which each finger or toe is touched and gently wiggled following the rhyme. After you wiggle each little "pig" (finger or toe), run your finger up each arm or leg and across the learner's body to his chin or nose saying, "wee, wee, wee, all the way home." This game is usually great fun for the learner and can often calm him when he is fussy. However, it may cause some learners with tight muscles to become too tense. If this occurs, discontinue and switch to a more calming activity.
TERMINAL BEHAVIOR:	Learner anticipates game by offering hand or foot, watching the facilitator, and showing increased excitement as the time to go "all the way home" approaches.

UNIT:	**I 4 / Sensory Integration**
EPISODE:	**E / Swinging**
PURPOSE:	Learner will accept new movements which help to prepare the balance system for movement.
ENTRY BEHAVIOR:	Learner has difficulty moving self around in environment and displays negative responses, such as crying, grimacing, etc., to movement by the facilitator that is different in some way.
MATERIAL:	Large beach towel or blanket and two facilitators.
PROCEDURE:	A learning facilitator places the learner lengthwise in the center of the blanket. Each facilitator takes two corners of the blanket and raises the learner slowly off the floor. The facilitators swing the learner gently from side to side. The facilitators should watch for changes in expression, color, and tone, including rapid breathing, stiffening of body parts, arching backwards of the head, pale skin color, or rapid movement of eyes. Rocking should be discontinued if any of these occur or if fussing persists. The speed of the rocking can be varied according to the learner's toleration.

Variation

1. Movement can also be up and down instead of side to side. While moving up and down, bounce learner's bottom gently on the floor.
2. Roll the learner from side to side by each facilitator simultaneously raising the same side, then lowering it and raising the other side of the blanket.

The facilitators should label the movement, e.g., "We're going side to side," "back and forth," "up and down," "bump, bump," etc.

TERMINAL BEHAVIOR:	Learner shows enjoyment of 2 to 5 minutes of rocking by smiling.

UNIT:	I 4 / Sensory Integration
EPISODE:	F / Thermal Awareness
PURPOSE:	Learner will develop awareness of and respond to different temperatures in order to become more alert to body sensations.
ENTRY BEHAVIOR:	Learner shows little or no awareness to heat and cold.
MATERIAL:	Ice (cubes, popsicles, ice cream), warm and hot foods and beverages, two or three 3- or 4-ounce flat plastic bottles, film roll containers, washcloths or sponges, bath water — warm, cold, and tepid.
PROCEDURE:	The facilitator will remove the learner's clothes before all of the following activities, which may be done at different times throughout the day. The learner should always be placed in a relaxed position.

1. The facilitator will allow the learner to rest in tepid bath water for a few minutes after bathing. The facilitator will remove the learner from the tub, cool the water, and place the learner back in the tub for a few moments, covering the learner with the cool water. The facilitator will remove the learner from tub and run hot water into the tub until it is quite warm, then place the learner back in the tub, covering the learner with warm water and keeping him in it for a few moments. Each time the learner is removed from the water, he should be wrapped in a towel and lightly patted dry, but should not be stimulated by vigorous rubbing. Vigorous rubbing and active tactile stimulation may be done a few minutes after the last dip in the water (Learning Episode I3A).
2. The facilitator may fill a bottle with cold water, wet a sponge with cold water, or wrap an ice cube in a plastic bag and rub one of these on the learner's back, particularly between the shoulders, on the back of the arms, hands, and sole of the feet. The facilitator may also allow the learner to lick or mouth the ice cube or popsicle.

   The facilitator may then apply warmth to the learner's chest, back, hands, and feet, 2 or 3 minutes after applying the cold application, by using a small bottle filled with warm water or a warm washcloth.

   During all of these activities the facilitator should label the temperature for the learner, e.g., "The bottle is cold," "Now the bottle is hot," etc.

TERMINAL BEHAVIOR:	Learner will know when he is feeling hot or cold and respond by a change in facial expression or looking around.

UNIT:	I 4 / Sensory Integration
EPISODE:	G / Localization of Touch
PURPOSE:	Learner will localize to touch and build body awareness.
ENTRY BEHAVIOR:	Learner can look at different parts of his body.
MATERIAL:	Variety of textured cloths and materials — rough/smooth, hot/cold, etc. Bottles filled with hot, warm, cool, and cold water.
PROCEDURE:	The facilitator will undress the learner and place him in a relaxing position. Then the facilitator will touch the learner on his skin at a point where he is not looking at the moment. The facilitator will continue touching the learner until he looks at the spot where he is being touched. If there is no response, the facilitator should try a rougher texture or more extreme temperature. The most sensitive areas are the hands and feet, while the least sensitive is the back area. Therefore, the facilitator should start with encouraging the learner to localize touch on his hands and feet, and gradually move to the trunk for localization. In the same way the stimulation may become more challenging, from being rough to being smooth and from being warm or cool to being neutral.
TERMINAL BEHAVIOR:	Learner will consistently look at the spot where he is touched by objects of various textures and temperatures.

COGNITIVE / AFFECTIVE EPISODES

Unit I 5 / PROCESS — SPATIAL RELATIONSHIPS

> Cognitive processes are those that provide experience for the learner in developing understanding of, and the ability to control, his environment. These are "processes" because they are not specific events, but means to develop intellectual capabilities from the standpoint of solving all kinds of problems and developing all kinds of strategies for effective information processing.
>
> Understanding spatial relationships means learning about one's place in the world and developing an efficient means of understanding and predicting the different effects and actions of objects in space. It includes understanding of depth, volume, equilibrium, and distance, among other properties. For young learners spatial understanding is somewhat dependent on movement, and learners who have movement deficits are at a disadvantage. For these learners the facilitator must be especially conscientious to provide visual experiences and to manage to involve the infants in alternative modes of experiencing movement that are acceptable to them and that develop understanding of spatial movement.
>
> These and the other cognitive learning episodes are based on the theories of Jean Piaget and are placed in a sequence suggested by the Uzgiris-Hunt Ordinal Scales of Infant Development. (Uzgiris, I. C., and Hunt, J. McV. 1975. *Assessment in Infancy: Ordinal Scales of Psychological Development.* University of Illinois Press, Urbana).

UNIT: I 5 / Process — Spatial Relationships

EPISODE: A / Knocking a Toy Off a Surface, Taking Turns Putting It Back

PURPOSE: Learner learns the concept of gravity and understands the path of falling objects.

ENTRY BEHAVIOR: Learner has demonstrated ability to follow a slowly moving object with his eyes and to find an object with his eyes on the basis of the sound that it makes. Learner can swipe with his arm.

MATERIAL: Variety of favorite toys; appropriate surface such as crib railing or high chair tray.

PROCEDURE: While the learner is sitting at his table or standing in his crib, balance a toy on the edge of the table or on the crib rail. Encourage the learner to knock it off. When he does, say "Down it goes, down goes the _____," and pick it up for him from where it has fallen. Learners often start this game themselves and will continue until you get tired. You could then trade places with the learner. Sit in a chair and knock the toy off the arm of the chair to the floor. Ask the learner to pick it up for you. You can show him how to do it while saying, "Hand the _____ to me, give the _____ to me, thank you," etc.

TERMINAL BEHAVIOR: Learner participates actively in knocking down and picking up toys. Learner anticipates place of landing with gaze.

UNIT:	I 5 / Process — Spatial Relationships
EPISODE:	B / Anticipating Movement of Objects
PURPOSE:	Learner will develop awareness of how an object moves or will move so that he can actually predict this movement.
ENTRY BEHAVIOR:	Learner has some vision and follows objects or people.
MATERIAL:	Colorful toy which is a favorite of the learner and which makes noise, or one which is a novel noisemaker.
PROCEDURE:	Sit the learner in a relaxed position in a quiet room. The facilitator should hold the toy at the learner's eye level, 7 to 12 inches in front of the learner's face and where the learner can see it. When the learner is looking at toy, the facilitator slowly moves toy around the learner's head in a clockwise direction. The learning facilitator continues moving the toy in a slow circle around the learner's head until it returns to the starting point in front of the learner. If the learner does not track it, encourage him by making noise until he follows it to the limit of his ability to turn his body. Then pause, making noise at the other side of the learner's head. The learner will not follow the toy with his eyes all the way around the circle by turning his trunk/body, but instead will turn his head to the left while the toy is still moving past the back of his head, in anticipation of the toy's reappearance on the left side of his head. Then repeat, moving around the other way. When the learner is able to anticipate the toy's reappearance, move the toy around the learner's head in the same way more rapidly, playing a type of chasing game.
Variation	The learner is seated in a comfortable position. The facilitator gets the learner's attention by talking to him and makes eye contact with learner. Standing a few feet away from the learner, the facilitator walks slowly around the learner in a circle in a clockwise direction. If the learner does not track the facilitator he can call the learner from a position at the other side of the learner's head. The learner will not follow facilitator with eyes all the way around the circle by turning trunk/body, but instead should turn his head to the left while the facilitator is still moving in back of the learner, in anticipation of the facilitator's reappearance on his left side. When the learner is able to anticipate the facilitator's reappearance, the facilitator will move around the learner more rapidly, alternating directions. A chase game can result which is fun for both.
TERMINAL BEHAVIOR:	Learner will turn his head to the side of the oncoming toy or person to anticipate the reappearance of the toy or person.

UNIT:	**I 5 / Process — Spatial Relationships**
EPISODE:	**C / Mirror Play: Facilitator, Learner, Toy**
PURPOSE:	Learner increases understanding of position of body and object in space.
ENTRY BEHAVIOR:	Learner has previously demonstrated discrimination between the mirror images of himself and of the facilitator.
MATERIAL:	Upright mirror large enough to permit viewing full length of learner, the upper part of facilitator's body, and a toy to be shown to the learner; several attractive toys with noisemaking qualities.
PROCEDURE:	As with other mirror games, hold the learner in your arms or stand him before a mirror so that both of you can see each other clearly. Hold a toy or other object in various positions (high or low, close or far away, one side or the other of you and the learner) so that the learner can see the object in the mirror but has to search to find where it actually is in the space around him. At first you can use a toy that makes a noise to direct his looking. Later encourage the learner to find the toy by looking only, without being helped by the sound of the toy.
TERMINAL BEHAVIOR:	Learner can turn and reach directly for toy anywhere in the space surrounding him after seeing it in the mirror.

UNIT:	I 5 / Process — Spatial Relationships
EPISODE:	D / Put and Take Different Objects from Different Containers
PURPOSE:	Learner will understand the relationship between a container and the things that fit into it.
ENTRY BEHAVIOR:	Learner has voluntary reach, grasp, and release and will remove objects from containers.
MATERIAL:	A number of containers of different sizes and shapes, such as buckets, coffee cans, etc.; toys or objects having different sizes and shapes, such as necklaces, blocks, cotton balls, etc.
PROCEDURE:	Start with a small object and a wide-mouth container. Show the learner how to drop in and take out the objects from the container, and encourage him to do it himself. In the beginning the learner may put in and take out one object at a time from the container, or he may just take it out and you may have to put it in again. As his skills and attention increase you can make the game more and more difficult by using larger and larger objects that have to be put in smaller and smaller openings of the containers. You can also encourage the learner to put more and more objects in a container before he turns it over and dumps them out.
TERMINAL BEHAVIOR:	Learner can place many closely fitting objects through the opening of a container into the container, and then dump them out to repeat the process.

Unit T 5 / PROCESS — SPATIAL RELATIONSHIPS

UNIT: T 5 / Process — Spatial Relationships

EPISODE: A / Dump and Fill

PURPOSE: Learner understands relationship between different size containers and material to be contained.

ENTRY BEHAVIOR: Learner can reach, grasp, and release. Learner has removed objects from containers in play. Learner has shown interest in dropping objects and observing results.

MATERIAL: As many different size containers and fillers as possible: pails, boxes, jars, pots, etc., for containers; dry beans, water, sand, rice, etc., for fillers.

PROCEDURE: You can vary this popular game by using different size containers and different kinds of fillers. Use pails, boxes, jars, pots, etc., as containers at different times and dried beans, water, sand, rice, etc., to show the learner filling and dumping, refilling and pouring. Just as you can use different materials to keep the game from boring the learner, you should also use different words and a different approach to the game from time to time. You can say, "dump," "pour," "turn over," "spill out," etc. To develop a clear understanding of the concept of quantity, encourage the learner to place as many items as possible in the container to fill it up before he dumps them out.

TERMINAL BEHAVIOR: Learner can fill any size container with material, dump the items out, and refill the container.

UNIT:	T 5 / Process — Spatial Relationships
EPISODE:	B / Water Play: Pouring, Object Properties
PURPOSE:	Learner understands nature of a liquid and its relationship to spaces. Learner understands the effect of a liquid on different items.
ENTRY BEHAVIOR:	Learner has demonstrated eye-hand coordination sufficiently to hold container and to fill and pour water from the container. Learner can discriminate edible from inedible substances. Learner has demonstrated interest in dump and fill activities.
MATERIAL:	A basin of water, several containers of different sizes, items that demonstrate different characteristics when placed in water, such as tissues, sponges, floating soap.
PROCEDURE:	Place a basin of water and several containers of different sizes in front of the learner. Undress the learner or cover him up. Also cover the area around him with waterproof material so that you do not have to worry if he spills the water. Besides helping the learner splash and pour the water from one container to the other, show him the effect of the water on several different objects. You could use things that float, sink, absorb, fall apart, etc., when placed in the water. Encourage the learner to handle these things and describe them to him as he plays. You can show the learner many surprises. For example, you can press a floating object under the water and then let it go so it pops to the surface. You should also encourage the learner to experiment on his own; praise his efforts and describe the results using the agent-action construction, i.e., "The soap floats," "The paper tears," etc.
TERMINAL BEHAVIOR.	Learner shows good control over the water when pouring and systematically experiments with effects of the water on different objects. For example, he repeatedly squeezes and fills up a sponge, repeatedly presses floating objects under the water and watches them rise, etc.

UNIT:	**T 5 / Process — Spatial Relationships**
EPISODE:	**C / Block Building**
PURPOSE:	Learner will understand the effect of gravity and balance and will better understand the concept of size.
ENTRY BEHAVIOR:	Learner can reach, grasp, and release and has combined two activities in play, such as performing pat-a-cake while playing with blocks.
MATERIAL:	Any kind of smooth-surface blocks, either homemade or commercially available.
PROCEDURE:	Blocks are one of the best toys you can give to the learner because they can be used in so many ways. Not only can you take turns in building towers and knocking them down, but you can also encourage the learner to copy different designs that you make and sometimes you too can copy his designs. You can also pretend that the blocks are "cars" on the road, "beds" for little dolls, and many other imaginary things. You and the learner should use the blocks in as many different ways for as many different activities as you both can think of. Start off by showing the learner towers of two or three blocks and encouraging him to build while leaving your model for him to copy. Then move on to other building and pretend games after he has built towers of four or five.
TERMINAL BEHAVIOR:	Learner can imitate simple forms, such as towers, bridges, and trains. Learner can also construct similar forms on his own. Learner can use blocks imaginatively in pretend play.

UNIT:	**T 5 / Process — Spatial Relationships**
EPISODE:	**D / Form Board Play**
PURPOSE:	Learner will develop an understanding of spatial relationships and goal-directed behavior.
ENTRY BEHAVIOR:	Learner has sufficient fine motor coordination to place a regular shape into its space. Learner will imitate the behavior of the facilitator.
MATERIAL:	Commercially available or homemade form boards with simple shapes, such as a circle, square, and triangle.
PROCEDURE:	Form boards with different shapes can be used, but if form boards with more than one shape are used they must be simplified by removing just one form (the circle) which will be used for placing. Later the more difficult forms, such as the square or triangle, can be removed to be replaced. Still later more than one shape at a time can be removed for replacement. The boards with three different shapes of different sizes can help the learner discover how to arrange shapes by size as well as learning to match the shape to the form. Even simple form boards can help the learner to find new solutions if the facilitator will rotate the board after the pieces are removed. You can use your imagination and your facilitating ability to demonstrate and encourage the learner to use the form boards in different ways, gradually making the games more and more difficult as the learner learns the easier tasks. Make sure you label the shapes as you use them and emphasize the verb, i.e., "*Put* the square in the hole."
TERMINAL BEHAVIOR:	Learner can remove and replace a variety of shapes from form boards directly even if the form board is rotated or its position is otherwise changed from the first presentation.

Variation

ENTRY BEHAVIOR:	Learner has demonstrated understanding of placement of simple forms, such as the circle and square, into spaces in form board.
MATERIAL:	Commercially available shape sorter boxes or Tupperware Ball.
PROCEDURE:	This game is a combination of the form board (Learning Episode T5D), and the dump and fill game (Learning Episode T5A). You can start off by handing the learner a circle or cylinder, which is the easiest form to put in the space. Then you can move on to the squares and other shapes which are more difficult to place in the spaces. You can also help the learner to learn to wait if you gradually encourage him to put more and more shapes in before he opens the box or ball to take or dump them out.
TERMINAL BEHAVIOR:	When placed in a random array in front of him, the learner can place all the various shapes in the shape sorter, remove the shapes, and replace them.

Unit I 6 / PROCESS — OBJECT PERMANENCE

The child's demonstration of understanding that an object or person does not cease to exist simply because it or he can no longer be seen is the first indication of representational thinking on the part of the young learner. This capability interacts with, and is related to, spatial relationships. The development of object permanence is also related to later language development. Language is a symbol system and is dependent on representational thinking. Therefore, when a learner signals that representational processes have begun by finding a hidden object, an enormously significant developmental milestone has been reached. There is a new level of awareness and a new opportunity for lesrning.

Learners who are mentally handicapped will be slower in the acquisition of cognitive processes, and the learning facilitator must take care to provide a wide variety of these experiences to enable slower learners to generalize this understanding to many situations.

UNIT: I 6 / Process — Object Permanence

EPISODE: A / Disappear/Reappear

PURPOSE: Learner learns to anticipate the direction of movement of a slowly moving object and to predict outcome.

ENTRY BEHAVIOR: Learner is able to watch an object moving anywhere in his field of vision and will linger at the point of disappearance of this object.

MATERIAL: Sheet of plywood or heavy cardboard about 12″ × 15″, small doll, car, or other interesting toy.

PROCEDURE: This game is another variety of the hide and seek games. Hold a sheet of plywood, about 12″ × 15″ in size, horizontally on the floor or table between you and the learner. "Walk" a doll, push a car, etc., toward and then behind the sheet of plywood, and continue pushing the toy along in a straight line until it reappears on the other side of the plywood. The learner will begin to show that he understands that the object or toy is traveling in a straight line behind the screen by following it as if he can see it, and watching for the toy where it reappears. Once he does this, start the toy moving in the opposite direction and proceed behind the barrier. Do this game until the learner can guess where the toy will reappear no matter what toy you use or from which direction it starts.

TERMINAL BEHAVIOR: Learner anticipates place where toy will emerge from behind the screen when pushed in a straight line from point of entry, no matter where that original point of entry was.

UNIT:	**I 6 / Process — Object Permanence**
EPISODE:	**B / Hide and Seek: Getting Partly Hidden Object**
PURPOSE:	Learner learns to recognize object even though its appearance has changed.
ENTRY BEHAVIOR:	Learner has shown by his behavior that he recognizes familiar objects in different positions. Learner can coordinate reach and grasp.
MATERIAL:	Small cloth, like a diaper, about 12″ × 15″; variety of small toys that do not make noise and that have a definite top and bottom, such as a small doll.
PROCEDURE:	Position the learner across from you at a low table in such a way that he can reach easily across the surface of the table in front of him with his arms. Place a small and desirable toy or a piece of food within easy reach of the learner on the top of the table. As the learner begins to reach for the object or food, partly cover it over with a cloth, making sure that part is still visible. Encourage the learner to take away the cloth and find the object, or to reach under the cloth and get the object. If the learner hesitates, you can demonstrate this for the learner until he gets the idea. Repeat this game at different times, using several different cloths and several different objects.

Variation

ENTRY BEHAVIOR:	Learner has shown by his behavior that he recognizes familiar objects that are in different positions. Learner can make swiping motions with his arms.
MATERIAL:	Piece of cardboard in a triangular shape (bend triangle in center so that it can stand on its base); variety of small toys that do not make noise.

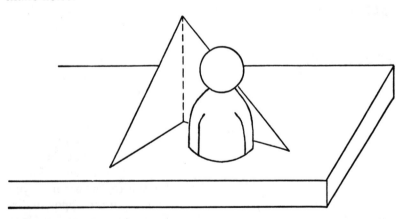

PROCEDURE:	Position the learner on his stomach over the facilitator's thigh so that the learner's underarms are supported by the thighs (Learning Episode I22A). In this position the learner's hands will be in his visual field. Place a small and desirable toy or a piece of food

within easy reach of the learner. As the learner begins to reach for the object or food, partly cover it by placing the cardboard between the toy and the learner. The cardboard should be at least 11″ at the base and 8″ on the sides. Of course the size of the cardboard may vary depending on the size of the toy, but most of the toy should be hidden so the learner can see only a part of it. Encourage the learner to knock over the cardboard, and find the object. You can demonstrate this for the learner until he gets the idea. Repeat this using different objects and sizes of cardboard.

TERMINAL BEHAVIOR: Learner immediately reaches for any covering of a desired item, removes it or knocks it over and grasps or indicates the item.

UNIT:	**I 6 / Process — Object Permanence**
EPISODE:	**C / Barrier Game: Object in View**
PURPOSE:	Learner learns to overcome obstacle and move in an indirect path to solve a problem.
ENTRY BEHAVIOR:	Learner can coordinate reaching and grasping. Learner has learned to move obstacles in order to get what he wants.
MATERIAL:	Small piece of Plexiglas about 10″ × 12″; attractive toys or bits of food.
PROCEDURE:	Sit the learner on your lap in such a way that he can reach around in front of him easily. Put an attractive toy within the learner's reach. As he reaches for the toy, place a piece of Plexiglas between him and the toy, and encourage him to get the toy. Make sure that you place the barrier and the toy in such a way that it is possible for the learner to reach around the barrier in order to get the toy. At first you can praise the learner for getting the toy in any way, whether it be knocking down the barrier, pushing it aside, etc. However, gradually encourage him to reach around the barrier for the object, by demonstrating and holding the barrier firmly to make it more difficult to move.
TERMINAL BEHAVIOR:	When presented with a barrier he can see through, the learner reaches around the Plexiglas and grasps the object without hesitation.

UNIT:	**I 6 / Process — Object Permanence**
EPISODE:	**D / Hide and Seek: Finds Object that Has Disappeared**
PURPOSE:	Learner develops imagery and ability to remember.
ENTRY BEHAVIOR:	Learner has shown that he understands objects will reappear by looking to the point at which they will appear and by looking for things that have fallen.
MATERIAL:	A large, clear-plastic refrigerator container with a plastic lid the learner cannot see through. A slit or hole should be cut in the lid big enough for small toys to fall through easily. A number of small and attractive toys, such as cars or animals.
PROCEDURE:	Sit the learner across from you on the floor or at the table, and show the learner how to play with the toys (small cars, animals, etc.) by pushing them or "walking" them on the top of the container described above. As each toy falls through the lid, show the learner where it is by lifting up the box and pointing out the toys through the clear bottom of the box. When all the toys have fallen through, remove the lid, let him pick up the toys and play over again. This learning episode fits nicely with Dump and Fill (Learning Episode T5A) and Form Board Play (Learning Episode T5D).
TERMINAL BEHAVIOR:	Learner begins to pick up the box to search for the toys himself after they have fallen through the hole.

Unit T 6 / PROCESS— OBJECT PERMANENCE

UNIT:

T 6 / Process — Object Permanence

EPISODE:

A / Find Object under Box

PURPOSE:

Learner develops ability to imagine objects and remember them without a visual hint.

ENTRY BEHAVIOR:

Learner can remove soft covering from hidden object. Learner can coordinate reaching and grasping or knocking over a cup or container.

MATERIAL:

Several small boxes that the learner can grasp, or cups with handles; small toys that do not make noise and that will fit under the boxes or cups.

PROCEDURE:

Put a favorite toy or piece of food in front of the learner. As the learner reaches for the toy or food cover it with a box or cup. Encourage the learner to take the box away to get the food or toy. Allow him to play with the toy or eat the food when he gets it, and be sure to praise him for his success. Repeat with different boxes and toys.

TERMINAL BEHAVIOR:

Learner immediately grasps or knocks over box covering toy, lifts it, and picks up toy.

UNIT:	T 6 / Process — Object Permanence
EPISODE:	B / Unwrap a Toy
PURPOSE:	Learner learns to keep the image of an object in mind while solving a problem using a complex motor act.
ENTRY BEHAVIOR:	Learner has solved hide and seek problems using cloth and box. Learner has ability to hold, grasp at midline with both hands, and release.
MATERIAL:	Several kinds of paper, ranging from very soft paper like tissue to stiff paper like tin foil; small and interesting toys.
PROCEDURE:	Take a toy that is a favorite of the learner's and, while he is watching you, wrap it up in a piece of paper. Then hand it to him and encourage him to "unwrap the toy," "find the toy." At first you can use paper, like tissue, that unfolds easily. Later you can use paper, like tin foil, that is more difficult and takes more effort to unwrap. Always allow the learner to play with the toy he unwraps for a few moments. He can do this while you are wrapping up another toy to hand to him.
TERMINAL BEHAVIOR:	Learner grasps offered and wrapped toy and unwraps it with ease.

UNIT:	**T 6 / Process — Object Permanence**
EPISODE:	**C / Searching Game: Alternating Two, Then Three, Covers**
PURPOSE:	Learner learns to make correct choice to solve a problem while remembering an object.
ENTRY BEHAVIOR:	Learner can pick up or indicate the correct one of two cloths when object is always placed under a cloth.
MATERIAL:	Two or three cloths that are similar and about 12″ × 15″ in size. Two or three cloths that are different and about 12″ × 15″ in size. Several small toys that do not make noise.
PROCEDURE:	In this hiding game you would first put the toy under one cloth for the learner to find. After he finds it, hide it the next time under the other cloth. After he finds it there, reverse the order of hiding. The game can be made more and more complicated by adding more cloths or by making it harder to tell the difference between cloths. Instead of using cloths with three different patterns, for example, three diapers can be used and you can hide the toy randomly under each of the three diapers.
TERMINAL BEHAVIOR:	Learner makes correct choice each time and removes cloth to pick up or indicate object directly.

UNIT:	**T 6 / Process — Object Permanence**
EPISODE:	**D / Searching Games: Two, Then Three, Times Hidden**
PURPOSE:	Learner learns to keep the image of an object in mind while problem solving in a distracting situation.
ENTRY BEHAVIOR:	Learner can find and pick up an object hidden under any single covering.
MATERIAL:	Two pieces of cloth about 12″ × 15″ that are similar in appearance and two pieces that differ in appearance; several interesting toys that do not make noise.
PROCEDURE:	Sit the learner at a table so that he can reach confortably all around in front of him. Put two different cloth towels on the table in front of the learner. Take a favorite object or toy and, while the learner is watching you, put it under one of the cloths. While the learner is still watching you, and making sure he can still see the object in your hand, take the object out from under the first cloth and move it underneath the second cloth. Leave it there and take your hand away. Encourage the learner to find the toy or object. If he seems confused, show him where the toy is and repeat the sequence several times. Then encourage him again to find the toy. If the learner still seems confused, return to the "Hide and Seek: Getting Partly Hidden Object" game (Learning Episode I6B) so he can have more success, and try this episode later. If he does manage to find the toy, praise him for his success and allow him to play with the toy for a little while. Do not forget to use different toys for the learner to find and different cloths under which to hide the toy so the idea can generalize.
Variation	When the learner can do this episode with success every time, add a third cloth and move the toy in the same way from the first to the second to the third cloth, leaving it finally under the third cloth. You can also vary the game by moving the toy from one cloth to the other in different directions, still leaving it visible in your hand between each move.
TERMINAL BEHAVIOR:	Learner reaches directly for toy after removing correct cloth.

UNIT:	T 6 / Process — Object Permanence
EPISODE:	E / Find Toy Moved from One Hiding Place to Another
PURPOSE:	Learner searches for objects that are not in their original hiding places and realizes toys can be moved without him seeing them being moved.
ENTRY BEHAVIOR:	Learner can find a toy hidden under one cover.
MATERIAL:	Small toy with which the learner enjoys playing; hiding materials, such as small washcloths; plain containers or boxes that are not see-through and one that is.
PROCEDURE:	The learner should indicate an interest in the toy to be hidden by playing with it for a minute or two. As the learner watches, the facilitator takes the toy and places it in a container. The facilitator then lifts the cover and dumps the toy from the container directly under the cover so that no part of the toy can be seen. The learner should go for the toy under the cover. If he does not, the facilitator can show him where the toy is and try the activity again until the learner gets the idea. If the learner is frustrated with this learning episode, the facilitator should make it easier to find the object by first hiding it in a see-through container and then demonstrating the hiding process to the learner.
TERMINAL BEHAVIOR:	Learner can find a toy moved from one hiding place to another without actually seeing the toy moved.

Unit I 7 / PROCESS — CAUSE AND EFFECT

Infant and toddler learners need to practice what makes things go and work in their environment and to discover their own role in those actions. As the infant comes to understand that he can be effectively causing events to occur reliably in his environment, a sense of competency and self-reliance develops.

For learners with movement deficits, it is especially important to take extra time to provide them with experiences that will lead them to understand their potential for causation and to develop their sense of mastery.

UNIT: I 7 / Process — Cause and Effect

EPISODE: A / Repeat an Interesting Act

PURPOSE: Learner learns that he can cause his environment to react reliably according to his movement.

ENTRY BEHAVIOR: Learner can focus with his eyes on an object 8 to 10 inches away.

MATERIAL: Commercially available or homemade "cradle-gym," attached to crib rails in such a way that it hangs about 8 to 10 inches away from the learner's face.

PROCEDURE: Place the learner on his back in his crib so that either his hands or his feet are close to the cradle-gym which has been stretched across the rails of his crib. Bring the learner's attention to the cradle-gym by shaking it, pointing to it, bending down so that your face is behind it, etc. As the learner gets excited, his movements will become more vigorous and he will wave his arms or kick his feet. As he does this, bounce the mattress near the cradle-gym so that it moves and the learner gets the idea that his movements cause the cradle-gym to react. At first smile and encourage the learner's movements to increase so he activates the cradle-gym. Then, as he regularly hits or kicks the gym, gradually move away so that he cannot see you. In this way he can give his full attention to the cradle-gym and continue his efforts to move it, building awareness of the relationship between his actions and the reaction of the cradle-gym.

TERMINAL BEHAVIOR: Learner moves vigorously enough to make the cradle-gym move, watches the effect, then repeats the action on his own.

Variation

ENTRY BEHAVIOR:

Learner looks at moving objects with interest and can direct his hand or arm movements.

MATERIAL:

Toys with parts that move when hit with little effort such as Three Men in a Tub, ball, balloon, and toys with rocker bottoms.

PROCEDURE:

With the learner in a proper position for optimal arm movement (Learning Episodes I22B, I22C, I22D), the facilitator places a toy in front of the learner. If the learner does not try to get or move the toy, the facilitator demonstrates how the toy moves and encourages the learner to imitate the movement through voice or manual guidance. At first, praise the learner for a movement toward the toy and move it yourself if necessary. As the learner begins to move the toy, gradually withdraw your praise and guidance to let the reaction of the toy itself reward the learner for his movements.

TERMINAL BEHAVIOR:

Learner repeats a movement over and over to see the resulting reaction of a toy.

UNIT:	**I 7** / Process — Cause and Effect
EPISODE:	**B** / Different Toys, Different Ploys
PURPOSE:	Learner discriminates the responses that are appropriate to specific toys and playthings and is able to carry out these appropriate responses.
ENTRY BEHAVIOR:	Learner is able to reach, grasp, poke, hit, or perform a specific response demanded by the toy presented to him. Learner shows interest in the actions of the facilitator.
MATERIAL:	Several toys, each of which demands a specific response on the part of the learner. These toys could include bells, a Surprise Box, a Busy-Box, a squeeze toy, or a roly-poly bear.
PROCEDURE·	Place the learner in a position that is relaxing and allows free movement of his arms and hands. Place a particular toy in front of the learner and demonstrate the response necessary to activate the toy. For example, if it is the bell, pick up the bell, ring it, and then put it down in front of the learner. Encourage the learner to imitate you. If the learner does not comply, either ignoring the bell or picking it up without using the specific response (ringing), perform the appropriate response again for the learner. This may have to be done several times before the learner imitates your response. Initially these demonstrations may also have to be followed by manual guidance of the learner's actions. Some toys are particularly good for this activity because they are self-correcting. For example, the Surprise Box cannot be activated unless the learner performs the required act. With these toys the reinforcement for performing the action is built into the response of the toy. With other less structured toys, such as the bell, the facilitator may have to be more active in reinforcing the learner for performing the action himself.
TERMINAL BEHAVIOR:	Learner assesses the required response of any particular toy or play material presented to him and performs that response appropriately.

UNIT:	**I 7 / Process — Cause and Effect**
EPISODE:	**C / Playing with One Toy in a Variety of Ways**
PURPOSE:	Learner interacts with one object in a variety of ways, exploring and exploiting the properties of the object.
ENTRY BEHAVIOR:	Learner watches or imitates the facilitator.
MATERIAL:	A pull toy or other toy that displays some action when handled.
PROCEDURE:	While the learner is seated comfortably at a table, present the toy. Encourage the learner to examine the toy in different ways by demonstrating some of these, such as pushing the toy back and forth on the table top like a car, spinning a wheel, pulling the toy by a string. Encourage the learner to imitate your actions by verbal directions or manual guidance.
TERMINAL BEHAVIOR:	Learner spontaneously interacts with a new toy in a variety of ways, exploiting the many properties of the toy.

UNIT:	I 7 / Process — Cause and Effect
EPISODE:	D / Getting Toy by Pulling Cloth
PURPOSE:	Learner learns to use things in his environment to get what he wants.
ENTRY BEHAVIOR:	Learner can reach and grasp from a sitting position. Learner has shown goal-directed behavior.
MATERIAL:	Several pieces of cloth about 1 foot in width, varying in length from 1 to 3 feet. Several small, attractive toys.
PROCEDURE:	Put the learner on your lap in front of a table so that the table is the right height for him to easily reach his arms across it. Put a large, attractive toy or piece of food big enough for the learner to see clearly on a piece of cloth. Encourage the learner to "get the food" or "get the toy," pointing to the item. If the learner reaches for the toy or food directly and fusses because he does not understand that he can pull it toward him on the cloth, show him how he can pull the object toward him by pulling on the cloth for him. Without letting the learner have the toy or food the first time, put it back on the cloth in the original position and repeat your demonstration two or three times. However, do not allow the learner to become so frustrated that he does not enjoy the activity. After two or three times of showing the learner how to get the toy or food on the cloth, encourage him to do it himself and to play with the toy or eat the food that he gets.
TERMINAL BEHAVIOR:	Learner smoothly pulls the cloth toward him and reaches directly for the toy or food as soon as it is within range.

UNIT:	**I 7 / Process — Cause and Effect**
EPISODE:	**E / Pull the String to Get the Toy: Horizontally, Vertically**
PURPOSE:	Learner learns to make a connection between the toy he wants and the string attached, to overcome his impulse to reach directly for what he wants, and to use problem-solving abilities effectively in all spatial areas, including overcoming gravity for getting things vertically.
ENTRY BEHAVIOR:	Learner has thumb and finger grasp and has had experience handling lengths of string.
MATERIAL:	Several interesting toys or favorite foods to which strings of different thicknesses can be tied. Lengths of string, from 2 to 4 feet, of different thicknesses.
PROCEDURE:	Sit the learner on your lap at a table approximately level with his chest so that he can reach easily all around him. Attach strings of different lengths to several of the learner's favorite toys. Put one of these toys beyond the learner's reach and lay the attached string out toward the learner's hands so it is within easy reach. Encourage the learner to pull the toy toward him with the string by demonstrating, giving verbal directions, pointing to the string, or providing manual guidance. When the learner can solve this problem on the table top by pulling the toy toward him smoothly without demonstration, place the toy on the floor with the string arranged in front of the learner on the top of the table. It might be necessary to hold the string on the table with your finger, without the learner noticing if possible. Point out the toy on the floor, and encourage the learner to "pull in the *toy*." If the learner hesitates, show him how to pull the object up by the hand-over-hand method. Do not forget to let him play with the toy he gets after pulling it in with the string.
TERMINAL BEHAVIOR:	Learner grasps string immediately with good pincer grasp, and, using hand-over-hand technique if necessary, pulls toy toward himself and grasps effectively to play with it.

UNIT:	**I 7 / Process — Cause and Effect**
EPISODE:	**F / Wind Up an Action Toy**
PURPOSE:	Learner learns that mechanical activities have an outside source for powering their action.
ENTRY BEHAVIOR:	Learner can focus on, and attend to, a moving stimulus.
MATERIAL:	Several toys that move by themselves after being wound up, pushed, or poked. Some examples include commercially available Surprise Boxes, jack-in-the-boxes, clowns that spin along parallel bars, wind-up frogs that jump, motor cycles that move, roly-poly clowns that rock when pushed.
PROCEDURE:	Wind up or push the toy as appropriate to start its action. Encourage the learner to watch the toy as it performs, until it stops. Then show him how to start it up again. A wind-up toy will usually be too hard for a young learner to do himself, so you can ask him to give it to you whenever it needs to be wound. The other types can be activated by the learner, and the facilitator should wait several seconds to give the learner a chance to try to activate the toy himself before restarting the action for the learner.
TERMINAL BEHAVIOR:	Learner attends to toy throughout its activity, then either restarts the action himself and waits until the action subsides or hands the toy to the facilitator for restarting.

Unit T 7 / PROCESS — CAUSE AND EFFECT

UNIT:	T 7 / Process — Cause and Effect
EPISODE:	A / Peg Pound
PURPOSE:	Learner learns to coordinate hands and use tools. Learner also learns effect of different strengths and weights on objects.
ENTRY BEHAVIOR:	Learner can grasp toy hammer and has begun to relate two separate objects.
MATERIAL:	Commercially available peg pounder. Some peg pounders have removable pegs or balls, some do not. For younger learners, those without removable parts are more effective. For older learners who can persist with a task and enjoy novelty, the kind with removable pegs or balls are more interesting as they must put them in and observe where the pegs exit at the end of the bench to retrieve them.
PROCEDURE:	Present the pounder to the learner after placing him in a relaxed sitting or kneeling position at a table. If the learner does not begin to hit the pounder by himself, you can show him how you hit the pegs through the holes and point them out on the other side of the "bench." Turn the bench over or replace the ball. Then let him try, and praise him for his efforts. You can guide his hand, but do not expect him to be accurate right away. At first he will just want to bang the hammer against the bench. Later you can work at showing him the purpose of accurately hitting each peg or ball.
TERMINAL BEHAVIOR:	Learner can effectively knock pegs or balls through holes, observe the resulting action, and turn toy over to repeat knocking action or to indicate to the facilitator that repositioning of the pegs is necessary.

UNIT:	T 7 / Process — Cause and Effect
EPISODE:	B / Using Stick to Drag in Toy
PURPOSE:	Learner learns to use implements in the environment not connected to a desired item to extend his own reach and solve a problem.
ENTRY BEHAVIOR:	Learner has demonstrated understanding of pulling a string to retrieve a toy. Learner can grasp a stick with his hand and swing it in an arc.
MATERIAL:	Dowel stick about 3/8″ in diameter and 12″ long. Small, attractive toys that do not roll too easily so that their movement can be controlled by the stick.
PROCEDURE:	Sit at a table holding the learner on your lap so that he can reach easily across the table, and place an attractive toy just out of his reach. Then place a stick so that one end of the stick is in easy reach of the learner's hand and the other end is next to the toy that the learner cannot reach with his hand alone. Show the learner how to solve the problem of dragging in the toy with the stick if he does not do it by himself. You may have to demonstrate this several times. Once he gets the idea of pulling the toy toward him with the stick, put the toy in all positions on the table that are possible for him to reach. In the beginning use an easy toy for the learner to get and one that he really likes. Do not forget to encourage the learner for his efforts, because this episode is often hard on his coordination and concentration and can be frustrating to a learner eager to get the toy. Also, do not forget to vary the problem by using different toys and sticks, and also by putting the learner and toy on the floor or in other situations.
TERMINAL BEHAVIOR:	Learner immediately grasps stick and effectively drags toy toward him with a sweeping motion, grasping the toy as soon as it is within range.

Unit T 8 / COGNITIVE CONTENT — CLASSIFICATION, SERIATION, GENERALIZATION

For the older toddler learner who has already demonstrated the beginning of the development of concepts and the use of symbols, this unit is designed to help him use these processes to solve various problems involving understanding of class membership (what goes with what), seriation (beginning understanding of number values and numerical sequences), and generalization (the ability to apply solutions experienced in one situation to another). These activities will give the learner practice in developing useful concepts that are precursors for many skills usually performed in formal schooling.

For the learner who seems to be slower in the learning process than his peers, it may be necessary to break these and the other cognitive learning episodes into smaller steps so that terminal behaviors can be achieved more readily. If this is done, each task involved in the learning process becomes easier to understand and do; then, neither the learner nor the learning facilitator should become discouraged.

UNIT:	T 8 / Cognitive Content — Classification, Seriation, Generalization
EPISODE:	A / Learner Opens Jar to Take and Put
PURPOSE:	Learner learns to combine fine motor skills with cognitive concepts about volume and space in order to solve problems.
ENTRY BEHAVIOR:	Learner can hold a jar with one hand and turn the lid with the fingers of the other hand. Learner has demonstrated previously an interest in dump and fill activities.
MATERIAL:	Clear plastic or heavy glass jars with openings large enough for a number of small toys to be placed inside and dumped out, but small enough for the learner's hands to be able to grasp. These can be formula bottles, plastic honey jars, etc. The lids should require only one or two turns to screw or unscrew. The objects or toys selected for putting in and taking out of the jars should correspond with the size of the jars: larger items for larger jars, smaller

items for smaller jars. Jars and objects with as wide a range of sizes as possible should be selected.

PROCEDURE:

When you start this game encourage the learner to drop some of the objects you have selected into the jar. While he watches you, screw the lid on the jar just enough so that it will come off easily when it is turned. Hand the jar back to the learner and tell him to "open the jar and dump out the buttons" ("beans," "checkers," or whatever you have used). You may have to show the learner how to turn the jar top several times and then hold his hand and guide him in the twisting motion. After the learner can manage to take the lid off and dump the objects out, encourage him to "put the buttons *(or other item)* back in the jar," and after he has done this to "screw on the lid." There are many variations you can play with this learning episode. It is especially good for changing roles and letting the learner be the "teacher" who selects the jar and objects to be used, puts them in the jar, screws on the lid, and hands the jar to you to open it up and start the process again.

TERMINAL BEHAVIOR:

Learner can select objects of appropriate sizes to be placed in the jars, put them in, screw the lid on, screw the lid off, and dump out the objects.

UNIT:	T 8 / Cognitive Content — Classification, Seriation, Generalization
EPISODE:	B / One- or Two-Piece Puzzles
PURPOSE:	Learner learns to place irregular forms in correct alignment with background, using cues of color and shape to form a coherent whole. Learner develops understanding of part/whole relationships.
ENTRY BEHAVIOR:	Learner has demonstrated adequate eye-hand coordination and finger dexterity to manipulate irregular forms. Learner has demonstrated understanding of filling spaces by doing dump and fill and/or simple form board activities.
MATERIAL:	Commercially available puzzles having irregularly shaped, one- or two-piece, meaningful forms, such as fruit, toys, etc. Puzzles can also be made by the facilitator by gluing magazine pictures on a cardboard background and cutting these into two pieces.
PROCEDURE:	First show the learner how the puzzle pieces fit into the spaces or fit together. Then take one piece out and hand it to the learner and wait expectantly for him to replace it in the space. If he does not do it, demonstrate yourself saying, "Put the *(item)* in." You can show him in this way repeatedly until he gets the idea. After he knows where the piece goes you can hand the puzzle to the learner with the piece in place, then take the piece out for him to replace. When he can take the piece out and put it back in himself one at a time, you can do the same thing taking out two pieces. Finally, hand him the puzzle with the pieces in place and show him how he can turn it over, dump the pieces out all at once, and replace them. Demonstrations, instructions, praise, encouragement, etc., should be given to the learner at each step.
TERMINAL BEHAVIOR:	Learner can dump pieces out of a puzzle deftly and directly and can replace them. Learner can put together homemade puzzle pieces that have no frame when the pieces are presented in order.

UNIT:	**T 8 / Cognitive Content — Classification, Seriation, Generalization**
EPISODE:	**C / Stacking Rings**
PURPOSE:	Learner practices eye-hand coordination and learns to order according to size.
ENTRY BEHAVIOR:	Learner can grasp donut-shaped ring and place it over a pole.
MATERIAL:	Commercially available stacking rings with cone base.
PROCEDURE:	Sit the learner in a relaxed position. Place a set of the commercially available graduated stacking rings which come in a cone in front of the learner with the rings in place. Take all the rings off the cone for the learner and hand them to him one at a time in their correct order for the learner to replace. Demonstrate or manually guide the learner as needed. Praise him for any effort toward replacing the rings. Then either you or he can take the rings off the cone. Let him replace them in any order at first. Continue alternating the "correct" one-at-a-time procedure with the one he does himself. As he begins to put the rings on the cone without any difficulty, you can stop the one-at-a-time procedure, place all the rings out for him to choose, and begin to help him select the correct size. Later, the graduated size of the cone will be self-correcting and the learner will not need to be guided.
TERMINAL BEHAVIOR:	Learner can select the correct ring from large to small from a complete range of rings and place them in order on the stacking cone.

UNIT:	**T 8 / Cognitive Content — Classification, Seriation, Generalization**
EPISODE:	**D / Attribute Blocks**
PURPOSE:	Learner is introduced to concepts of size, shape, and color.
ENTRY BEHAVIOR:	Learner has demonstrated intuitive understanding of differences in shapes and sizes by correctly solving shape sorters and form boards or by discriminating size, color, or shape.
MATERIAL:	Commercially available Attribute Blocks consisting of circles, squares, triangles and rectangles, which are each red, yellow and blue, thick, medium, and thin, and small, medium, and large.
PROCEDURE:	These are special blocks for teaching size, shape, and color. Even before learners can use the words that describe the blocks, they can use them for sorting and matching games. At first, you should be careful not to confuse the learner with too many different blocks. You might start by selecting one dimension (shape, color, or size) and encouraging the learner to pick out from several additional blocks the one that matches the one you are holding in your hand or have put in front of him. You can demonstrate to the learner what you want him to do and correct him simply by selecting the right block while saying, "The square block goes with the square block." When he gets the idea of matching you can make the episode a little harder by getting him to choose among more blocks or blocks that are more similar.
	You can also show the learner how to sort, and could start by placing all the blocks of one color in one place or container, and all the blocks of another color in another place or container, etc. Make sure that you do not confuse one attribute, for instance, shape, with another, like color. For example, if you were sorting shape, you initially would keep color, size, and thickness constant. Then, when the learner gets the idea of piling the blocks in different places, depending on the chosen attribute, you can show him how he can separate them by another attribute. Again, when you are teaching the learner about shapes, do not confuse him by using different colors or sizes. Stick to the one attribute you are trying to teach the learner. Later you can move on to two dimensions (shape and color). There are many creative ways you can use these blocks for helping the learner to develop concepts.
TERMINAL BEHAVIOR:	Learner correctly selects matching block on basis of single, common attribute. Learner can place all blocks with single, common attribute in piles correctly, following a single example of the facilitator's, or on his own initiative.

UNIT:	**T 8 / Cognitive Content — Classification, Seriation, Generalization**
EPISODE:	**E / Correctly Choosing the String with Toy Attached**
PURPOSE:	Learner solves more complex problems by combining simpler behaviors.
ENTRY BEHAVIOR:	Learner has demonstrated ability to pull toy attached to a string toward him in order to get the toy.
MATERIAL:	Two or three pieces of heavy string or yarn about 3 feet in length. (The decorative kind used to tie packages is ideal.) Several toys that are attractive to the learner, or the kind of cookie or apple ring with a hole in it.
PROCEDURE:	Place one toy, or a piece of food, with a string tied to it on the table in front of the learner. Place another empty string, which is different from the correct string, next to the string that is attached to the toy. Encourage the learner to "get the toy." Praise him if he pulls the correct string, or direct him toward the right string if he does not get it himself. When the learner pulls the correct string of two parallel, different ones, make the problem more and more difficult by adding another string, by crossing the strings over, by using similar strings, etc. Let the learner play with the toy for a few moments or take a bite of the food each time he gets it.
TERMINAL BEHAVIOR:	Learner can choose the correct string without trial-and-error methods by following each string with his eyes to its source and thus selecting the correct string to pull. The pulling is then done directly and assertively, and the toy or food is grasped immediately.

Unit I 9 / SELF-IMAGE

> The learner's self-image is important for development because it guides his perception of himself among people and his judgment of his capabilities to perform according to his own and others' expectations. If the learner develops a realistic understanding of his body and its capabilities, the learner generally will gain positive feedback from his performance in activities that appropriately tap his capabilities. If the learner begins to show an awareness of the perception of his body and engages in activities that are too difficult for him, thereby providing him with almost constant negative feedback from the social and physical environment, he may develop a poor sense of his own self and his capabilities. The learner's accurate awareness and understanding of himself and his capabilities are critical to his overall development, and activities that foster a realistic self-concept will ultimately be beneficial to optimal development in all areas.

UNIT: I 9 / Self-Image

EPISODE: A / Pat-a-Cake: Hands and Feet

PURPOSE: Learner learns to use two hands together and to imitate social behavior.

ENTRY BEHAVIOR: None.

MATERIAL: None.

PROCEDURE: This is the traditional "pat-a-cake" game, which is fun for both learner and facilitator. Make sure you use the learner's name and your own name as well as the pronouns "me" and "you," when you say, "Pat-a-cake, pat-a-cake, baker's man. Bake me *(or facilitator's name)* a cake as fast as you *(or learner's name)* can. Roll it, and pat it, and mark it with a 'B'. Put it in the oven for Baby and me." Repeat using the feet of the learner.

TERMINAL BEHAVIOR: Learner anticipates actions of the facilitator from his language and participates in "pat-a-cake" motions spontaneously.

UNIT:	I 9 / Self-Image
EPISODE:	B / Naming and Touching Body Parts
PURPOSE:	Learner learns to know position and limits of body parts and to recognize their names.
ENTRY BEHAVIOR:	None.
MATERIAL:	Pieces of cloth or other materials of various textures or temperatures.
PROCEDURE:	This game is like many of the other games that involve touching parts of the learner's body, but, even with young learners, the emphasis can be on the word rather than on just the sensory stimulation alone. While you have always talked to the learner while touching his body with this game, it is now very important to emphasize the name of the body part as you touch that part of his body. You can emphasize the word by saying it a little louder than the other words you use and by repeating it frequently. For example, "This is your *hand, hand, hand,*" while grasping the learner's hand and squeezing it or stroking it with a terry cloth towel or other material. (This language can also be used for Learning Episode I22E.)
TERMINAL BEHAVIOR:	Learner shows recognition of the name of a body part by pointing to, or holding out, the part of his body that the facilitator names.

Unit T 9 / SELF-IMAGE

UNIT: T 9 / Self-Image

EPISODE: A / Body Parts: Function

PURPOSE: Learner learns the capabilities of each named body part.

ENTRY BEHAVIOR: Learner will tolerate having a sense momentarily closed off. Learner recognizes the name of body parts. Learner has visual or auditory acuity that is sufficient to allow discernment of differences between a free sensory condition and one that is partially closed off.

MATERIAL: None.

PROCEDURE: This is another game of touching and naming the body parts of the learner. This time, however, the emphasis is on *what* the body part *does*. First, touch the learner's ears and name them, then cover his ears so that your voice is slightly muffled and say again, "You *hear* with your ears." Then take your hands away and repeat, "You hear with your ears." As you touch the learner's mouth say, "This is your *mouth*," and pat it gently. Usually the learner will then make a sound and you can say, "You *talk* with your mouth." Continue this game, saying such things as, "You *pat* with your hands," after you pat; "You *stamp* with your feet," after stamping; "You *wiggle* your fingers," etc.

TERMINAL BEHAVIOR: Learner can show he understands the function of a body part by either naming what the part can do in response to a question such as "What do you do with your ears?" (hear), or by performing an action in response to a question like, "What do we do with our feet?" (stamp).

UNIT:	**T 9 / Self-Image**
EPISODE:	**B / Mirror Play with Pictures of Learner and Facilitator**
PURPOSE:	Learner learns to tell the difference between the real self, the mirror image, and pictures of himself and the facilitator. This way he learns that real things can be represented many ways.
ENTRY BEHAVIOR:	Learner shows understanding of difference between himself and mirror image and between facilitator and facilitator's mirror image by turning to the actual facilitator in response to a question while viewing himself and the facilitator in the mirror.
MATERIAL:	Colored pictures, such as a Polaroid snapshot, of facilitator's head and shoulders and learner's head and upper body together. Mirror large enough for upper part of facilitator's body and most of learner's body to be reflected when facilitator is holding learner or when the learner is standing next to the facilitator in such a way that both their heads are level.
PROCEDURE:	Tape a picture of the learner and yourself to a mirror. Hold the learner in your arms up to the mirror so that he can see both himself and you in the mirror as well as the pictures of himself and you. Point to the learner's reflection in the mirror. Use the learner's name and encourage him to pat or point to his own reflection. Then point to the picture of the learner, and encourage him to point to or pat the picture. In this way the learner can see the difference between a picture which does not move and his own mirror image which moves as he moves. You can then do the same thing with yourself and with your picture, having the learner touch your own face, your face as reflected in the mirror, and the picture of your face in turn.
TERMINAL BEHAVIOR:	Learner demonstrates comprehension of difference between photograph and mirror image by moving in response to mirror image or by performing, and by simply pointing to, or looking at, photograph.

UNIT:	T 9 / Self-Image
EPISODE:	C / "Mary Wore Her Red Dress"
PURPOSE:	Learner's self-awareness is increased by hearing and/or singing a song incorporating his name and a description of an item of his clothing.
ENTRY BEHAVIOR:	Learner has normal hearing, with amplification, if necessary, and recognizes his name.
MATERIAL:	No special equipment is needed. The facilitator should practice chanting or singing the suggested song (or another of his own choosing) until he can chant or sing it, incorporating each learner's name and a possible item of clothing, with ease. One song is given; others could be used.

We suggest limiting the description of the clothing to naming the color and the item, that is, *red* dress, *brown* shoes, *green* and *white* shirt, and so forth. Color is a relatively easy attribute or characteristic for the learner to identify, so it is a good place to start. Also, if the learners do not already know the color names, the concept of "color" will be confused if the facilitator sings about Mary's *red* dress, Jerry's *striped* shirt, Nita's *white* socks, and Marcos' *corduroy* slacks. Make it easy for the learners to form the concept of particular colors and color in general by singing about only one attribute of the clothing — color.

Perhaps at a later time, when there is less chance of confusion, the whole grouping could be changed to *plaid* shirt, *striped* slacks, *dotted* dress, *checked* shirt, etc.

Many songs of this type suggest singing about *new* shoes and a *new* dress. This should be used cautiously with any group since we want Marcos to feel good about himself and his brown slacks, whether they are new or not.

PROCEDURE:

"Mary Wore Her Red Dress" can be used with an individual learner, a small group of learners, or a larger group. Procedures for all these are discussed below.

Use of the song with individuals or small groups would probably arise spontaneously in response to something a learner (or group of learners) did in his activities. For example, a learner might come to the facilitator to show his cowboy boots. After he has shown and told about them, the facilitator can share his pride by singing, "Terry wore his brown boots, brown boots, brown boots...."

The song might be used at group time in a variety of ways. It could be used as a song to invite the learners to story time, as an extra song to help form the content of story time (perhaps combined with opening a suitcase full of clothes, identifying and talking about them), or as a song to tell each learner he can go outside.

One suggested procedure for using the song to help form the content of story time follows: Have the learners and facilitator seated in chairs or on the floor. A circular or amphitheater arrangement is an ideal setting for such activities.

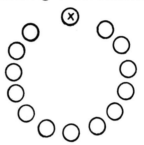

This arrangement is suggested so that each learner can see every other learner and so that the facilitator can stay in one place and sing the song, just looking at the learner whose name he is saying. However, it is far more effective to move around from learner to learner, kneeling or sitting beside him as you sing about him. If the facilitator kneels slightly to the side of the learner, facing into the group, he can establish the desired rapport with one learner without losing the attention of the other learners. In addition, moving to the learner you are singing about helps the other learners identify him and the item of clothing that is being mentioned.

As the facilitator sings about blue jeans, or a yellow shirt, he can lightly touch the item mentioned, so the learners know what it is he is talking about. This should only be done however, if he feels the learner will welcome it. Some learners do not like to be touched in this fashion, and their feelings should be respected. If in doubt, do not touch. The rapport and warmth that comes from personal contact will have to be established in other ways with these learners.

If the learners seem to be losing interest, the song can be shortened by singing only the last line.

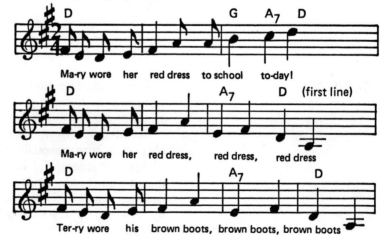

Nita wore her blue dress to school to-day!

A shortened version of the song, perhaps the last line, could also be sung to those learners who sometimes feel uneasy when a song is addressed to them.

As mentioned in the introductory material, the specific materials recommended to develop a learner's positive self-image are really only reflections of the genuine respect and affection that the learning facilitator must have for each learner. Much of this is communicated in ways other than words — a smile, a shared pleasure, a pat on the shoulder, a tolerance of shortcomings, pride in accomplishment. Some of it can be communicated through this song.

TERMINAL BEHAVIOR:

When the learner's name and an item of his clothing occur in the song, he indicates that he realizes the song is about him: he may smile, sit up and look at the facilitator, or hang his head, turn away, or leave.

UNIT:	**T 9 / Self-Image**
EPISODE:	**D / "Where, Oh, Where Is Dear Mario?"**
PURPOSE:	Learner's spoken name is used in a song to invite him to come to the group time or storytime. The learner indicates his recognition by coming to the group or by indicating that he does not want to come.
ENTRY BEHAVIOR:	Learner must have normal hearing and recognize his name.
MATERIAL:	No special material is needed. The facilitator should practice chanting or singing the suggested song (or another of his own choosing) until he can sing it, incorporating each learner's name with ease. An audio tape recorder can be helpful in perfecting this. It is also suggested that the facilitator practice some of the suggested variations so he can use them to be more responsive to the particular situation that develops. One song, to the tune of "Paw, Paw Patch," is given:

Where, oh, where is dear Ma-ri-o, where oh, where is

dear Ma-ri-o, where, oh, where is dear Ma-ri-o?

Here he is right here.

PROCEDURE:	This learning episode is very flexible and can be altered to meet the varying physical facilities, routine schedules, and learner capabilities that are found in an individual learning environment.
	If the learning environment is the flexible, active place that is recommended, the learners will probably be engaged in a number of activities when the approximate time for group time arrives. Although group time should be placed in the schedule at an hour when it interferes least with the learner's self-directed activities, perhaps just after a snack, some learners will be quite involved in their own activities. Rather than trying to get everyone to stop what they are doing, try getting a learner or two to help put the area for group time in order. Arrange what chairs or rugs are free, and start the song. The aim is to pull the learner to the group time, using his name to catch his attention.
	Start the song, "Where, Oh, Where Is Dear Mario?" using the names of the learners who are there. If only two or three are there, sing the whole song to each learner. This will give the other learners in the room time to finish their activities and come if they want to. As each learner comes, he is helped to find a place to sit,

and is sung to. Be sure to smile, to communicate to the learner that you are pleased he is there. If there are eight or nine learners in the group from the very beginning, the song may be shortened to keep them from losing interest.

Where, oh, where is dear Ma-ri-o, where, oh, where is

dear So-phi-a, where, oh, where is dear lit- tle Ruth?

Here they are right here.

Those learners who do not come to the group time can be included by changing the last line to something like, "In the other room," or "Playing with the clay." Do not insist that the learner come to the group time. The use of his name, active songs and games, and interesting stories at his level of understanding will, it is hoped, attract him to come because he wants to.

Learners exhibit a variety of reactions to hearing their names used in a song. Some smile broadly, look straight at the facilitator, and enjoy having the facilitator smile at them. Some hang their heads and will not look at the facilitator, giving him the clue that the learner may not want him to look straight at him. Others giggle and duck their heads, but continue to smile. Most of the learners will tell you if you accidentally omitted them or one of the other learners.

It is suggested that this song be used without accompaniment, so that the facilitator can be free to help a learner find a chair, rearrange a mat, remove distractions, and in other ways prepare the learners for what is to follow in group time.

Learners who are confident and have the language capability can be encouraged to supply the last line of the song, "Here I am right here," or "Building with the blocks," but be cautious about introducing this too soon. The step from listening to speaking out on one's own is a large one; some learners have to grow a lot, both in confidence and in competence, before they are able to take this step.

TERMINAL BEHAVIOR:

When his name occurs in the song, the learner realizes that he is being referred to and can indicate whether or not he wants to come to the group.

UNIT:	**T 9** / Self-Image
EPISODE:	**E** / "Bunny Blackears"
PURPOSE:	Learner is helped to develop a positive self-image and to improve the learner's ability to coordinate motor movements with the words of a song.
ENTRY BEHAVIOR:	Learner must have beginning ability in imitating and coordinating motions with a song.
MATERIAL:	A large cardboard poster with the words of the song "Bunny Blackears" printed in large letters. You should draw pictures to represent the important nouns. The poster might look like the one below:

A rabbit hand puppet, either homemade or purchased; a carrot for each learner (optional).

PROCEDURE:
Display the large "Bunny Blackears" poster and allow the learners to show interest in it. When a small group has gathered around the poster, put the rabbit puppet on your hand and have the puppet sing the "Bunny Blackears" song and give a carrot to each learner. After singing the song, the bunny might spend some time talking about carrots. Not too much time need be spent on this unless the learners seem particularly interested — this is just one illustration of how the facilitator should feel free to digress from the principal objectives of a learning episode in order to take advantage of any opportunity to enhance the learner's cognitive growth.

Have the puppet say to the group, "I have told you my name and I would like to know your name. What is your name?" Then have the bunny go to each learner and ask him his name, praising him for saying his name clearly. If the learner is unable to say his name, have Bunny Blackears say the child's name and ask the child to repeat it. The bunny can express further interest in the learner by commenting approvingly on what he is wearing or by asking him some questions about himself. The bunny might also draw attention to his own attributes and habits in order to increase the learner's understanding of rabbits. For example, the puppet could say, "Look at my long, black ears. Would you like to feel them? They're furry. You have short, small ears. I can wiggle my ears. Can you wiggle yours?"

After spending some time talking about himself and relating his anatomical features to those of the learner, the bunny might say, "I like to sing songs, do you? See the words of the song on that big piece of cardboard? There's a picture of me. Your teacher will sing the song and show you things to do as you sing. Do just what she does." Then the facilitator can sing the "Bunny Blackears" song, modeling the motions for the learners and encouraging them to join in the activity. The words and their corresponding motor actions are written below. The tune is that of "Bunny Pinkears" and can be found in *The Kindergarten Book* (Wenthen, Amy (ed.), 1956, Ginn and Company, Lexington, Mass.). You may make up another tune to fit the words.

> "Bunny Blackears"
> I am Bunny Blackears
> *(hold up one finger on each side of the head)*
> How do you do?
> *(wiggle fingers up and down)*
> Here's a little carrot
> *(outline the form of a carrot)*
> I have brought for you.
> *(extend palm in front of body)*
> Thank you, thank you
> *(hop on one foot)*
> Pretty Bunny Blackears.
> *(hop on the other foot)*

Variations

This learning activity provides a good starting point for a unit about rabbits. You might have the learners listen to records or books about rabbits. Allow the learner to become *actively* involved in the listening or reading by encouraging him to act out the story he hears, to guess what will happen next, or to describe the pictures he sees. Below are listed some books about imaginary rabbits. These should be supplemented with books about real rabbits, and you should help the learners understand the difference between real and storybook animals. For example, when reading *My Hopping Bunny*, you should explain that bunnies do not really hop over buildings or hop to the moon.

Bright, Robert. 1971. *My Hopping Bunny*. Doubleday & Co., New York.

Brown, Margaret Wise. 1947. *Golden Egg Book*. Golden Press, New York.

Brown, Margaret Wise. 1972. *The Runaway Bunny*. (new ed.). Harper & Row, New York.

Kunhardt, Dorothy. 1962. *Pat the Bunny*. Golden Press, New York.

Potter, Beatrix. 1902. *The Tale of Peter Rabbit*. Frederick Warne & Co., New York.

Potter, Beatrix. 1909. *The Tale of the Flopsy Bunnies*. Frederick Warne & Co., New York.

Scarry, Richard. 1976. *The Bunny Book*. Western Publishing Co., Racine, Wis.

Williams, Garth. 1958. *The Rabbits' Wedding*. Harper & Row, New York.

You might cut out pictures of rabbits and make them into puzzles by pasting them onto pieces of cardboard and then cutting them into unit pieces, each one representing a certain body part.

The learner will enjoy making his own rabbit puppet. Let your imagination run wild as you select a variety of materials with which the learner can create a puppet. A puppet could be very simply made by drawing a rabbit face on a paper sack and pasting on pipe cleaners for whiskers. Two holes could be cut at the top to allow the learner to poke his fingers through and make rabbit ears. Allow the learner to sing songs, tell stories, and play games with their puppets.

You might bring live rabbits into the classroom or take the learners on a field visit to a farm or other places where rabbits are to be found. Talk about the similarities and differences between real rabbits and storybook bunnies. Any of the above ideas can also be used to increase the learner's appreciation of the habits and habitats of animals other than rabbits.

TERMINAL BEHAVIOR: Learner is able to say his first and last names at the puppet's request, sing the song, and perform the associated motor actions.

UNIT:	T 9 / Self-Image

EPISODE: F / Make-A-Face Game

PURPOSE: Learner develops better self-awareness and a positive self-image. He becomes more familiar with facial attributes, their names and functions.

ENTRY BEHAVIOR: Learner knows the names and functions of the parts of the face.

MATERIAL: A circular piece of felt material 10 inches in diameter for each learner and the facilitator; a complete set of facial features (ears, eyes, nose, mouth, hair, and eyebrows) cut from felt for each participant.

Felt facial features
(10-inch face)

PROCEDURE: This learning episode is broken down into five steps for clarity:

Step 1. Place the materials on a table or on the floor and allow the learners to freely explore and play with them as they wish.

Step 2. When you feel that the learners have had sufficient time to become familiar with the materials and to discover for themselves how to play the game, begin to introduce more structure by placing the "face" or "head" (large circular piece of felt) in front of you, and arranging the pieces of one set of facial features in random fashion in the center of the table or in the center of the group circle if the game is played on the floor. Say, "I'm going to make a face. First, I need a mouth. Who can look at the parts of the face and find a mouth that I can put on my face?" If the learner is unable to select the designated feature, demonstrate making a face, naming the features and describing them in terms of size, shape, color, function, and emotional expression, as you place them in their appropriate positions on the head. You may also ask the learner to point to the part of his face or others' faces that corresponds to the one you have placed on the felt circle.

Step 3. Give each learner a circular head and a set of facial features and suggest that he make a face. If a learner is unable to position the features correctly on the head, place your felt face before him as a model, or encourage him to watch other learners who are able to play the game correctly. It is a good idea to verbally describe the attributes and functions of the facial features throughout the entire learning episode.

Step 4. After the learner has built a face, ask him to point to various facial features as you name them. For example, say, "Kevin, show me where the mouth is."

Step 5. As you point to the various features, ask the learner to name the feature and to state its function. As you point to the mouth, for example, say, "What part of the face is that? What all can you do with a mouth?"

TERMINAL BEHAVIOR: Learner is able to construct a face by placing cutout facial features in their proper positions on the large round piece of felt. The learner can point to the feature designated by the facilitator and name the feature the facilitator points to. He can state at least one thing that can be done with each part of the face.

Variation I After the learner has constructed his face, you may continue the game by telling him to remove a specific facial feature.

TERMINAL BEHAVIOR: Learner is able to remove the feature designated by the facilitator.

Variation II To make the game more challenging, you could display a face with one feature missing, and ask the learner to name the missing feature and to state one of its functions. Say, for example, "What part of the face is missing? Yes, the mouth is missing. Tell me something you can do with your mouth." There are a variety of acceptable answers to the question about the function of the various features.

TERMINAL BEHAVIOR: Learner is able to name the missing feature and state at least one of its functions.

Variation III You can provide an opportunity for the development of language and the ability to perceive and express emotion by encouraging the learner to make a "happy" or "sad" felt face with either an upturned or a downturned mouth. Some ways in which you might help the learner understand the concept "happy" would be to smile and say that you are happy, show pictures of people who look happy, or talk about what kinds of things make someone feel happy.

By saying, "You've made a happy face. I wonder why the person is happy," you create a situation in which you might assume that the learner will project his own feelings onto the face and that as he tells why the face is happy, he is actually telling what makes *him* happy. You may also encourage personal expression of feelings in a more direct manner by asking the learner to tell what things make him feel happy or sad.

Variation IV The "Make-A-Face" Game may be played using materials other than felt. Various fruits, vegetables, or paper sacks could serve as faces, and buttons, pegs, pieces of paper, crayons, or other materials could be used to make the facial features. The display below illustrates how you might use a pizza mix as a means of self-expression. Let the learners help you mix the pizza dough. Divide the dough among them and allow each learner to create his own pizza face by rolling out the dough and placing various foods (e.g., macaroni, green pepper, parsley) on top to represent the facial features. Describe the foods and facial features as the learner places them on the pizza face, and encourage the learner to relate them to his own facial features. The baked pizzas can then be served to the group at snack time.

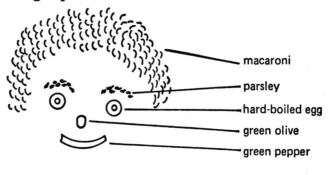

macaroni
parsley
hard-boiled egg
green olive
green pepper

"Pizza Face"

Variation V

To help foster a positive self-image more directly you can make the activity more personally relevant by proceeding as follows. Arrange for photographs of each learner to be taken and enlarged. Then make a puzzle by cutting each photograph into several pieces, each containing only one facial feature. Place each learner's own facial features in front of him in a random fashion. Ask him to put the pieces of the puzzle together to make his face, and then to name each feature as you point to it and ask, "what part of your face is this?" If the learner has difficulty putting the pieces of his puzzle together, you may provide him with a cardboard frame containing outlines of the shapes of the individual pieces, thereby giving him visual clues as to where the puzzle pieces belong. Help the learner glue the pieces of his completed puzzle to the cardboard frame and then place it in his personal cubbyhole at school, or construct a mobile by attaching each learner's puzzle to strings hanging from a circular wire or metal disc.

TERMINAL BEHAVIOR:

Learner is able to put the pieces of his face puzzle together correctly, name each feature, and take pride in the completed picture of himself.

Unit T 10 / CREATIVITY: ART ACTIVITIES

Art activities contribute vitally to learners' development. This unit, however, is concerned primarily with inspiring each child's creative thinking and self-expression through different art media which, in turn, will promote his emotional and intellectual development. However, before this can happen the facilitator must understand and respect the value of using art. The facilitator must recognize the value of art as a personal experience. Art helps the young child to discover and express his own unique individuality and ideas. It helps the young child to discover and appreciate what he knows and how he feels toward his environment. Art helps the young child recognize that other learners see and react to their environment in many different ways. The art process, rather than the finished product, contributes important learnings and satisfactions.

The art activities should allow the learners to explore and invent freely, using a large variety of art materials and tools. Consideration for the young child's incomplete motor development must affect the choice of basic materials and tools — they must permit freedom of movement. Because most young learners have brief attention spans, the art activities should be short, uncomplicated, sensory oriented, and varied. Maturational levels, capabilities, and interests will vary from learner to learner. Therefore, materials and tools and how they are used must differ.

All learners proceed through certain developmental stages in regard to art. Your learners will represent many different stages since individual growth patterns differ. Here are brief descriptions of each stage:

1. Scribble stage: The learner explores materials and tools, learning about their possibilities and how to manipulate them.
2. Controlled scribbling stage: The learner scribbles in a more intentional way, and repeats simple lines and shapes. At the end of this stage, the child names his marks.
3. Representational stage (4 to 6 years old): The drawings relate to the child's thoughts and feelings. Drawings are more realistic and recognizable from an adult's point of view. The child will draw something as it appears to him, often distorting or omitting details.

Developmentally delayed or disabled children often move through these stages more slowly than normal peers and, if there is considerable gross/fine motor involvement, their creative artwork may always seem quite primitive. Nevertheless, practically every child enjoys and benefits from such relatively unstructured opportunities for creative expression.

Guiding Children's Growth in Art Experiences...
Some Simple Do's[1]

1. Do not weary the children with too many new things within a given time (especially at first).
2. Create an atmosphere of freedom of expression. This means freedom in *use* of materials, not *abuse*.
3. Establish an attitude of "try it."
4. Help the child with the "how to do" not the "what to make."
5. Stimulate the child's own creative ideas by accepting and respecting what he produces.
6. Use the children's ideas for creating experiences in your school or center.

continued on next page

---

[1]From Thomas, Sister Mary, 1965. Creative Art Experiences. Chicago. p. 3. Reprinted by permission.

UNIT: T 10 / Creativity: Art Activities

EPISODE: A / Modeling Media (Play Dough)

PURPOSE: Learner gains new sensory experiences as he explores what can be done with this modeling medium. He develops manipulative skills (dexterity, motor control) and is stimulated to use his creativity and self-expression in using the dough many different ways.

ENTRY BEHAVIOR: Learner is interested in and curious about handling and exploring play dough.

MATERIAL:
1. Play dough recipe (pliable): 1 cup flour; 1/2 cup salt; several drops of liquid soap or 1 tablespoon salad oil; 1/2 cup water; food coloring. Combine the dry ingredients. Slowly mix in the water, soap, and coloring. Play dough will keep for some time if stored in a covered jar or plastic bag in the refrigerator.
2. Play dough recipe (self-hardening): 1 cup flour; 1 cup salt. Add water slowly to make a pliable dough. Omit liquid soap or salad oil.

PROCEDURE:
Play dough (pliable): The toddler's early experiences with dough should center upon exploring and experimenting, using hands and fingers. Pieces of oilcloth or wax paper will protect the table. Start the learner with a ball of dough, omitting additional embellishments at first. Fill a large aluminum salt shaker with flour for the learner to use on his hands, in case the dough becomes too sticky. Do not show the learners what to make, but encourage each one to explore how the dough can change as *he* manipulates it in various ways (pounding, squeezing, patting, rolling, pushing).

Young learners enjoy using rolling pins and cutting out forms with cookie cutters of various shapes. On another occasion add "imprinting" objects such as tongue depressors, shells, macaroni, buttons, and spools. You can add texture to the dough by adding Cheerios, Rice Krispies, spaghetti bits, dried peas, sand, pebbles, etc., to the original mixture.

With added experience and age, the learners first will name their crude attempts (unrecognizable to adults) and gradually will start to use the play dough in a more realistic manner (making forms such as simple containers, people, animals, etc.). At this time you might introduce additional objects for the learner to embellish his play dough form with (such as colored toothpicks, pipecleaners, straws, etc.). This will present new challenges for him and encourage imaginative ideas.

Play dough (self-hardening): If you want a play dough material that dries hard, leave out the salad oil. The play dough pieces can be painted with tempera paints and then shellacked. The learners might want to decorate their pieces with odds and ends before painting them.

TERMINAL BEHAVIOR:

Learner is more familiar with the properties of pliable and self-hardening play doughs and knows more what his different body parts can do in shaping or modifying its forms. He has greater dexterity in manipulating the dough and has discovered new ways to use it.

UNIT:	T 10 / Creativity: Art Activities

EPISODE: B / Sculpture Media (Wire and Box)

PURPOSE: Learner discovers new ways to express himself and be creative through three-dimensional materials. The learner gains skill in working with three-dimensional materials.

ENTRY BEHAVIOR: Learner has had previous satisfactory experience in using paste, white liquid glue, tape, paper punch, and scissors. He is interested in exploring three-dimensional materials.

MATERIAL: Wire sculpture: electrician's wire that is coated with different colored plastics; other varieties of narrow width wires; wooden blocks or cardboard squares; U-shaped nails or strong staples; decorative odds and ends (straw bits, colored tape, clay beads, macaroni, colored paper bits, aluminum foil).

Box sculpture: all kinds of empty boxes (differing in shape, size, color, texture); egg cartons, different kinds of cardboard tubes, empty spools of thread; ribbon bits, yarn, colored toothpicks, pipe cleaners, noodle products; tempera paint (basic colors); easel brushes; paper punch; four or five pairs of scissors; white all-purpose glue; Q-tips; small paper cups; tape.

PROCEDURE: *Wire sculpture*: Fasten the wire, which the learner has selected from the variety available on the table, to a wooden or cardboard base. A strong stapler and staples or U-shaped nails will secure the wire to its base.

During early experiences, allow the learners to explore what they can do with the wire (such as bending, twisting, or looping it, and shaping the wire into different positions and forms). Later suggest that the learners add different odds and ends decorations to their wire creations.

Box sculpture: On a table spread out a large variety of empty boxes, tubing, and other containers. Set out four or five pairs of scissors. Dilute white liquid glue with water, and pour a small amount into paper cups. The learners can use Q-tips to apply the glue.

At first you might hold up two or three different kinds of boxes, asking, "What way might you put this and this together?" Or, "How could you fasten together these two things?" Initial experiences should focus upon encouraging the learners to try out different means of organizing, selecting, and combining the various three-dimensional materials presented. Encourage each child to express *his* original ideas, and, at all times, leave out facilitator-made models. Tempera paints, crayons, colored chalk, collage items, and odds and ends should be provided to encourage further creative self-expression. When the learners have worked with box sculptures for some length of time, their sculptured inventions will probably show more complexity or more realistic representation. The facilitator, at this time, might stimulate the learner to explore the materials more carefully, in a different way, or more specifically (i.e., you could make a mean, scary monster, build yourself a boat to live on, etc.).

TERMINAL BEHAVIOR: Learner has done initial exploration and has learned some ways of working and building with wires (bending, twisting, shaping, intertwining, and decorating wires) and boxes (organizing, selecting, combining, and fastening boxes of all shapes, sizes, colors, textures). The learner has better small motor control and coordination and, judging *on an individual basis*, each learner shows individual growth in the areas of creativity and self-expression.

UNIT:	T 10 / Creativity: Art Activities
EPISODE:	C / Pasting Collages
PURPOSE:	Learner develops further means of creative self-expression through pasting and arranging collage materials that vary in textures, colors, shapes. The learner increases his sensory awareness through combining paste and collage materials in all kinds of ways, and further increases his small motor abilities.
ENTRY BEHAVIOR:	Learner, through previous activities, knows how to paste and use scissors. The learner is familiar with the collage materials presented, although he now will be working with them in new, different ways.
MATERIAL:	Homemade paste (or use white all-purpose glue or commercial paper paste). Combine 1/2 cup flour and enough cold water to produce a creamy quality. Stir the mixture continually for 5 minutes, while it slowly boils. Cool. Add a few drops of clove or wintergreen oil (this prevents spoilage). Store the paste in a covered jar and refrigerate.
	Background paper (large sheets that vary in shape, size, texture, color); scissors; *all kinds of collage materials* (the list is endless), for example, clear and colored cellophane drinking straws; all kinds of yarn and string (long pieces); cereals (uncooked); rice; spaghetti products; eggshells; dried beans, peas; grasses, seeds, tree bark, weeds, flower petals; sand, pebbles, small seashells; sawdust; salt; sugar; glitter and sequins; cornmeal; feathers; vinyl and Christmas tapes; Christmas and other holiday wrappings; ribbons and laces; sandpaper; cloth scraps; felt scraps; pipe cleaners; toothpicks and tongue depressors; cotton and Q-tips; buttons; stick and gum things (stamps, stars, reinforcements, etc.); rickrack; cardboard, cut paper; aluminum foil scraps; bottle caps; magazine scraps and newspapers; wallpaper scraps; paper bags; tissue; confetti; popcorn; corrugated paper.
PROCEDURE:	At first, limit the selection of collage materials that you offer to the learners. Perhaps present one, two, or three different collage materials that offer contrasting textures or colors or shapes and that appeal to the eye. Collages can vary from the simple to the elaborate. The following activities present some ways to proceed from simple collage work to more challenging, varied creations.
	As the learners become familiar with making collages, offer them different kinds of background paper that vary in shape, color, size, and texture. Later the learner might try pasting collage materials on three-dimensional items such as cardboard boxes, paper plates, painted coffee cans, wood scraps, etc.
	Paper-tearing collages: This activity is fun for all learners and provides a successful collage experience for those who have not yet learned to cut with scissors. Paper-tearing promotes fine motor skills and provides a freeing kind of experience. The pieces of torn paper might suggest such forms to the learner as animals, people, etc. (or they may be enjoyable in themselves *without* reminding the learner of anything specific).

Give each learner a small cup of paste or glue, or dab some paste on pieces of paper towel. Each learner should be given a large sheet of manila or colored construction paper on which to paste. The colored paper pieces, which vary in shape, color, and size, are arranged in a low container (such as shoebox lid) and placed in the middle of the table. This activity will provide sufficient challenges for the learner as he chooses, tears, organizes, and pastes the different paper pieces. Later, introduce colorful magazine illustrations, Christmas cards, or holiday wrapping paper for the learners to tear, paste, and combine with the other solid color scraps.

String and/or yarn collages: Place long yarn or string pieces in several low containers. The lengths of yarn should not be so long that they are unmanageable and produce a frustrating experience for the learner. The yarn should vary in color and width. Perhaps combine the yarn pieces with lengths of string, fishing line, or twine. At a table give each learner a small cupful of paste or glue, as well as a large sheet of manila or colored construction paper on which to paste. Have the learner paste the long yarn pieces down on his paper while discovering how many different kinds of shapes he can make with it. Much later, the learner might want to develop the yarn shape that suggests a specific thing to him (i.e., he might see a truck in his ⊂⊃ shape string). He might add chalk, paint, magic marker, crayons, or other collage materials in developing his specific or abstract idea.

Straw collages: Use both the opaque and colored cellophane straws, and put them in shoebox lids. Place three or four pairs of scissors on the table. Have small white glue jars for each child, as well as background paper for gluing. Ask, "What different kinds of things might be done with the straws?" Steer the learners toward exploring such possibilities as cutting the straws, buckling them, intersecting them, twisting them, cutting the straws open and then pasting them flat, making a picture or shape with the straws, etc. How might the learners "draw" using the straws? Can the learner make something tall and skinny, or enormous and fat? Let the learner discover how he can alter the width and produce a three-dimensional effect, by pasting a large, medium, or small pile of straws together.

Texture collages: Select collage materials with particular emphasis on textural variations. You might want to use only fabrics, or only natural things, or only cereal items, or only Christmas materials that vary in texture. In the activity described here, a nonthematic selection of items with contrasting textures is offered. The list includes scraps of velvet and silk, aluminum foil, cotton, buttons, small seashells, dried beans, feathers, glitter, sugar, small crayon bits, and yarn (substitute your ideas). The textures should include soft, silky, rough, grainy, bumpy, and crinkly qualities. Place the textured materials in containers on the table, and have the learners select, organize, and glue them on colored construction or manila paper. Use white glue, rather than paste, because it provides better strength for the heavier weight collage materials used. This activity presents an opportune time for fostering language growth. As the learner works, he can feel and verbally describe the different textured items used. He can discuss the different colors and shapes in his collage creation. Can the learner identify different collage items, or remember certain experiences by looking at specific materials (for instance, going to the beach to collect the shells he is using)? An emphasis on language development *at no time* should stifle the learner's enthusiasm and creativity in working with the materials.

Certain textures or colors of different items might make one feel angry, itchy, happy, etc. If the learner has done a lot of previous collage work, encourage him to make an "angry" picture, for instance, by selecting collage materials that make him feel mad (i.e., using rough textures, jagged shapes, or vivid colors). Other motivating ideas for collage creations might include "My Daddy at Work," "My Baby Brother," "Me Playing in the Snow," "What I Liked Doing Most this Summer," "Me on My Birthday."

TERMINAL BEHAVIOR: Learner has explored the possibilities offered by all kinds of collage materials and has developed his capacity for imaginative thinking and self-expression through collage art work. Collage materials, and resulting collage inventions, have promoted growth in the descriptive language area. The learner has developed better motor control and coordination through such activities as pasting, using scissors, manipulating different collage materials in different ways, and tearing paper.

UNIT:	**T 10 / Creativity: Art Activities**
EPISODE:	**D / Painting Activities (Tempera and Soap)**
PURPOSE:	Learner discovers how paint, soap, and items from the environment can be used in new ways.
ENTRY BEHAVIOR:	Learner has had many previous experiences in painting and using a paint brush.
MATERIAL:	"Thing" painting: background paper (white or colored construction paper or large sheets of newsprint); two or three cans of tempera paint (two or three different primary colors); "thing" — twigs, tongue depressors, paper clips, string, cotton (for dabbing and patting) or feather duster (thinner paint is required). Potato printing (or substitute fruit and/or vegetables): several different colors of tempera paint; shallow pan with several paper towels; background paper (newsprint, colored construction); vegetables (potatoes, corn cob, carrots, turnips, lettuce, green peppers); fruits (apples, lemons, oranges). Painting with whipped soap flakes: mild soap flakes, tiny leftover soap bits, water, eggbeater; several aluminum salt shakers filled with one or two different basic colors of powdered tempera; large, dark-colored sheets of construction paper; large men's shirts or vinyl aprons.
PROCEDURE:	Each learner will need freedom to explore each of the three following activities. At first the beginner probably will scrub with his painting or printing tool. Let him. Later he will explore different strokes, lines, printmarks, and designs which he might make by using different items and/or his body parts.

Thing painting: Have the beginner start by using only one kind of painting tool, such as twigs and sticks, which vary in shape, length, etc. Introduce only one basic color paint. On a flat surface, pour paint in shallow pans, and place two or three twigs and sticks in each one. The learners may stand or sit while working. Have him dip his stick into the paint and then explore the different marks and lines he can make. He might make contrasting designs and marks by twisting his stick, by dragging it, by rolling it on its side, by dotting with it, or by dripping paint from it. Let him be the explorer and creator as he paints with his twig and finds out about its many possibilities. Other "things" can be substituted, used individually at first. Cotton produces interesting marks because it can be patted, dabbed, and scrubbed over the paper in many ways. Later combine different "thing" painting tools that produce contrasting marks. At this time several basic color selections should be added to the original one chosen.

Potato printing: With the beginner, start with one kind of vegetable — a potato is good. Cut the potato into halves and then into a variety of smaller forms and shapes. At first, present one primary color of tempera paint. Pour the paint into one or two shallow pans, which have been lined with several layers of paper towels. Now you have a homemade stamp pad. The learner dips his potato shape into the paint and then presses it onto his paper. Initially the beginner will scrub instead of print.

As he is given numerous opportunities to print over an extended time, he should turn his attention from scrubbing toward discovering how he might repeat different marks and designs with the various potato pieces. Now present other basic paint colors and use other kinds of printing backgrounds, such as cloth, cardboard, or tissue. What other sliced vegetables and/or fruits do you think might produce interesting, contrasting effects? Under the "Material" section, there are a few suggestions as to kinds of vegetables, fruits, etc., that you might use. What can you add to this list?

Painting with whipped soap: With an eggbeater combine the mild soap flakes, small bits of soap, and a small amount of water until the mixture reaches a finger paint consistency. Have several large salt shakers on the table, containing one or two different colors of powdered tempera. Give each learner a large, dark sheet of construction paper. Put 2–3 tablespoons of soap mixture on each child's paper, perhaps showing on a separate sheet how to spread it out with the hands and other body parts. More important than the end product is the wonderfully free sensory experience offered by the soapy mixture. Encourage the learner to explore the different effects produced by using the fingers, elbows, knuckles, palms, fingernails, arms, etc. After initial explorations put out several aluminum salt shakers containing two different colors. Let the learners sprinkle the paint over their white soapy mixture, mixing paint combinations onto their papers. On another occasion add textured substances to the soap, such as sand, seeds, or glitter. Another variation would be to add spices to the soap mixture for scent.

TERMINAL BEHAVIOR: Learner is comfortable using a messy, finger-painting type of medium. His means of individual expression, his creativity, and his visual awareness have been increased through involvement with these art activities.

UNIT:	T 10 / Creativity: Art Activities
EPISODE:	E / Chalk and Crayon Activities
PURPOSE:	Learner discovers new ways to use chalk and crayon. He gains further sensory awareness and discrimination ability by appreciating the differences in colors, organization, lines, textures, and shapes that he uses.
ENTRY BEHAVIOR:	Learner has done basic crayon explorations before trying out crayon-resist activities.
MATERIAL:	Dry colored chalk work: thick, soft, colored pieces of kindergarten chalk; background paper with varied surfaces such as black, colored, and white construction paper, large sheets of newsprint, finger-paint paper, and sandpaper. Chalk on wet paper: wet paper such as paper towels, construction paper, paper bags, or sandpaper. Wet colored chalk work with buttermilk: buttermilk; variety of background paper. Crayon resists: large crayons, broken in half and peeled; diluted tempera paints (black, white); black, white, and colored construction paper.
PROCEDURE:	*Colored chalk on dry paper*: Chalk and crayons are used in similar ways. However, chalk allows more opportunity to experience because its colors blend more easily and, generally, it presents a freer, softer medium. Place colored chalk in low containers on the table. Have the learners draw on large sheets of newsprint or black construction paper. After initial chalk explorations, introduce other background papers that vary in their textural surfaces (rough, smooth, etc.). For instance, you might use glossy finger-paint paper, sandpaper, colored or white construction paper, corrugated cardboard, or different kinds of fabrics. *Colored chalk on wet paper*: Surface paper that is rough in texture works well (such as large paper bags, sandpaper, manila paper, or paper towels). Soak the towels or paper in the sink, or sponge the paper with water. Smooth out the wet paper on a table or floor surface. Soak the chalk in cold water. When the wet chalk is applied to a wet surface, it will glide more easily, producing vivid, interflowing colohs. If the learner wishes to preserve his chalk picture, you can spray on a fixative. Hair spray or commercial fixatives may be purchased, or you can use the following homemade recipe: 1 part shellac, 2 or 3 parts alcohol; combine the two ingredients, spraying it on with a fly-sprayer. *Wet colored chalk using buttermilk*: Use a variety of background papers, as mentioned in the two previous chalk activities. Spread buttermilk over the paper, using a clean easel brush. Soak the chalk in cold water. The vivid colors can be mixed on the paper with the fingers. These marks will not rub off of the buttermilk surface (a solution of sugar and water produces similar results). On another occasion vary this activity by having the learner dip his dry chalk into a bowlful of buttermilk and then draw on dry paper.

Crayon resists: Combining crayon and diluted tempera is fun for preschoolers. Resists do require a certain amount of physical strength from the learner. He must press firmly on his crayon in order to make heavy waxy marks that will "resist" the coat of diluted tempera paint. Place broken, unwrapped large crayons in containers on the table, and have each learner take a sheet of white construction paper. After the learner has crayon coated his paper, have him cover his crayon design with *black* water-diluted tempera paint (paint must be thin). The results are exciting for the crayon markings alone will show through the wash of black paint.

Other interesting crayon resist combinations include:

1. Black paper/colored crayons/white paint
2. Colored paper/colored crayons/paint (any color)
3. Colored paper/black crayon/white paint
4. Colored paper (*not* black)/white crayon/paint (any color)

TERMINAL BEHAVIOR:
Learner's artwork reflects uninhibited, creative qualities, expressing his own personal ideas and feelings. The learner has encountered new kinds of sensory experiences and his visual awareness and discrimination abilities have become sharper through working with a variety of colors, textures and shapes.

Ideas in this unit come from the following resources:

Association for Childhood Education International. 1957. *Creating with Materials for Work and Play.* ACEI, Washington, D.C.

Cherry, C. 1969. *Motivational Curriculum Chart for Early Childhood.* Fearon Publishers, Belmont, Cal.

Pitcher, E., Losher, M., Feinburg, S., and Hammond, N. 1966. *Helping Young Children Learn.* Charles E. Merrill Books, Columbus, Ohio.

Saunders, E. 1966. *Painting.* Whitman Publishing Co., Racine, Wis.

Smith, C. S. 1971. *A Preschool Teacher's Handbook in Art Activities.* Education Personnel Development Act, Individual Study Project, Denver, Col.

Thomas, Sister Mary. 1965. *Creative Art Experiences.* Field Enterprises Educational Corp., Chicago.

Unit T 11 / EMOTIONAL DEVELOPMENT: FEAR (Fear of the Dark)

The overall purpose of this unit is to help the young learner explore, identify, and verbally express some of his personal fears that pertain to the dark. It is not uncommon for toddlers to have fears of the dark, fears of being alone at night, and fears of imaginary monsters in the dark. The young child exercises his imagination with a mixture of what he knows and does not know about his environment. The extent to which these normal fears are felt largely depends upon how well that young learner's basic needs have been satisfied. The parent, the educator, and other adult figures first need to support the young child by understanding and accepting the child's feelings. Then the young child needs help and encouragement in learning constructive ways to express his fears and cope with fearful situations (through language, dramatic play, painting, music) plus some active, successful experiences in conquering his fears. This unit focuses on the ways of exploring and overcoming some fears related to the night. In addition, auditory and visual discrimination are exercised in the following activities.

UNIT:	T 11 / Emotional Development: Fear (Fear of the Dark)
EPISODE:	A / "Bedtime for Frances"
PURPOSE:	Through this story activity the learner is encouraged to talk about his fears of the dark and to look more closely at situations involving darkness so that he can find successful ways to overcome nighttime fears.
ENTRY BEHAVIOR:	Ability to hear and understand spoken language and satisfactorily express reactions. Learner has demonstrated fear of dark, monsters, noises, etc.
MATERIAL:	Picture book: Hoban, Russell. 1960. *Bedtime for Frances*. Harper & Row, New York.
PROCEDURE:	Read *Bedtime for Frances*. The facilitator's voice should dramatize the imaginary sights, strange sounds, and fears that Frances feels. This picture book should initiate discussion about the child's own fears of the dark at bedtime. Do not read the book straight through. Stop as Frances encounters each new fear, and involve the learners, through verbal means, in sharing her fear and exploring its origin. First, Frances thinks she sees a tiger in the corner of her bedroom. Show the picture of Frances looking for the tiger, while asking the learners if they spot a real tiger

anywhere in the picture. Proceed with the story, stressing how the parents give Frances reassurance. Next, Frances thinks she sees something big and dark — she thinks it might be a giant who is out to get her. Ask learners if they can find a giant in the picture; they probably will say that they see a coat thrown over the chair. The facilitator, with each of Frances' imaginary fears, helps the learners distinguish reality from the imagined at nighttime. Have the learners carefully look at details of the picture and tell about what they really see (versus what Frances imagines).

Next, Frances spots a crack in the ceiling over her bed — maybe a spidery animal with lots of legs will emerge. Ask the learners if they see any bugs coming out of the crack. Next, Frances thinks that there is something moving the bedroom curtains. Ask the learners if they think Frances might be afraid of that — why? What might be moving the curtains? Next, Frances hears a noise at the window — a bump and a thump, as if something were out to get Frances. "Was Frances afraid? Did she wake her parents? Look out the window with Frances — what could be making that noise?" (Show moth beating against glass.)

This book is excellent in telling about Frances' anxieties, how her parents reassure and encourage her to describe and investigate her imagined fears. The story shows how Frances succeeds in conquering a fear on her own (she looks carefully at the windowpane noise and finds that her fear was a moth beating against the glass). Ask the learners, "How do you feel when you get into bed at night?" "Do you hear and see things in the dark like Frances?" "How do you feel when someone hugs and kisses you?" The facilitator should jot down the learner's responses and declarations. The learner's expressed fears can be used in the following learning episodes. The facilitator's attitude must show the learner that his fears and feelings are understood and respected, before he embarks upon verbally expressing his nighttime fears. The facilitator's purpose is to help the learner investigate and talk about what he thinks he hears or sees, so that he can gain more control and knowledge over what he *knows* does exist in his environment at night.

Variations

A hand puppet, tape recorder, and screen. Record indoor and outdoor sounds of the night (feet on sidewalk, dripping water faucet, crickets, wind blowing, refrigerator). Play back these sounds, coordinating them with a made-up story (using a puppet) which is similar to Frances' story (except about a little boy or girl going to bed). Each time the puppet settles into bed, he hears a new scary sound (on tape). The puppet says to the learner, "I hear something — I think it will hurt me. What do *you* think it is?" The facilitator should *not* try to scare the learner, but should try to encourage him to identify and describe the scary sound to the puppet, thus offering the puppet reassurance. Thus, the learner has another experience of talking about and perhaps relieving fears about nighttime sounds, and through offering reassurance and explanation to the puppet, may be better able to reassure himself.

TERMINAL BEHAVIOR:

Learner has begun to express verbally different fears of the dark shared by Frances. The learner looks more closely at situations involving darkness and is learning actively to examine and differentiate real fears from imagined fears.

Learner can tell how Frances successfully conquered a nighttime fear alone, and thus shows some awareness of how one can cope with scary situations.

Learner can talk more about (and investigate at home) fearful noises, shapes, etc., that he thinks he sees or hears at night.

Learner also feels support from the facilitator in talking about nighttime fears and thus has gained more knowledge, confidence, and control over what he knows does exist in his environment at night.

UNIT:	**T 11 / Emotional Development: Fear (Fear of the Dark)**
EPISODE:	**B / Story Completion**
PURPOSE:	Learner is provided with the opportunity to use language to express his fears of the dark.
ENTRY BEHAVIOR:	Facilitator must assess whether the learner has any nighttime fears. (If he has none, this learning episode will not meet his needs and interest.) If he does, the facilitator must also assess whether the learner is sufficiently secure, emotionally, for this episode.
MATERIAL:	None.
PROCEDURE:	The facilitator begins a story about a little boy or girl (same sex as the learner) who is going to bed. The learner must continue and complete the story. The facilitator encourages, but does not push the learner by asking questions; the learner might be able to add more scenes to the story, to use visual imagery in describing nighttime silhouettes, and to produce nighttime sound effects (tongue clicking, squeaky voice, nails scratching on chair, imitation of squeaky door). The story should approximate the child's home environment and, if possible, focus upon those fears and words that the learner might have expressed in Episode A ("Bedtime for Frances").

> Once upon a time there was a little boy named Billy. He had a mother and father, but no brothers or sisters. After supper, it got very dark outside. Billy knew it was time to get ready for bed. He put on his pajamas, brushed his teeth, and had a story read to him by his Daddy. *But*, you know, Billy really didn't want to go to bed . . . he was kind of afraid of the dark. (*To learner*) Now, it is your turn to tell the rest of the story."

Here are various guidelines in drawing out the learner's feelings, and incorporating them into the story:

1. Why was the little boy afraid?
2. What was he afraid of after bedtime?
3. Maybe you can tell how he felt when he heard (or saw) that particular noise (or thing)? How might you help him find out what that noise (or thing) really was?
4. Can you find out what that noise is and comfort that little boy?
5. What do you think he did, feeling scared? (Did he turn on the lights, look more closely at the lumpy monster, listen carefully to the strange sound, wake up his parents, climb in his parent's bed, take more stuffed animals into his bed, stay awake all night?)
6. How should the story end?

Facilitator, make sure that the learner can offer the little boy at least *one* successful way to overcome a nighttime fear — the learner might need your help!

TERMINAL BEHAVIOR: Learner has found at least one way to help the story character cope successfully with his nighttime fears. (This may have transferred to the learner's handling of some of his personal nighttime fears.) The learner is better able (through storytelling) to verbalize his fears.

UNIT:	T 11 / Emotional Development: Fear (Fear of the Dark)
EPISODE:	C / "Cat at Night"
PURPOSE:	Learner identifies nighttime silhouettes in a picture book and indirectly gains more skill and confidence in figuring out what scary nighttime forms might really be in his home environment.
ENTRY BEHAVIOR:	Learner is familiar with and can identify and name the book's daylight picture scenes (containing rabbits, chickens, flowers, cat, trees, houses). The learner has beginning skill in visually perceiving, discriminating, and naming silhouettes.
MATERIAL:	Picture book: Spear, Dahlov. 1969. *The Cat at Night.* Doubleday & Co., New York.
PROCEDURE:	Use only the pictures with this activity. Encourage participation from the learners, and have them figure out what Goliath, the cat, can see in the darkness. Explain that cats have very good eyes and can see things much better than people in the darkness. The story goes that the farmer prepares for bedtime and puts Goliath out on the porch. See if a learner can find the cat on the porch. In the darkness, how does the learner know that thing (silhouette) is Goliath? (It looks like a cat, has whiskers, long tail, four legs, etc.). This might be a good time for the facilitator to explain that, although at nighttime people have a hard time seeing such details as color, mouths, eyes, etc., we often know what something is well enough to be able to guess what it is by its form or silhouette. Ask the learners to tell what they think Goliath can see standing on the porch in the darkness. Elicit as many responses as possible. Then turn to the next daytime page (tell learners that this is the exact scene in the daytime), and let the learners find out if their responses were right. Did they overlook some things? Flip back and forth between both day and night scenes, so the learners can explore, identify, and name more forms in both. Can the learners tell the color of the flowers in the darkness? Could the learners see the doghouse and dog? How many house windows could the learner see in the darkness? How many *really* were there? Proceed through each nighttime/daytime pair of scenes in this manner. Encourage the learners to identify and name as many nighttime silhouettes as possible and have them find out whether they were right or not by looking at the daytime page. Have the learners locate and tell about the outdoor things and their details which either were overlooked or could only be seen in daylight. In terminating this activity, the facilitator might ask the learners what kinds of dark outlines they see from their beds at nighttime. Encourage the learners to describe how the thing looks at nighttime and what it really is in daylight. Does this silhouette look scary, friendly, or funny to the learner? Pursue a discussion along these lines *if* picked up by the learner.
Variation	If the facilitator owns a Polaroid camera, he might take daytime and nighttime duplicate pictures of different parts of the classroom, toys, and equipment. The daytime/nighttime duplicates can

be put on the bulletin board in random order or used in a Lotto game. Have the learners identify and match the nighttime/daytime pairs. Have the learners tell what they can see and cannot see in the nighttime photo as opposed to what they can see in the daytime one. Encourage verbal reactions from the learners. (Does a specific toy look different at nighttime and how? Do some things look scary in the darkness and why?)

TERMINAL BEHAVIOR: Learner can identify and name nighttime forms in the picture book; this skill may indirectly increase the learner's ability and confidence in figuring out fearful nighttime forms in his own home environment. The learner is better able to perceive and discriminate silhouettes. He is better able to identify and tell what cannot be seen at nighttime, such as details, colors, some forms. He is better able visually to imagine nighttime forms (imagining the silhouette in its entirety, including details, colors, etc.). The learner can verbalize the nighttime forms which he sees from his bed at night, and is beginning to describe and identify what he sees and to tell about how that item looks to him at night (scary, friendly, funny).

Additional books dealing with nighttime:

Depaola, Tomie. 1967. *Flight the Night.* J. B. Lippincott Co., Philadelphia. (About a little boy's fear of the night.)
Ressner, Philip. 1967. *At Night.* Harper & Row, New York. (Magnificent black and white photos depict nighttime and darkness in story form.)
Schneider, Nina. 1958. *While Susie Sleeps.* William R. Scott, New York. (This story book offers reassurance and knowledge concerning what goes on at nighttime.)

Unit T 12 / ROLE PLAYING

> The toddler spends a great deal of his time in the world of imagination and make-believe. He often pretends to be other than who or what he is. He plays many roles. Besides serving as diversion and play, role playing also helps the learner acquire new skills and behaviors, and prepares him for the variety of roles (family, occupational, and social) required of an individual in the present day. In addition to helping the learner acquire new behaviors, role playing has also been shown to be quite effective in modifying existing behavior and thus is an excellent technique of behavior change. It has been used in such diverse fields as social, educational, industrial, and clinical psychology. Different explanations have been offered for the technique's effectiveness. Among them are: 1) the objectifying of experience, or helping an individual see his behavior as others do, 2) the acquisition of new skills, or the correction of skills after seeing them as they appear to others, and 3) the providing of a cathartic release, by having the individual become totally involved in the role-play situation.

UNIT: T 12 / Role Playing

EPISODE: A / Role Play

PURPOSE: Learner's imagination is stimulated and the learner gains practice in taking the point of view of another. Depending on how it is used, this episode can help the learner acquire new skills and behaviors, help prepare him for the variety of roles demanded of each individual in today's society, indirectly modify his behavior, or provide an emotional release by permitting the learner to become involved in the role playing of emotionally laden scenes.

ENTRY BEHAVIOR: Learner can take the role of another person and can communicate satisfactorily with peers and/or facilitators.

MATERIAL: None.

PROCEDURE: The role playing technique has widespread applicability. It can be used to familiarize the learner with family, occupational, and social roles, and can also be used to help him acquire new skills and behaviors in these areas. Here are examples of how role playing might be used as part of a unit on the Family.

     You might begin by saying, enthusiastically, "Today is a Let's Pretend Day. I'm going to pretend to be a mother. Yes, I shall play the role of a mother. Who wants to play the role of my child?" Then spend about 3 minutes in a role-play situation in which you talk and act like a mother. Encourage the learner to be the child.

You might model the entire role-play situation before you ask the learners to participate. This will depend on your evaluation of the learner's ability to role play. You might make props (e.g., tools, clothing, housekeeping materials) available to make the role play more realistic.

After you play the role of the mother and one learner plays the child, switch roles. Then talk about his feelings during each of the role playing situations and discuss the behaviors of the people involved. You could then encourage the learner to play the role of other family members, or you might have two learners pretend to be two different family members. After the role playing, ask them how they felt when they were role playing, how they feel about their own family members, and ask them to describe their families (e.g., the number of people in the family, their names, what they look like, what they do, and the learner's feelings about each of the members). You might extend the role play into a unit on the Family (see Unit T 13).

You might have the learners make a book on "What Is a Father?" or "What Is a Mother?" They could cut out pictures from magazines or draw pictures of their parents. They could also dictate stories about their families and you could write down each learner's story and put them together in a book. You might even reproduce copies of the book and make one available to each learner.

The same basic procedures could be followed to teach occupational and social roles. Role playing can be effective in preparing a learner for a variety of everyday behaviors and social skills. For example, you might encourage him to role play going on a shopping adventure, making purchases, going on a vacation, going camping, staying with a babysitter, or visiting a doctor. You might visit a firehouse, bakery, airport, market, etc. Then have the learners decide which roles they want to try out.

As an agent of behavior change, role playing has been shown to be quite effective. It has been used to help resolve interpersonal problems with peers, teachers, siblings, and parents, to increase or facilitate social interaction, and to help an individual become more assertive in his behavior. If two learners are involved in an interpersonal hassle, you could have them first reenact the problem situation or event. Next, have them put themselves "in the other's shoes" and switch roles. Follow this with a discussion of the problem event and their feelings while they were playing such roles. If you feel the learners are not mature enough to role play on their own, you could play the role of one learner and the other learner could play himself.

Another procedure to help resolve hassles might be to first have the learners play themselves, reenacting the situation as it occurred and expressing their own feelings. Then have them reverse roles and role play an ideal situation, how they wish it would have occurred. Again, follow this discussion of the situation, their behavior, and their feelings, and how they might resolve the situation.

Having a learner engage in role play forces him to interact with another. It is hoped that this will serve to stimulate him to interact with others in a variety of situations.

One form of play acting of prescribed behavior is known as behavior reversal. Take, for example, an inhibited and withdrawn learner. The facilitator takes the role of another person with whom the learner has played a passive, withdrawn role. The two enact some scene or incident which the facilitator describes in advance. It may be an incident involving the child asking another child to play with him. The learner first plays himself and the facilitator plays the role of the other child. Then they switch roles. This time the facilitator may overdramatize the desirable assertive behavior, thus giving the learner an opportunity to learn adaptive responses by modeling or imitation.

Variation

Dramatic play has been used for centuries as a way of acquainting children with the various folk models of their society or cultural subset. In addition to using dramatic play for the open-ended development of their cognitive/affective domain, it is being increasingly used in a therapeutic manner to assist children in favorably altering their feelings and belief systems so that they are more positive about and comfortable with them. Although it is beyond the scope of this curriculum guide to further elaborate on such techniques, the following references will supply the learning facilitator with numerous guidelines and helpful learning episode suggestions.

Axline, V. M. 1947. *Play Therapy.* Houghton Mifflin, Boston.
Dorfman, E. 1958. Personality outcomes of client-centered child therapy. *Psych. Monogr.* 72:1-22.
Fuchs, N. R. 1957. Play therapy at home. *Merrill-Palmer Q.* 3:89-95.
Ginott, H. 1961. *Group Psychotherapy with Children.* McGraw-Hill Book Co., New York.
Moustakas, C. E. 1953. *Children in Play Therapy.* McGraw-Hill Book Co., New York.
Moustakas, C. E. 1959. *Psychotherapy with Children: The Living Relationship.* Harper & Row, New York.
Moustakas, C. E. (ed.). 1966. *Existential Child Therapy.* Basic Books, New York.
Prescott, D. A. 1957. *The Child in the Educative Process.* McGraw-Hill Book Co., New York.
Rubin, A. I. 1960. *Projective Techniques with Children.* Grune & Stratton, New York.

TERMINAL BEHAVIOR:

Learner is able to participate in the role playing situation, by acting his and the other person's parts, and by talking about his feelings during the role playing.

Unit T 13 / EMOTIONAL DEVELOPMENT: FAMILY IDENTITY

The family unit's primary goal is to nourish each child's identity. The young child establishes his identity by relating to and identifying with others — in other words, this comparing process helps the child to know his own self better. The young child initially compares the self to his immediate family and later expands out to the neighborhood and larger community. How well the family gives the child a sense of worth, acceptance, and love has a profound impact on how the child feels about himself and how well he will be able to relate later to outside groups. Let us assume that the young child has developed a positive self-image and feels secure within his family group — his family has helped him in feeling secure and valued for his uniquenesses. When the young child feels this sort of respect, he then is ready to recognize and value each family member's uniquenesses. When the child enters preschool he will be ready to reach out to peers and value them for their differences and similarities. At a later time the family unit will help each child to realize differences and similarities between his own family and families of other peers, but first the child must feel secure, accepted, and valued by his own immediate family.

This unit helps the young child transfer his feelings of being accepted to accepting, respecting, questioning, and talking about differences in the composition of the family. For example, one child might see a family group from his own life experience as including mother and father, whereas his best friend might perceive the family group as having a mother and eight siblings. The following unit will help the learner to establish a more healthy self-identity by more openly comparing himself and his family with other peers and their families. Such broader social understanding and acceptance are desperately needed to tackle today's and tomorrow's social dilemmas and prejudices.

UNIT:	**T 13 / Emotional Development: Family Identity**
EPISODE:	**A / "Home" Visits**
PURPOSE:	Through first-hand "home" visits, the learner develops beginning awareness that his own family has differences from and similarities to families of his peers.
ENTRY BEHAVIOR:	Before presentation of this unit the learner needs many varied experiences that have centered upon individual uniqueness of "the self" and on how each learner shares both differences and similarities with other classmates. The learner needs previous experience with field trips and must be aware of accompanying safety rules.
MATERIAL:	At least one photograph of each learner's family (these are displayed to initiate interest, questions, and discussions); illustra-

tions of many different families engaged in different activities (eating, preparing food, doing daily routines, engaging in fun activities); wall display of illustrations with different family members fulfilling different family roles (cooking, caring for baby; going to work; going to school, playing, quarreling); two or three learners' families who live nearby who will volunteer to have the facilitator and four to six learners as visitors for approximately one hour around snack time.

PROCEDURE:

Before snack time the facilitator gathers the whole group together. She reads Lois Lenski's *Papa Small* and asks, "Who lives in the Small house?" (Papa Sam, Mama Sam, Paul, and Polly). "How many Smalls are there?" The facilitator goes through the pages again, encouraging the learners to talk about the illustrations of the Smalls doing different activities. The facilitator then asks the learners, "Who lives in your house?" The facilitator tallies the learners' responses on a small sheet of paper and uses this information later in forming Learning Episode T13C. It is important that the facilitator encourage the learners to talk about their own families. The facilitator asks, "Do you think that all families are alike?" "Is each family of the same size?" "Juan, is your family similar to the Small family?" If the learner does not understand or does not respond to the facilitator's question, he can modify it by asking, "Juan, how many children are in your family?" If Juan replies "five," the facilitator should repeat his response in a complete sentence — "Your family has five children." The facilitator asks Juan how many grownups live in his house and encourages him to name them (father, mother, aunt — and their specific names). Throughout the facilitator points out ways in which the learners' families might be different from and/or similar to the Small family. (Keep the book open showing the Small family!) Be sure to elicit a response from the learner whose house each subgroup will visit. The facilitator informs the learners that they will be visiting a learner's house within the next 3 days. The subgroup will find out if and how the family they visit might be different from or similar to their own families (and the Small family). *All* learners will have a turn to visit a house! At this time either the facilitator or the aide and the four visiting learners depart, walking to the house. During the walk the facilitator encourages the subgroup to talk about how they might find out who lives in L's family, whether L's family is large or small, and what kinds of work and fun things his family might do together. A "visiting" learner might come up with the idea that the group count the people in the house (F: "What if everyone is not at home?"). The facilitator could suggest, "Might we find out some answers to our questions by asking L's mother?" As long as interest persists in this discussion, the facilitator can repeat the questions that the learner might want to ask and find an answer to.

At L's house, the mother-hostess shows the "visiting" learners around the house. The facilitator should beforehand prepare each mother-hostess to tell about her family (makeup, size, activities). Perhaps the mother can tell what she prepared for breakfast, what particular house chores she must do on this day, what she is cooking for dinner and what kinds of special fun activities and work projects their family will partake in this weekend. The facilitator might ask the mother to ask the learners about their own families, what their mothers were doing today, what they ate for breakfast. Whether the learners have carried juice and cookies to the house or whether it is being provided, the learners can help the mother set the table (or set up for snacks outdoors). The facilitator might ask the learners how they think the learner helps his father (raking, mowing, carpentry). Allow for discussion to develop among learners, and perhaps have L's mother tell about how he is an important contributor in helping his dad. The facilitator might read *Mommies Are for Loving* or *The Little Family*. At this time, on the return walk, and on successive occasions the facilitator stimulates discussion from learners as to how their own families are similar to and different from L's family.

TERMINAL BEHAVIOR: Through first-hand experience of visiting a learner's house, the learner has begun to develop some awareness that his own family has differences from and similarities to another family (especially in regard to family composition, size, and activities).

UNIT:	**T 13 / Emotional Development: Family Identity**
EPISODE:	**B / Making Family Books**
PURPOSE:	Learner is provided with a stronger awareness of his own family's uniqueness in regard to family makeup, size, and activities.
ENTRY BEHAVIOR:	Before presentation of this unit the learner needs many varied experiences that have centered upon individual uniqueness of "the self" and on how each learner shares both differences and similarities with other classmates. The learner needs previous experience with field trips and must be aware of accompanying safety rules.
MATERIAL:	Black magic marker or black crayon; large sheets of paper (manila, newsprint, brown wrapping paper); stapler; colored cardboard or construction paper or manila folders; crayons, paint, or colored magic markers.
PROCEDURE:	The facilitator can use one of two different approaches with the learners. The first is to create a homemade book by having the learner dictate his story to the facilitator. The facilitator records the words on large pages. The second way is a picture storybook. The learner either draws a picture on the upper part of the newsprint or pastes a family photograph on the upper portion of the pages. The facilitator can stimulate ideas by talking with the learner about his family, individual family members, family size, family activities, etc. The facilitator might suggest that the learner draw portraits of different family members, draw ways in which the learner helps his mother or father, draw family fun and work activities, or draw activities with various siblings, grandma, or grandfather. One picture can relate an entire story, or several pictures together can tell a story in sequential style.

After the learner draws a picture, he tells the facilitator about its contents and the facilitator records his words. The facilitator uses the black marker or crayon on newsprint and prints, using both upper and lower case letters. This project can continue over a period of weeks. If the pages are threaded together with yarn, the learner can add additional pages about his family throughout the school year. The learner selects and tells the facilitator which color cardboard he wants to cover his book. The facilitator prints the learner's name on the front of the book, and the learner decorates the cover. Each book becomes an important addition to the learner's library, and remains there for other learners to look at and to read with an adult or by themselves.

These family picture books can be read and discussed between two or three learners. The learner can show his book and tell about his family, using the pictures. Since the facilitator wants to develop further awareness in the learners of differences and similarities among families, he encourages the learners to compare each others' families in terms of size and makeup: "Julia, let's go back to Duane's book and find out whether his family might be similar to or different from your own family." (Look at makeup in terms of brothers, sisters, babies, adults, pets. Look at size in terms of counting siblings, counting adults, counting sisters, counting the total members included in that specific family group.)

Variation

A similar goal can be achieved if learners convert a grocery carton into a homemade TV set.

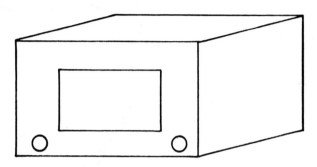

On white pages taped together into a long rolled strip, individual learners or learners together can draw (produce) a TV program about their families. Maybe the TV program's title could be the name of the learner's street, like Sesame Street. The learner narrates his family story for the audience, working the paper roll so that the pictures coincide with his story. He might need an adult's help with this.

TERMINAL BEHAVIOR:

Learner has developed more awareness of differences and similarities among families by reading, discussing, and comparing his family with other learners', using each learner's picture book.

UNIT:	T 13 / Emotional Development: Family Identity
EPISODE:	C / Family Lotto
PURPOSE:	Learner first identifies and later talks about family similarities and differences in playing this family lotto game.
ENTRY BEHAVIOR:	Learner must have a beginning ability to distinguish differences and similarities among different family groups.
MATERIAL:	Duplicate Polaroid camera shots of each learner's family or duplicate magazine photo or drawings of family groups (Polaroid shots of learners might be impossible to acquire, so be prepared to substitute duplicate illustrations or hand-drawn examples); four cardboard sheets for lotto boards; smaller cardboard cards for picture duplicates.
PROCEDURE:	The facilitator prepares family portrait Lotto sets in advance. From the tally sheet information in Learning Episode T13A, he makes sure that every learners' family size and composition is represented on one of the four boards. The combination of family units is endless. The facilitator may present his own family as an example (P=parent, R=relative, O=child).

The facilitator mounts each duplicate family picture on a smaller, individual card. The game is put in close proximity to the bulletin board of the learner's family photographs. If photographs are not available, the facilitator might use the four learners' homemade picture books, or else discuss the families of each of the four learners. The point is for the facilitator to review his family with each learner and compare the four learners' families. For example, the facilitator might ask the learner, "Who lives in your house?" The facilitator asks each learner, about his family, especially in regard to makeup and size. He helps the learners to talk about family size (grownups and children) and who they are (brother, sister, grandma, etc.). Of course, the facilitator is somewhat handicapped in this discussion if he is unable to refer the learner to his family photo (or his family picture book). The facilitator asks learner #1 if his family is similar to learner #2's family. He goes around the table this way and helps each child to tell how his family is like and/or different from another learner's family. Family Lotto is begun by playing it in regular lotto style. Each child has a board. The small cards are stacked face down. The facilitator picks up the top one, shows it to all four learners and asks, "Who has one that looks like this?" The learner is asked to match only the duplicates. The facilitator makes the game harder by asking the learner to tell *why* his picture is similar to the one he is holding. The learner responds by saying, for example, that both have a mommy, or both have a relative grownup, or both are alike because they show one child.

The facilitator asks the learner to show him a picture on his card that is not like the one he (the facilitator) is holding. The facilitator asks the learner to tell how the two family pictures differ from one another. If one learner is unable to respond, encourage aid from other learners.

The facilitator asks the learners to see if they can find a family picture on their board that is similar to their own family in makeup and size (some learners will not have the appropriate model picture on their board). First, the learner must point to the family picture that corresponds to his own family. Then the facilitator has him tell how that picture is like his family and how it is different from his family.

The facilitator can spread the small cards face up on the table and have each learner find a family that approximates his own.

Variation I

Pictures of family work activities, individual family members, and family fun activities can be substituted for the above family portrait lotto game.

TERMINAL BEHAVIOR:

Learner can identify and tell about similarities and differences among family groups, using picture representations.

Variation II — Ideas

1. Invite a grandparent to visit the class and talk about his or her own family.
2. Invite a mother and her infant to preschool and have the mother actually show the group how she cares for the baby — bathing, diapering, feeding.
3. In imitating the parent's household roles, set up a cooking project, buy ingredients at a store, make the item, have the learners set tables, and eat the final product at snack time.
4. In a household corner prepare different family prop boxes. Each box of clothes and accessories represents different family members.
5. Use family unit puppets in dramatic play, make family sock puppets, or have learners paste magazine cutouts of different family members on tongue depressors. Cut out family flannel figures to use on a flannel board.
6. For outdoor play set out a small imitation lawn mower, small gardening tools, and carpentry equipment, and a tub for washing dolls and clothes.
7. In the household corner have a real vacuum cleaner, broom, cooking equipment and sewing equipment with oversized, blunt-end needles and all kinds of cloth.
8. Make an outline of the learner on large paper. The learner can elaborately clothe his outline, using any art media, including paint, colored chalk, collage pasting, crayons. This activity should stress the importance of the learner in his family.

Variation III — Action Songs

1. "Mulberry Bush": The learners role play mother and father's activities while singing..."This is the way we wash the clothes/sweep the floor/rake the leaves/(etc.)"
2. "Rockabye Baby": The learners pretend to rock an infant in their arms. (From Chanian, P. (compiled by). 1956. *Favorite Nursery Songs*. Random House, New York.)
3. "Do, Do, Pity My Case":

   Do, do, pity my case. In some lady's garden,
   My clothes to wash when I get home, in some lady's garden.
   — my hands to wash when I get home.
   — my dog to feed

— to set the table
— to rake the lawn
— my nap to take
— to see my Dad

The learners improvise by substituting endless kinds of family activities to the second line of the song. (From Seegar, Ruth. 1948. *American Folk Songs for Children*. Doubleday & Co., New York.)

Variation III — Records

1. "Daddy Comes Home": Children's Music Center, Inc., Los Angeles, Cal. (C601A) 45rpm.
2. "Home and Family": Children's Music Center, Inc., Los Angeles, Cal. (R6) 45rpm.

Variation IV — Rhymes

1. "In a Helping Way"

   Helping Mother, helping Mother,
     It is just like play...
   Washing dishes, washing dishes
     In a helping way...
   Helping Daddy, helping Daddy,
     It is just like play...
   Raking leaves, raking leaves
     In a helping way.

   The learner pretends to wash, rake, cook, etc.

2. "Skippity-Skip"

   Oh, it's skippity-skip to bed!
     I'd rather stay up instead
   But Mother says, "Go,
     And please don't be slow!"
   So I skippity-skip to bed.

   The learners skip around the room while chanting. (From Richoux, George. 1960. *Follow the Leader: Book of Action Rhymes for Young Children, III.* David C. Cook Publishing Co., Elgin, Ill.)

TERMINAL BEHAVIOR:

Learner can deal with more abstract representations. The learner shows awareness that his own family is similar to and different from other learners' families in makeup and size by identifying and describing these qualities.

Children's books on the child and his family:
Amoss, Bertha. 1968. *Tom in the Middle*. Harper & Row, New York. (sibling conflict)
Bauer, Helen. 1951. *Good Times at Home*. Melmont, Chicago.
Borack, Barbara. 1967. *Grandpa*. Harper & Row, New York.
Buckley, Helen. 1959. *Grandfather and I*. Lothrop, Lee & Shepard, New York.
Buckley, Helen. 1961. *Grandmother and I*. Lothrop, Lee & Shepard, New York.
Carton, Lonnie. 1960. *Mommies*. Random House, New York.
Carton, Lonnie. 1963. *Daddies*. Random House, New York.
Colman, Hila. 1963. *Peter's Brownstone House*. Morrow & Co., New York.

Cooke, Barbara. 1961. *My Daddy and I.* Scott, Foresman & Co., Glenview, Ill.

Coombs, Patricia. 1958. *Waddy and His Brother.* Lothrop, Lee & Shepard, New York. (new baby in the family)

Flack, Marjorie. 1973. *The New Pet.* Doubleday & Co., New York. (new baby in the family)

Guy, Anne. 1967. *A Baby for Betsy.* Abingdon Press, New York. (adoption)

Higgins, Don. 1966. *I Am a Boy.* Golden Press, New York.

Higging, Don. 1966. *I Am a Girl.* Golden Press, New York.

Hoban, Russell. 1976. *Baby Sister for Frances.* Harper & Row, New York. (new baby)

Keats, Ezra. 1967. *Peter's Chair.* Harper & Row, New York. (new baby)

Kessler, Ethel, and Kessler, Leonard. 1964. *All Aboard the Train.* Doubleday & Co., New York.

Lenski, Lois. 1932. *The Little Family.* Doubleday & Co., New York.

Lenski, Lois. 1944. *Let's Play House.* Oxford University Press, New York.

Lenski, Lois. 1951. *Papa Small.* Henry Z. Walck, New York.

Penn, Ruth. 1962. *Mommies Are for Loving.* G. P. Putnam's Sons, New York.

Pner, Helen. 1946. *Daddies: What They Do All Day.* Lothrop, Lee & Shepard, New York.

Schick, Eleanor. 1970. *Peggy's New Brother.* Macmillan, New York. (new baby)

Zion, Gene. 1968. *No Roses for Harry.* Scholastic Book Services, New York.

Zolotow, Charlotte. 1966. *Big Sister and Little Sister.* Harper & Row, New York. (sibling conflict)

MOTOR / EXPRESSIVE / SOCIAL EPISODES

Unit I 14 / GROSS MOTOR

The gross motor area is an extremely important one for the young learner because he learns a great deal through feedback from this expressive ability. The ability to move around means the ability to explore his environment in a way that promotes intellectual development. The presence of motor competency also positively affects the self-image and the independence of the child, because moving around successfully through the environment enhances the learner's self-image, and having the movement capability to go from one place to another on his own develops a sense of independence in the learner. Many learning episodes listed in the Gross Motor Unit could be included with other units on information processing, but they are included here because they do demand movement as a primary capability. Before beginning to teach the learning episodes in this unit, the learning facilitator can consult Unit I 22, which provides some preparatory learning episodes for learners who have deficiencies in the motor area. Consultation with a physical therapist is often helpful for children with movement handicaps. A valuable resource is: Finnie, N. 1975. *Handling the Young Cerebral Palsied Child at Home.* E. P. Dutton & Co., New York.

For learners who have other sensory and cognitive deficits, many movement activities are acquired more slowly because of the disruption of the learner's ability to gain full feedback from his environment as he acts upon it. As a consequence the learning facilitator may need to encourage movement by providing the learner with extra feedback and, for visually impaired learners, by keeping the physical environment constant so that the learner comes to know the placement of natural obstacles in the environment and can avoid these while using them to monitor his progress around the environment.

UNIT:	I 14 / Gross Motor
EPISODE:	A / Arm and Leg Flex and Stretch
PURPOSE:	Learner practices symmetrical movements and feels free and easy movements of arms and legs.
ENTRY BEHAVIOR:	Learner's arms and legs have no tendency to feel too tight or to resist passive movement.
MATERIAL:	None.
PROCEDURE:	Place the learner on his back on a floor or other roomy area with a fairly hard surface. Put your thumbs in the learner's palms so that his fingers close around your thumbs and you can then close your fingers around his hands. You can then move the learner's arms in toward his body, folding his arms across his chest, and then gently moving his hands away from his body, stretching his arms out wide. Next raise the learner's arms straight over his head, then down and in alongside his chest, then straight down toward

his tummy. As the learner begins to smile and show excitement in response to this activity you can become more and more vigorous. However, you should always be sensitive to how much movement the learner really likes, and stops when you sense the learner becomes tense or uncomfortable.

When the learner's knees are bent you can also press your hands away from his body with his feet. If he does not push away you can take the lower part of the learner's legs in your hands and, while holding one leg bent, straighten out the other leg. Then straighten the bent leg while you gently bend the straight leg.

TERMINAL BEHAVIOR: Learner cooperates in activities by actively participating in bending and stretching arms and legs.

UNIT:	I 14 / Gross Motor
EPISODE:	B / Roughhousing
PURPOSE:	Learner will be able to feel that his body is in different positions and show enjoyment of these positions.
ENTRY BEHAVIOR:	Learner accepts being carried in different positions without showing fear. Learner has never had a tendency toward seizures (convulsions).
MATERIAL:	None.
PROCEDURE:	Many activities can be good exercise and lots of fun for both facilitator and learner, as well as a means of preparing the learner for self-directed movement. The facilitator should *always* hold the learner firmly while doing the following:

1. Swinging him around like an "airplane" while grasping him under the arms or by the hands.
2. Holding learner's feet to play "wheelbarrow," with his hands on the floor.
3. Swinging him under the facilitator's legs, while grasping the learner's hands or holding him under the arms.
4. With the learner's legs around the facilitator's waist, and face to face, the facilitator can hold the learner at his waist and tip him over backward by bending over himself.
5. The facilitator will assume a crawl position and place learner on his back for a "pony ride" by crawling forward or bouncing up and down.
6. Do the "piggy-back." The facilitator will place the learner on his back with the learner's arms around his neck, or the facilitator will hold the learner in position on his back by reaching back and firmly holding the learner against him by grasping the learner's waist.
7. The facilitator will lie on the floor with the learner stretched out beside him. The facilitator will play "roll over" by pushing learner over and over as he rolls over beside learner, saying "Roll over" each time.

TERMINAL BEHAVIOR:	Learner will show awareness that his body is in different positions by balancing correctly.

UNIT:	**I 14 / Gross Motor**
EPISODE:	**C / Tick-Tock**
PURPOSE:	Learner will be able to hold his head vertically despite his body being moved about.
ENTRY BEHAVIOR:	Learner has difficulty holding his head up and may show floppiness in the joints of his body.
MATERIAL:	None.
PROCEDURE:	The facilitator will pick up the learner under the arms with a firm grasp, hands encasing the rib cage, holding the learner in a vertical position so that they are face to face. To the words "Tick-Tock goes the clock; Tick-Tock, Tick-Tock, Tick-Tock, Bong!" the facilitator will tilt the learner to the right ("Tick") then to the left ("Tock"). On the word "Bong" the facilitator will lower the learner rapidly, then bring him back to position for more "Tick-Tock." During the "Tick-Tock" the facilitator will try to establish and maintain eye contact with the learner.

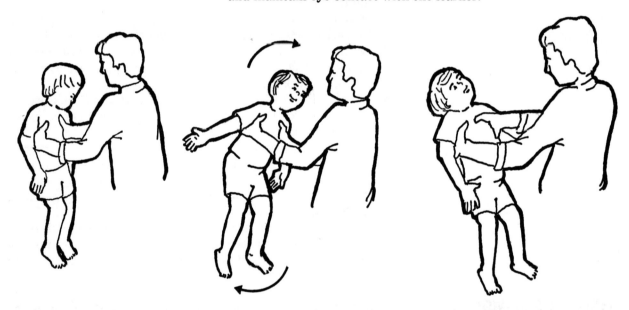

TERMINAL BEHAVIOR:	Learner will maintain his head in a vertical position when his body is tilted in any direction.

UNIT:	**I 14 / Gross Motor**
EPISODE:	**D / Weight Shifting on Elbows**
PURPOSE:	Learner will improve shoulder stability and control while lying on his stomach.
ENTRY BEHAVIOR:	Learner has developed some head control lying on his stomach and on his back.
MATERIAL:	A favorite toy.
PROCEDURE:	Place the learner on his stomach and prop him upon his elbows. Then shift his weight from side to side by tapping his shoulders gently from the side, one after the other. Put a toy in front of the learner and entice the learner to reach out toward it with the arm that is not bearing the weight of his body.

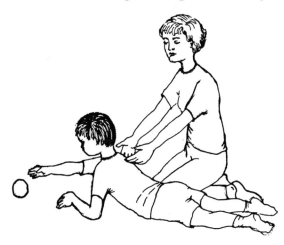

TERMINAL BEHAVIOR:	Learner can shift his weight to one side and reach out purposefully for a toy with the other arm without collapsing or stiffening up all over.

UNIT:	I 14 / Gross Motor
EPISODE:	E / Scooter Board Play
PURPOSE:	Learner develops arm coordination and head and trunk control.
ENTRY BEHAVIOR:	Learner can support himself on his arms with his head raised 90° when placed on his stomach.
MATERIAL:	Gym dollie or commerically available "Crawligator."
PROCEDURE:	Put the learner on his stomach across a gym dollie or Crawligator. The learner will usually hold his head up and put his feet out behind him. Hold his lower legs just enough to help him balance on the gym dollie or Crawligator so he uses his own muscles as much as possible. If he turns his body, secure him with a belt. You can steer him around the floor by guiding his feet as he moves himself forward and backward by pulling or pushing with his hands.
	Another way to move the older learner around and help him practice balance is to secure him on the dollie with a belt and have him hold onto a heavy rope or hula-hoop so that you can pull him along the floor on the scooter board. You can move him backward, forward, sideways, and also around in circles, as you describe the direction in which you are going. You can also play "train," "truck," etc.
TERMINAL BEHAVIOR:	Learner can move himself about the floor freely and effortlessly in any direction. Learner will grasp hula-hoop or rope and participate in pretend games.

UNIT:	I 14 / Gross Motor
EPISODE:	F / Roll Over in a Blanket
PURPOSE:	Learner experiences how it feels to roll over.
ENTRY BEHAVIOR:	Learner has head control with little head lag. Learner can extend arms above head and grasp an object.
MATERIAL:	Blanket (folded to at least twice the size of the learner). Small toy.
PROCEDURE:	1. Place the learner on his back in the center of the blanket. Wrap the blanket loosely around the learner's body. One facilitator holds the learner at his wrists, which are extended above his head. A second facilitator holds the learner at his ankles. At the count of three, both facilitators will roll the learner clockwise, making each complete roll last five counts. The facilitators will roll the learner six times in each direction. Gradually the facilitators will increase the speed and the number of rolls per session. 2. Place the learner on his back in the center of the blanket. The learner will reach his arms above his head and hold onto a small toy. One facilitator rolls the learner holding onto his shoulders. A second facilitator rolls the learner holding onto his calves. At the count of three, both facilitators will roll the learner six rolls in each direction, making each complete roll last five counts. Gradually the length of the session and the speed of the rolls increase, or the learner may be rolled up and down an incline or over rough surfaces.

Variation

ENTRY BEHAVIOR:	Learner is attempting to roll back to his stomach from his back but is not turning his body sequentially and is too stiff.
PROCEDURE:	Place the learner on his back. Bend the right hip by holding the calf and pushing the knee up; present an interesting toy to the learner's left side. Turn the learner slightly toward the left by twisting over his legs, encouraging him to reach for the toy with his right arm. Help him to roll all the way over to his tummy. He may roll on his left arm and you may have to help him to free it. Reward the learner with toy play and then continue the game, helping him roll over from his back in the opposite direction. Throughout the day you can roll him this way from stomach to back rather than lifting and placing him.
TERMINAL BEHAVIOR:	Learner will role in a position with his head held straight over his shoulders, shoulders in a straight position over hips, and hips in a straight position over feet with the parts of the body moving in sequence.

UNIT:	**I 14 / Gross Motor**
EPISODE:	**G / Pull to a Sit**
PURPOSE:	Learner strengthens back muscles and develops head and trunk control.
ENTRY BEHAVIOR:	Learner can keep head from falling back or forward when held upright but does not have a tendency to stiffness in the neck and trunk muscles.
MATERIAL:	None.
PROCEDURE:	Place the learner on his back on a non-skid surface. Lean over the learner and put your thumbs in his palms so that he will grasp them. Fold your hands over his so that you can hold his hands firmly if you feel his grip loosening. Slowly raise the learner to a sitting position, making sure that his buttocks do not slide along the surface. When the learner is sitting straight up with his head balanced and is comfortable in his sitting position, let go of his hands and grasp him firmly around his hips, pressing his buttocks firmly into the surface of the table or floor. This will allow the learner to use his own muscles to balance in a sitting position to the best of his ability. Be ready to give more support further up on the trunk so that the learner does not fall either backward or sideways, since at this point you will not be supporting his back, but holding his hips enabling him to balance on his own.

Variation I

ENTRY BEHAVIOR:	Learner sits independently momentarily. He cannot assume sitting and shows no attempts at balancing. With support he sits with a fairly straight back and good control.
PROCEDURE:	The facilitator starts by talking to the learner who is lying on his back facing the facilitator. The facilitator holds the learner's upper arms above his elbows and very slowly pulls the learner up to sit. During this movement, the facilitator tilts the learner from side to side, deciding on the amount of tilt according to the learner's ability to maintain his head in the middle and in line with his back.
	The facilitator may lie the learner back down with the same handhold and movements.

Variation II

PROCEDURE:	The facilitator places the learner in the long-legged sitting position (see Position 1). The facilitator grasps the learner's right leg and hand with his left hand and the learner's left leg and hand with his right hand. The learner's hand should be held between the facilitator's thumb and forefingers and the learner's leg by the facilitator's other fingers (see Position 2). The facilitator should develop a comfortable holding grip.

The facilitator gently tilts the learner's head and shoulders back as if lowering him to the floor. The facilitator should not lower the learner onto his back. Instead, the facilitator stops the backward tilts at the level at which the learner just about loses head control and before he drops his head back. If the learner loses head control, the facilitator should pull the learner's arms and legs forward until the learner regains control and can lift his head. The facilitator can repeat tilting the learner backward and forward.

If the facilitator wishes to tilt the learner from one side to the other, he can start by shifting the learner over to the learner's right side, tilting the learner slowly over the learner's right buttock and leg. Again the facilitator stops the tilt when the learner loses control of his head, and pulls the learner back to the starting position. The facilitator should shift the learner over the left buttock and leg slowly and return him to the full sitting position just as the learner loses head control. The facilitator should tilt the learner slowly in all directions as if rocking him so that the learner can gradually learn to hold his head upright in all positions (see Position 4).

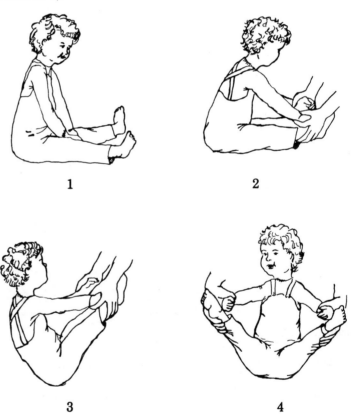

1   2

3   4

TERMINAL BEHAVIOR: Learner anticipates being pulled upright by tensing his arms and shoulders and shows no head lag as he is raised to a sitting position. Learner sits alone with good balance when placed. Learner is able to hold his head upright in spite of changes in his body position.

UNIT:	I 14 / Gross Motor
EPISODE:	H / Getting to a Sit
PURPOSE:	Learner will strengthen trunk and neck muscles and improve ability to get into a sitting position.
ENTRY BEHAVIOR:	Learner has some head control, some beginning ability to roll over, can prop himself on elbows when on his stomach, and can shift his weight in this position.
MATERIAL:	A floor pad.
PROCEDURE:	Place the learner on his back and bend his legs slightly. Raise the learner's right arm and shoulder, putting the learner's weight over to the left side, letting him lean on his left shoulder; as you pull him up by raising his right side, lean on his elbow, then lean on his hand with the left arm stretched out supporting the body weight in sitting. To help him lie down again, raise his right arm and shoulder to lean him on his left hand, then his elbow, then his shoulder, lowering him down. Repeat the maneuver on the other side.

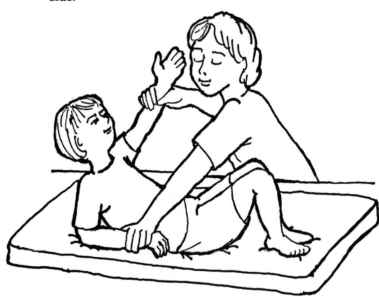

Variation

MATERIAL:	Large, soft, beach ball.
PROCEDURE:	The facilitator places the learner on his back on top of a large beach ball. The facilitator holds the learner's left arm close to his elbow, and encourages the learner to pull himself up by rotating him onto his right arm (see display) for support, while giving the learner as little facilitative support as possible. Holding the learner's right elbow, the facilitator encourages the learner to support himself on his left arm when lying down. Repeat procedure for other side.
TERMINAL BEHAVIOR:	Learner will be able to assume a sitting position by rotating over onto one arm and pushing up to sitting position with his hand.

UNIT:	**I 14 / Gross Motor**
EPISODE:	**I / Postural Shifting for Beginning Sitting Balance**
PURPOSE:	Learner will be able to shift positions while sitting to practice beginning balance in sitting.
ENTRY BEHAVIOR:	Learner has head control. He has some ability to use his hands for pushing support in sitting. He may sit with help by himself. There may be some floppiness or low tone, especially in the pelvis and lower back.
MATERIAL:	A favorite toy
PROCEDURE:	The facilitator sits on his heels on the floor or sits on a low couch. He sits the learner in a straddle position on one of his thighs close to his knee, and facing away from the facilitator (the facilitator should be looking at the back of the learner's head). The learner should be leaning forward slightly with feet flat and knees bent (Position 1). The facilitator places both of his hands on the sides of the learner's trunk, beneath the armpits. Slowly the facilitator lowers his hands down the child's trunk until the learner starts to lose sitting control by falling forward or to the side. At that point, the facilitator should place his hold slightly higher on the learner's trunk and move the learner slowly forward/backward, and side to side, but not too far from the learner's center of gravity. The facilitator also can bounce the learner gently on the facilitator's thigh and thus encourage him to keep his hands near the facilitator's knee.

Next, the facilitator should place a toy in front of his knee, within reach of the learner's hand (Position 2). The learner should bend forward to reach toward the toy while being held at his waist or pelvis by the facilitator on the facilitator's thigh. Encourage the learner to raise himself back to the initial sitting position. If the learner struggles, the facilitator should move his right or left hand onto the learner's chest and lift the learner. The facilitator also should encourage the learner to rock side to side or back and forth by himself, while providing support when needed.

1 2

TERMINAL BEHAVIOR:	Learner is able to sit and make attempts at preventing himself from falling.

UNIT:	**I 14 / Gross Motor**
EPISODE:	**J / Sitting with Straighter Back**
PURPOSE:	Learner will sit with straighter back using his arms in front of him for support.
ENTRY BEHAVIOR:	Learner has head control. He sits supported with a rounded back. Most of his trunk feels floppy and has low muscle tone. He can sometimes push up on straight arms when lying on his stomach.
MATERIAL:	None.
PROCEDURE:	The facilitator sits on his heels on the floor or sits on a low couch. He sits the learner in a straddle position on one of his thighs close to his knee, and facing away from the facilitator (facilitator should be looking at the back of the learner's head). The learner should be leaning forward slightly with feet flat and knees bent (see Position 1 in Learning Episode I14I). The facilitator places both of his hands on the sides of the learner's trunk, beneath the armpits. Slowly the facilitator lowers his hands down the child's trunk until the learner starts to lose control and falls forward or to the side. At that point the learner should automatically move his hands and arms forward or to the side and lean his head and shoulders away from the fall.

If the learner is just beginning to sit, these reactions may not appear, and the following should be performed by facilitator: The facilitator quickly catches the learner with the same hand holds on the sides of the learner's trunk. The facilitator should bounce the learner on his thigh *gently* while keeping the learner's hands in front of his body. This can be achieved by moving the facilitator's hands to the learner's shoulders. The facilitator's thumbs should be on the learner's back or shoulder blades, while his fingers are in front of the learner's upper arms. The facilitator pulls back, pushing the learner's arms forward until the learner's hands are near or on the facilitator's knees. The facilitator should lift his thumbs and pull the learner's shoulders backward (the learner is still leaning forward). If the learner's arms pull back too much so that his hands move away, the facilitator should bring his thumbs back onto the learner's shoulder blades. The facilitator maintains his hand position while the learner looks at interesting activities or scenes.

TERMINAL BEHAVIOR:	Learner can sit on a lap and straighten his back, propping his arms forward for support.

UNIT:	I 14 / Gross Motor
EPISODE:	K / See-Saw: Push and Pull
PURPOSE:	Learner will be able to sit squarely on his buttocks with a straight back while performing a learning episode or engaging in spontaneous play
ENTRY BEHAVIOR:	Learner can sit independently and reach out.
MATERIAL:	An action toy, such as a coin box or pop beads; a carpet or mat.
PROCEDURE:	The facilitator and the learner will sit on the floor face to face with legs spread apart and straight, back of knees flat on the floor. The facilitator's legs will be on top of the learner's legs near to the ankles to hold them in place. The facilitator will place coins opposite the learner's preferred side so that the learner will transfer weight to nonpreferred side and reach across for coin. The facilitator will ask the learner to "get the coin and put it in the box." The facilitator will hold the coin box with the slot at lap level first, then at shoulder level, and finally above eye level, which will require the learner to reach up with a good straight back.

Variation	The learner and the facilitator sit in the same position as above. The facilitator takes the learner's wrists, and the learner holds on to the facilitator's wrists, so that their wrists are locked. The facilitator then pulls the learner forward while saying "pulling" and waits for the learner to pull. The facilitator repeats the pull motion until the learner does it, repeating "pulling." The concept and motion of "pushing" is performed in the same manner. The facilitator pushes and pulls the learner gently and slowly, not lifting him off the ground.
TERMINAL BEHAVIOR:	Learner will be able to sit squarely with a straight back and bear weight on both hips to play spontaneously or "push and pull."

UNIT:	I 14 / Gross Motor
EPISODE:	L / Balancing Rock and Roll
PURPOSE:	Learner will improve sitting balance, and his fear of sitting off the floor will be reduced.
ENTRY BEHAVIOR:	Learner has the ability to sit unaided or with only slight support.
MATERIAL:	Heavy cardboard barrels 12 or 20 inches in diameter. Barrels may be covered with carpeting, or a terry cloth towel may be thrown over the barrel which will be on its side.
PROCEDURE:	The facilitator will straddle the barrel, sitting on the closed end, and place the learner straddling the other end of the barrel, facing the facilitator. If the learner is unstable his hands should be held at the level of his shoulders. The facilitator should roll the barrel about 4″ from side to side. The facilitator will encourage the learner to maintain his balance by shifting his body weight toward the center of gravity. The facilitator will release the learner's hands as soon as he is weight shifting. A learner who is too small to be secure facing the facilitator may be held around the trunk with his back to the facilitator. Some larger learners may be encouraged to ride a small barrel alone with feet well planted, rocking from side to side.

Variation I

MATERIAL:	Large (minimum of 2 feet in diameter) beach ball.
PROCEDURE:	The facilitator will sit the learner on the ball so that his hands are not touching the ball. The facilitator will grasp both ankles or lower legs of the learner and move him slowly back and forth and side to side. The facilitator will encourage the learner to attempt to keep his balance by shifting his body position toward the center of gravity.

Variation II

MATERIAL:	A swing in a park (large seat).
PROCEDURE:	The facilitator sits on the swing and places the learner facing him on his lap with legs around him. The facilitator braces the learner with his hand behind the learner's back. Gently the facilitator swings the swing, allowing the learner to regulate how fast and how high he wants the swing to go by his facial expression, i.e., with any sign of fear the facilitator will slow down, with any sign of pleasure he will increase his swinging pace.

Variation III

MATERIAL:	A rocking horse or animal in the park.

PROCEDURE:

The facilitator will place the learner, or the learner will climb, on the horse with as little assistance as necessary from the facilitator. The learner will hold the handle of the horse and rock back and forth with guidance from the facilitator. The facilitator will stand alongside and encourage the learner to rock back and forth. The facilitator will guide the learner by placing his hand behind the learner's back. This guidance will give the learner a sense of security and act as an aid to catch the learner if he looses his balance.

TERMINAL BEHAVIOR:

Learner is able to maintain sitting balance when moved and any resistance to being off the floor will be reduced so that the learner shows pleasure in climbing and other activities.

UNIT:	I 14 / Gross Motor
EPISODE:	M / Thrust to Floor
PURPOSE:	Learner protects himself when falling.
ENTRY BEHAVIOR:	Learning has voluntary movement of arms.
MATERIAL:	Large beach ball (at least 2 feet in diameter), or large barrel.
PROCEDURE:	First, the facilitator should briskly rub the learner's palms on the floor or carpet, using firm pressure. Next, the facilitator should place the learner on his stomach over the ball or barrel. the facilitator grasps him by the ankles and pushes him forward so that the learner's head goes toward the floor as rapidly as possible without frightening the learner. The facilitator may repeat this action, moving faster each time if there is no sign of fear (crying, stiffening, eye-widened facial expression) for 8 to 10 repetitions.
	The same effect can be achieved by picking the learner up, turning him upside down, and thrusting him quickly toward the floor in the course of roughhouse play.

Variation I

ENTRY BEHAVIOR:	Learner has voluntary movement of arms and is able to sit.
MATERIAL:	None.
PROCEDURE:	While the learner is in a sitting position, the facilitator should briskly rub the learner's palms on the floor or carpet, using firm pressure. While the learner remains sitting without the support of his arms, the facilitator should gently push the learner to the side. If the learner does not reach toward the floor when pushed, the facilitator should guide the learner's hand to the side toward which he leans with one hand, while pushing gently with the other.
TERMINAL BEHAVIOR:	When thrust or falling forward, the learner consistently reaches toward the floor so that his hands contact the surface before his head breaks a fall.

UNIT:	**I 14 / Gross Motor**
EPISODE:	**N / Creeping Up on All Fours**
PURPOSE:	Learner will be able to bear weight on his knees and will develop muscles in his legs and hips in preparation for creeping.
ENTRY BEHAVIOR:	Learner has been commando crawling.
MATERIAL:	Ace bandage; bath towel; entertaining toy upon which to focus.
PROCEDURE:	Begin the learning episode by rubbing the soles of the learner's feet with a towel. Tap the backs of the learner's thighs with your fingers rapidly for a few seconds. Then tie an ace bandage around the learner's thighs so that line of the upper leg is straight up and down from hip to knee. Place a towel under the learner's tummy, keeping a hand hold on each end. Lift the learner's torso with a towel until the learner is in a good knee/hand creeping position. Rock the learner's body with the towel to encourage knee contact and weight bearing with hands.

Variation I

MATERIAL: Entertaining toy upon which to focus.

PROCEDURE: Start the learning episode by positioning yourself behind the learner with the learner on his stomach. Encourage him to raise his head and rest on his elbows or hands by presenting a toy to him. From the back raise the learner's legs into a kneeling position by placing your fingers forward on his hip joint and lifting up, rotating his thighs forward. Holding firmly, gently rock the learner back and forth. Reduce the amount of control of the hips as soon as some weight bearing and voluntary movements by the learner are felt.

Variation II

PROCEDURE: After Variation I above, the learner assumes hands and knees position. Place a toy a few feet ahead of the learner and encourage the learner to "get the toy." As the learner creeps toward the reward, the facilitator should keep his hands on the hips of the learner to ensure that he maintains the position and that he transfers his weight from side to side, alternating hands and feet. The facilitator can help the learner to alternate hands and feet by gently and rhythmically rocking the learner from side to side.

TERMINAL BEHAVIOR: Learner will be able to position himself in a good knee/hand creeping position and to creep forward

UNIT:	**I 14 / Gross Motor**
EPISODE:	**O / Going over Obstacles to Get a Toy**
PURPOSE:	Learner learns to plan his movements to successfully overcome obstacles in his environment. Learner learns to persist in order to get what he wants. Learner will improve balance and become aware of his body in space.
ENTRY BEHAVIOR:	Learner can creep on all fours.
MATERIAL	Homemade obstacles, such as pillows, chairs on their sides, boxes with ends cut out, commercial flexible cloth and wire tunnel, five or six inner tubes roped together, a sheet thrown over a long narrow table or stretched between and over chairs, open-ended barrel, a bolster about 6 inches in diameter.
PROCEDURE:	Put a favorite toy or something else the learner likes on the floor so that the learner can see it. Put one or two obstacles in his way and then encourage him to move toward the toy. These obstacles should be things that the learner can go under, around, or over with some ease (for example, pillows, chairs on their sides, boxes with the ends out for crawling through). You will need to encourage the learner toward the toy to make it fun instead of frustrating. Once the learner enjoys the challenge, you can make it more difficult by using many obstacles or things that are difficult for him to get around.

When using a tunnel the facilitator may crawl into the tunnel to meet the learner, or he may crawl ahead of the learner, enticing the learner to follow.

Using a bolster, the facilitator helps the learner to take a crawl position over the bolster. The facilitator will encourage the learner

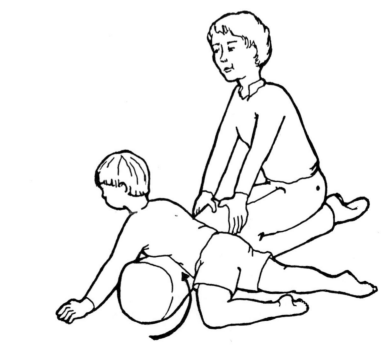

to lift his knees and crawl over the bolster to reach the toy by holding the bolster and rolling it slowly in the direction that would move the learner forward onto his hands (see illustration below). Do not let the learner become discouraged or he will simply crawl off to another, less troublesome, game.

TERMINAL BEHAVIOR: Learner crawls (or walks) easily through, around, under, or over whatever obstacles are placed in his way in order to get to where he wants to go.

UNIT:	**I 14 / Gross Motor**
EPISODE:	**P / Crawling Up and Down Steps for Toy or Reward**
PURPOSE:	Learner develops the ability to crawl up and down steps and to control his body when moving in a vertical direction.
ENTRY BEHAVIOR:	Learner can crawl across floor, successfully moving over small obstacles that are in his way.
MATERIAL:	Small flight of carpeted stairs or commerically available play steps; attractive toy or piece of food.
PROCEDURE:	Place a favorite toy of the learner's, or a piece of food, at the top of the play steps or short flight of stairs and, from the other side or top, encourage the learner to crawl up the steps to get the toy. You can reach over the top of the play steps and down to him to make sure that the learner does not fall, or you can stay next to him and guide his hands and legs. Help him to move into a sitting position at the top after he reaches the toy. After the learner has played with the toy at the top of the steps for a moment or two you can ask him for the toy and then place it at the bottom of the steps. Encourage the learner to move down the steps to get the toy. If the learner is fearful of crawling down the steps head first, you can help him discover that he can turn himself around at the top and come down safely feet first by guiding his body through these movement sequences.
TERMINAL BEHAVIOR:	Learner crawls up and down short flights of stairs spontaneously.

UNIT:	I 14 / Gross Motor
EPISODE:	Q / Ball Rolling and Chasing
PURPOSE:	Learner develops eye-hand control and purposeful movement.
ENTRY BEHAVIOR:	Learner has good sitting balance and visually directed reaching.
MATERIAL:	Large, colorful ball 6 or 8 inches in diameter, "Nerf" ball, or graspable baby ball.
PROCEDURE:	If the learner is sitting but not yet crawling, sit him in the middle of the floor and sit yourself opposite him spreading your legs so that it would be easy for you to capture a ball pushed by the learner in just about any direction. Roll the ball to the learner and tell him to "Get the ball." Make sure that you use a colorful ball, one which has soft thumb or finger holes in it. Encourage the learner to roll the ball back to you. You may have to push the ball back and forth yourself a few times before the learner gets the idea. Even after he understands he is to push it back, he may begin to hit the ball about in any direction. This is why it is important for you to sit with your legs apart so that you can capture the ball when he pushes it off. With a crawling learner, the learner can be encouraged to chase the ball. If you want, you and the learner can chase the ball together, sometimes with him "winning," sometimes with you "winning."
TERMINAL BEHAVIOR:	When sitting, learner pushes ball in the direction of facilitator and returns it directly when the facilitator pushes it to him. When moving, the learner races the facilitator to get the ball and cooperates in play.

UNIT:	**I 14 / Gross Motor**
EPISODE:	**R / Bouncing on Feet**
PURPOSE:	Learner will be able to stand holding on to something.
ENTRY BEHAVIOR:	Learner has some trunk and head control and the ability to straighten knees and straighten hips. Learner does *not* have a tendency toward stiff muscles.
MATERIAL:	Round hassock, large ball, or small barrel.
PROCEDURE:	1. The facilitator will hold the learner around his trunk under the arms in a standing position with feet touching the floor. The facilitator will lift the learner up and down so his feet bounce flat on the floor. Sing "Up and Down" as the learner goes up and down.
	2. A round hassock should be placed on its side so that it will roll. Hold the learner with his stomach against the hassock, feet touching the floor. Roll the learner forward and backward lifting his feet from the floor and returning them flat to the floor.
	3. A beach ball or small barrel may be used the same way as in 2.
Variation I	The facilitator will sit on the floor with legs spread straight out in a "V" shape. The facilitator will help learner to come to a stand from a crawl or sitting position by offering the necessary hand support. The facilitator will hold the learner in a standing position facing the facilitator with learner's feet firmly placed, heels down, between the facilitator's legs. Facilitator's hand, thumbs in front, will grasp the learner at the level of the upper hips. The correct position will be reached when the facilitator's thumbs rest on the point of the learner's hip bones. In this position the facilitator can give the learner support while he is talking to the learner face-to-face. The facilitator can also shift the learner's weight from side to side. As this activity is repeated from day to day in the course of any language interchange with the learner, the facilitator can slowly reduce support to the hips.
Variation II	
ENTRY BEHAVIOR:	Learner has tight or stiff muscles (high muscle tone), making movement very restricted. He stands holding on with knees knocking and feet turning inward (or outward).
PROCEDURE:	The learner stands facing and holding onto a table. The facilitator kneels behind learner and reaches for learner's feet. He carefully turns the learner's feet into a parallel position.
	The facilitator places his hands around and in front of the learner's knees. He places his hands on the child's knees and braces the back part of the learner's thighs with his thumbs. Pressure, applied to the knee with the fingers to the front, and to the back part of the thighs from the thumb, should straighten both knees and push the hips over the straightened knees. The feet should stay parallel.

The facilitator should gradually release his hold on the learner's knees, allowing the learner to keep his own knees straight.

Variation III

ENTRY BEHAVIOR: Learner bears weight primarily on the leg and foot.

MATERIAL: Towel.

PROCEDURE: The facilitator rubs the soles of the feet of the learner, using pressure, before standing him up. Extra rubbing should be given to the foot on which the learner tends not to bear weight. Walk the learner with both hands held up, holding his hands or upper arms.

TERMINAL BEHAVIOR: Learner will be able to stand with hands held, or leaning against something stable, with straight hips and knees and feet parallel.

UNIT:	I 14 / Gross Motor
EPISODE:	S / Cruising
PURPOSE:	Learner will be able to cruise, taking a few side steps in order to reach a goal.
ENTRY BEHAVIOR:	Learner is able to stand, holding onto a low support such as a table. Learner can reach for an object if placed within arm's length.
MATERIAL:	Cookie or favorite toy; table (about chest level in height).
PROCEDURE:	The learner stands holding onto a table. His feet are about 4 inches apart and his legs are in straight alignment. The facilitator places a cookie or toy 4 to 6 inches from the learner's maximum arm reach. Cookie should be placed to the side of the learner. The facilitator calls the learner's attention to the cookie or toy. The facilitator encourages the learner to "get the cookie," verbally as well as physically, by holding and pulling the learner's arm toward the cookie or toy. If no spontaneous leg movement occurs toward the cookie or toy, the facilitator releases the learner's arm and places his hands over the learner's hips. He slowly tilts the learner's body over the leg opposite the side on which the cookie was placed. This move should raise the leg on the side of the cookie or toy. The facilitator quickly moves one of his hands to the raised leg and places that leg about 6 inches away from the stationary leg. The learner should then be closer to the cookie. The facilitator holds the learner's hips and tilts learner's body over this newly placed leg moving the learner even closer to the cookie or toy so the learner gets the cookie or toy. Repeat this procedure with new reward placed farther away from learner in both directions.
TERMINAL BEHAVIOR:	Learner can cruise, using furniture for support if needed.

UNIT:	I 14 / Gross Motor
EPISODE:	T / Pull Ups
PURPOSE:	Learner will be able to pull himself to a stand.
ENTRY BEHAVIOR:	Learner stands holding onto a support. He cruises with suppport.
MATERIAL:	Favorite toy or cookie; couch or sturdy, low table.
PROCEDURE:	The learner is sitting on the floor. The facilitator calls the learner's attention to a favorite toy which is on a couch or low table and out of his reach (4 to 6 inches away). The facilitator encourages the learner to get the toy by holding one of learner's hands and pulling the learner up. The learner moves from sitting to kneeling with both knees or on one knee with the other leg bent and foot on the floor. Then the facilitator helps the learner to stand over one or both legs and straighten his body to an upright position. The learner should be standing, holding onto the facilitator's hand and to the couch. The facilitator encourages the learner to let go with one hand and grasp the top to play with it.
	During the next sessions follow the same procedure, but the arm-pulling action should become less and less until the learner pulls himself up, holding the facilitator's arm.
TERMINAL BEHAVIOR:	Learner pulls to a stand at a couch when reaching for a toy.

UNIT:	I 14 / Gross Motor
EPISODE:	U / Pulling Up to Stand on Knees
PURPOSE:	Learner straightens his hips and improves balance in readiness for walking.
ENTRY BEHAVIOR:	Learner has the ability to turn his shoulders over his hips. Learner also has the ability to extend his arm, grasp, and pull or push up.
MATERIAL:	A favorite toy (such as a doll with removable limbs or hat), pad or carpet, foam block.
PROCEDURE:	Learner will sit on his heels on a pad or foam block, face the facilitator, and lean down to pick up a toy piece (Position 1).

The learner straightens up to put a piece of the toy (which is being held at the learner's shoulder level by the facilitator) in its proper place (Positions 2 and 3). Positioning of the toy can then be changed so that the learner reaches high or low. The height to which learner reaches can be increased according to learner's balance.

3

TERMINAL BEHAVIOR: Learner is able to pull up onto his knees and extend his hips, bearing weight on his knees.

UNIT:	**I 14 / Gross Motor**
EPISODE:	**V / Weightshifting in Standing for Balance**
PURPOSE:	Learner will be able to shift his body weight between left and right legs when walking or stooping.
ENTRY BEHAVIOR:	Learner waddles in walking. He falls occasionally. In order to maintain straightness in the hips for balance, the learner often stiffens his knees and goes up on his toes. He sits in various positions and is able to turn his body.
MATERIAL:	A large balloon, string, and beans to put in the balloon.
PROCEDURE:	The facilitator encourages the learner to stand. The facilitator suspends a balloon in the air or ties it near the top of the back of a chair. The balloon should be up high enough so that the learner has to reach out to hit the balloon. The facilitator tells the learner to stand facing the balloon and to hit the balloon. The facilitator should place his hands around the learner's hips with fingers in front and thumbs at back on the learner's bottom. The facilitator slowly pushes the learner's hips over the left leg making sure the learner's right leg is no longer in contact with the floor. Also, the learner's trunk and head should curve away from the left side. The facilitator is to stop pushing the learner's hips toward the left when this response occurs. The facilitator shifts the learner's hips away from the left side toward the right and over the right leg. The left leg should lift up while the learner's neck and trunk curve toward the left. The facilitator stops at this point and returns the learner's hips squarely over both legs. The facilitator should repeat two more times over each side.

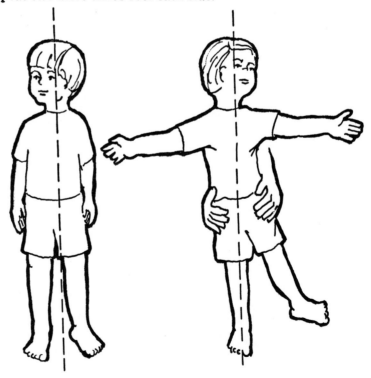

Variation I

The facilitator may do the procedure without a balloon or any toy. Instead, when walking, the learner's hips can be shifted over each weight-bearing leg.

The facilitator will place himself behind the learner, grasping the learner at the hips. As the learner steps forward the facilitator will rotate the leading hip forward, shifting the learner's body weight to the forward foot as it touches the floor, and alternating sides as the learner tips out. The forward motion must be initiated by the learner. The facilitator only guides the motion, rotating the hips and shifting the weight.

TERMINAL BEHAVIOR:

Learner shifts his body weight whenever he walks or stoops in order to maintain balance.

UNIT:	I 14 / Gross Motor
EPISODE:	W / Stoop and Pick Up
PURPOSE:	Learner will be able to stoop in order to pick up an object and recover his standing position.
ENTRY BEHAVIOR:	Learner is able to stand, holding on with one hand; is able to go from kneeling to knee standing; and is able to go from a squat to a stand with support.
MATERIAL:	A chair or low table to use as hand support; assorted toys, especially noise-making ones.
PROCEDURE:	The facilitator should capture the learner's attention with a toy on a playing surface. While the learner is paying attention, the facilitator makes the toy fall to the floor next to the learner. Encourage the learner to stoop down and pick up the toy. Then encourage the learner to place the toy back on the playing surface. Praise the learner and enter into his play sequence. If this is too difficult for the learner, place the object on an intermediate surface (between table and floor) for grasp and recovery. The facilitator can also support the learner by bending his knees to stoop and then offering an arm to raise with the learner for support.
TERMINAL BEHAVIOR:	Learner will stoop and recover toys during the process of playing.

Unit T 14 / GROSS MOTOR

UNIT:	T 14 / Gross Motor
EPISODE:	A / Pushing a Learner in a Cart
PURPOSE:	Learner improves strength and control of body. Learner practices walking. Learner learns to cooperate and take turns.
ENTRY BEHAVIOR:	Learner can walk steadily with hand held for support.
MATERIAL:	Commerically available cart with a handle the proper height for supporting the learner (about chest high) and ball casters or swivel wheels for easy turning; bricks; a doll.
PROCEDURE:	This episode, which is cooperative and imaginative, can be set up by you if you place one learner in the cart and then guide another learner as he pushes the riding learner around the room. You can encourage the imagination of the cooperating learners by going along making car noises, pretending you are outside on the street and describing it, etc. The learners should take turns riding and pushing as they become tired of each of their respective roles as pusher or passenger.
Variation I	Instead of another learner, heavy building bricks can be loaded into the cart (for stability) and the doll placed on top for a ride. The facilitator can then give the learner a chance to ride.
Variation II	While the learner is playing with a few favorite toys, the facilitator will bring out a wagon. The facilitator will encourage the learner to put the toys in the wagon and push them all around the room or yard. The facilitator will then encourage the learner to pull the wagon. The facilitator will demonstrate pushing and pulling the wagon; and saying the words "push and pull" during the activity as the wagon is pushed or pulled.
TERMINAL BEHAVIOR:	Learner spontaneously invites another learner for a ride in cart and pushes him about, planning his direction and moving him effectively, or learner pushes toys around in the cart.

UNIT:	T 14 / Gross Motor
EPISODE:	B / Playing Ball: Throwing and Kicking
PURPOSE:	Learner develops eye-hand and eye-foot coordination. Learner learns to interact with others in cooperative play.
ENTRY BEHAVIOR:	Learner has standing balance sufficient enough to enable him to lift one foot off the floor momentarily without holding onto something for support. Learner can clasp two hands together rapidly at the midline with good coordination. Learner can throw or push a ball in the general direction of the facilitator.
MATERIAL:	A large ball at least 6 inches in diameter; several other balls in graduating sizes down to the size of a tennis ball.
PROCEDURE:	Start this episode with a rather large ball. Toss it gently to the learner from a short distance. He will probably not catch it at first, so encourage him to "get the ball and throw the ball" back to you. After you throw it back and forth a few times, place the ball on the floor and, while the learner is looking at your feet, kick it in his direction. Encourage him not to pick it up but to kick it back to you. Be prepared for the ball to be kicked in any direction, even backward. Praise the learner for any contact between his foot and the ball. Kick the ball gently back to the learner from wherever it is after he has kicked it. When the learner seems to be tiring of kicking the ball, switch back to throwing and catching or fetching. Other learners can join in as in I17F.

Variation

PURPOSE:	Learner will balance on one foot with good extension of the opposite hip.
ENTRY BEHAVIOR:	Learner walks alone but with poor balance and without straight hips.
MATERIAL:	*Heavy* ball or cardboard box (with weights inside) with top higher than bent knee of the learner; or patches of carpet fastened to the wall.
PROCEDURE:	The facilitator will place a ball or box directly behind the learner's foot just far enough back so that his raised foot will kick it. (If a box is used, it will have to be weighted to give some resistance. Another alternative would be putting a patch of carpet on the wall behind the learner, which could be hit by the learner's foot when it is raised just a few inches above the knee.) The facilitator will stand in front of learner and hold his extended hand on the side of the foot that is to kick. The less preferred foot should kick first so that weight bearing is on the "preferred" side. It may be wise to ask the learner to kick without designating which foot first. Say, "Kick the ball hard." Then repeat, alternating feet several times.

TERMINAL BEHAVIOR: Learner plays catch and kick ball with facilitator or other children with good accuracy in kicking and throwing and is occasionally able to catch the ball when it is thrown to him. Learner will walk more rhythmically and with better balance.

UNIT:	T 14 / Gross Motor
EPISODE:	C / Tug of War
PURPOSE:	Learner will strengthen his grip, develop arm and leg muscles, and improve his balance.
ENTRY BEHAVIOR:	Learner can stand alone with good balance and walk backward.
MATERIAL:	Nylon rope, 1 inch in diameter and at least 6 feet long, with a large knot tied in each end.
PROCEDURE:	The facilitator and the learner stand facing each other. Each grasps the rope near the end in front of the knot, and the facilitator backs up slowly and pulls, encouraging the learner to "lean back, pull." The learner should stand by grabbing the rope in each hand with the dominant hand in front of the helping hand which is nearest the knot. The foot position should be the same with the dominant (preferred) foot placed a short space in front of the other foot. The facilitator and learner can also both back up slowly and pull. The facilitator will control his pressure on the rope to exert a steady pull to keep the learner leaning back, balanced, and pulling. The facilitator should be careful not to relax the pressure letting the learner fall back, but to end the episode by pulling the learner forward to stand fully upright.
TERMINAL BEHAVIOR:	Learner walks with strength and balance.

UNIT:	**T 14 / Gross Motor**
EPISODE:	**D / Walking Game**
PURPOSE:	Learner will change feet and shift body balance in a planned pattern, bearing weight equally on both feet.
ENTRY BEHAVIOR:	Learner has the ability to walk with toddler gait.
MATERIAL:	Large Kindergarten Blocks, or loops of string large enough for a foot to be placed inside easily, or large footsteps cut out of foam or colored paper and stuck to the floor; an interesting toy or treat.
PROCEDURE:	The circles (blocks, steps, etc.) should be placed for easy stepping, depending on the size of the learner. The facilitator will tell the learner to "match your feet to the steps," "step in the circle," or "step over the blocks" as he models the pattern. The goal may be a toy or a treat, or a hug from the facilitator.

Footsteps   String circles   Blocks

TERMINAL BEHAVIOR:	Learner will be able to walk with good rhythm and weight shifting.

UNIT:	T 14 / Gross Motor
EPISODE:	E / Stepping On, In, and Over[1]
PURPOSE:	Learner develops balance and confidence.
ENTRY BEHAVIOR:	Learner can walk on smooth surface with ease.
MATERIAL:	Commerically available balance beam placed on its wide side; or a plank, 1″ × 6″, about 6 to 8 feet long, and 2 bricks; or one or more old automobile tires; or a plain ladder 4 to 6 feet long.
PROCEDURE:	Set up the balance beam in a place familiar to the learner. Walk it once yourself calling the learner's attention to your feet. Ask him to step onto the beam. At first you can offer the learner both hands for support. Then use one hand only as he learns to balance better. First, encourage the learner to walk along the balance beam with one foot on the floor and one foot on the beam. You may need to help him bend his knee at first by pressing behind the knee until he gets the feel of the up/down movement by himself. When the learner is confident enough to move along with one foot on the floor and one foot on the balance beam, he can be encouraged to walk with both feet on the balance beam. Be sure to provide him with as much physical support and verbal encouragement as he

seems to need for this activity by offering your hands to be grasped by the learner. Try not to hold him but let him hold you. As he gains skill, move farther away from him, but not so far that he cannot reach you at all.

Variation I

Place a tire or ladder on the floor. Give the learner a soft toy or puppet to hug or hold. Stand in front of the tire or on the middle of the ladder. Say, "Step into the tire (*ladder*), take the puppet into the tire (*ladder*) with you. Watch me. Lift your foot up and over." Repeat to step out of the tire or ladder. When the learner can step in and out of one tire or the ladder, add more tires, one at a time, set about 1½ feet apart. When the learner can step in and out with ease while holding the toy, remove the toy and repeat the activity.

1. Learner walks forward with one foot on each side of each ladder rung.
2. Learner walks forward on the right side of the ladder with left foot inside ladder and stepping over each rung.
3. Learner walks forward on the left side of the ladder with right foot inside ladder and stepping over each rung.

TERMINAL BEHAVIOR:

Learner will walk with one foot on the balance beam and one foot off by himself. Learner will be able to step in and out of a series of tires or ladder spaces without hesitating or losing his balance.

---

[1]Ladder activities from Braley, W. T., Konicki, G., and Leedy, C. 1968. *Daily Sensorimotor Training Activities.* Reprinted with permission by Educational Activities, Inc., Freeport, N.Y. 11520.

UNIT:	**T 14 / Gross Motor**
EPISODE:	**F / Walking Up Steps to Get Reward**
PURPOSE:	Learner learns to ascend and descend stairs.
ENTRY BEHAVIOR:	Learner has ability to stand on one foot momentarily and has the confidence to go up and down stairs by creeping.
MATERIAL:	Short flight of carpeted stairs with railing, or commerically available play steps.
PROCEDURE:	Put a favorite toy of the learner's at the top of the stairs or on the platform at the top of the play steps. Hold your hands out to the learner just enough to support him for balance. His one hand should be on the railing if there is one. Encourage the learner to walk up the steps to the top, stoop and pick up the toy, and walk down the other side of the play steps or turn and go down the stairs holding you as needed. Repeat this activity immediately if the learner enjoyed the episode for the fun of climbing itself. Otherwise let him play with the toy for awhile and return to the climbing later.
TERMINAL BEHAVIOR:	Learner spontaneously goes up and down stairs, using only a railing for support on stairs or lightly holding facilitator's hand on steps without a railing.
Variation I	Place a tire or ladder on the floor. Give the learner a soft toy or puppet to hug or hold. Stand in front of the tire or on the middle of the ladder. Say, "Step into the tire (*ladder*), take the puppet into the tire (*ladder*) with you. Watch me." "Lift your foot up and over." Repeat to step out of the tire or ladder. When the learner can step in and out of one tire or the ladder, add more tires, one at a time, set about 1½ feet apart. When the learner can step in and out with ease while holding the toy, remove the toy and repeat the activity.

1. Learner walks forward with one foot on each side of the ladder.
2. Learner walks forward on the right side of the ladder.
3. Learner walks forward on the left side of the ladder.

TERMINAL BEHAVIOR:	Learner will be able to step in and out of a series of tires or ladder spaces without hesitating or losing his balance. Learner will walk with one foot on the balance beam and one foot off by himself.

Unit I 15 / FINE MOTOR

Learning episodes in this area are geared to promote development in the visual-motor-manipulative skills. As the young learner manipulates and organizes small play materials, many concepts are developed and consolidated. The learner becomes able to understand spatial concepts, to exercise his problem-solving skills with regard to the causal nature of events in his environment, and to discover essential properties about items in his world. For the learner with deficiencies in the fine motor area, the positioning techniques, which are designed to relax the learner and/or to directly facilitate hand use, are most important and are illustrated in the readiness section (Unit I 22). These enable the learner to function most efficiently when there are interferences with this developmental mode.

The learner with good fine motor abilities is also able to perform many of the self-help skills that enhance independence and self-image. For the learner with no fine motor developmental deficits, feeding, dressing, and other self-help skills are performed easily in the course of acquiring other fine motor skills. For other learners, however, special efforts should be made to encourage development of fine motor skills to facilitate self-help since these are so important from the standpoint of developing good feelings about oneself. An occupational therapist may often be of help in advising on additional and specific activities to promote good hand function and suggesting equipment that can facilitate the development of self-care activities.

UNIT: I 15 / Fine Motor

EPISODE: A / Holding Toys, Listening

PURPOSE: Learner will grasp and explore with hands, mouth, and eyes.

ENTRY BEHAVIOR: Normal grasping ability.

MATERIAL: A number of different toys and household objects that can be easily held by the learner. These things should be of different textures, such as rough versus smooth, and weights, such as heavy versus light. These items should also be interesting to look at and listen to. While such things as rattles shaped like dumbbells are easiest for the learner to grasp and mouth, there are many other interesting things in the household for the learner to play with which can also be held easily. These things include measuring spoons, keys, sponges, chain jewelry, and combs.

PROCEDURE: Position the learner comfortably in supported sitting position so he is relaxed. Place each object in the learner's hand, and tell him what it is as you give it to him. "This is a *comb.*" You may have to open the fingers of a young learner's hand by stroking the top of his hand firmly, from knuckles back toward the wrist, or rolling the object into his palm from his wrist downward toward his fingers. Smile at the learner whenever he moves the object about and describe to him what he is doing with the object: "*(Learner's* *name)* shakes the comb." At times, gently guide the learner's hand into his line of vision, and in this way help him to focus his eyes on the object as he holds it. When the learner drops a new object after only a moment, hand him the same object and repeat the sequence. If he has held the object often or explored it for some time, hand him another object, describe it, and encourage activity.

Repeat the activity for as long as the learner looks at what is grasped. Be sure to alternate hands, especially if the young learner seems to use one hand more than the other, so that each hand participates.

TERMINAL BEHAVIOR: Learner grasps object when placed in his hand and explores it through shaking, banging, mouthing, looking at it, pulling on it, etc.

UNIT:	I 15 / Fine Motor
EPISODE:	B / Reaching for a Dangling Object
PURPOSE:	Learner will develop eye-hand coordination and visually directed reaching.
ENTRY BEHAVIOR:	Learner has demonstrated purposeful grasp by opening his hand when things are placed near it or against it. Learner has started to wave his arm toward things that he wants.
MATERIAL:	Toys or objects that are easily grasped by the learner, such as rattles in the shape of tubes or cylinders, or large rings or teethers. Pieces of heavy elastic like that used for sewing in waistbands, about 12–18 inches in length, to be tied in the middle of each of the toys.
PROCEDURE:	While the learner is lying on his back or is propped sitting comfortably in a semi-upright position, take a toy that is easy for the learner to grasp, tie a piece of heavy elastic around it, and dangle the toy by the elastic within easy reach of the learner. Encourage the learner to "reach and get the *toy*." It is usually easier for the learner to grasp slightly to one side or the other while both his hands and the object are in his visual range. If the learner does not reach directly for the toy, you can help him by putting it against his hand while still dangling it with the elastic. Then the learner will usually take it in his hand. Once the learner has a hold of the toy, tug gently on the elastic, saying, "Let me have the *toy*" until the learner lets go. Then say, "I've got the *toy*. I've got the *toy*. Reach and get the *toy* again." Again, dangle the object well within the learner's reach. Since the object is on a piece of elastic, it will bounce up and down, and it will be especially fun for the learner if you pretend to be startled when he lets go and it bounces high in the air. Be careful that the object does not fly up and hit you in the face when the learner lets go.
	This episode may also be played out while the learner is on his stomach, propped on his elbows, by placing the toy within reach and dragging it away. Some learners will tend to use one hand more than the other at a very early age and may need special encouragement to reach with the non-preferred hand. Be sure to alternate hands, giving the learner an opportunity to use both.
TERMINAL BEHAVIOR:	Learner reaches directly for dangling object, grasps it, and either explores it extensively or pulls and releases it to participate in the give-and-take play of the episode with either hand.

UNIT:	I 15 / Fine Motor
EPISODE:	C / Paper Play
PURPOSE:	Learner will increase ability to grasp with one or both hands and begin to use hands in opposition to one another.
ENTRY BEHAVIOR:	Learner has begun to show a voluntary grasp and release.
MATERIAL:	Magazine pages or other attractive pieces of paper, e.g., wrapping paper, etc. (Using just the pages rather than the whole magazine will help insure against unintentional encouragement to the learner to destroy magazines you may want to keep.)
PROCEDURE:	Give sheets of paper to the learner and demonstrate crumpling, tearing, stretching, etc. Encourage him to imitate, and enjoy the activity along with the learner, sharing his excitement in the activity. Generally learners will not need encouragement to perform this episode, but if they do you can guide their hands as in Learning Episode I15A.
TERMINAL BEHAVIOR:	When presented with a piece of paper, learner demonstrates many activities using two hands together such as crumpling, tearing, stretching, etc.

UNIT:	I 15 / Fine Motor
EPISODE:	D / Reaching Up High
PURPOSE:	Learner will be able to raise his arms above shoulder level, straighten his back, and swing his arms in preparation for lifting overhead.
ENTRY BEHAVIOR:	Learner can sit unsupported and is able to grasp.
MATERIAL:	Two attractive rings about 6 inches in diameter.
PROCEDURE:	Sit the learner on the floor. Present the rings to him to grasp one in each hand at his lap or chest level. Take one ring in each of your hands and raise them to his shoulder level and then, with "so big," above his head. When the rings are above his head, pull upward gently so that he will have to stretch and straighten his back.

Repeat, raising the rings higher each time for the first grasp so that the learner begins to stretch up himself. |

Variation I

ENTRY BEHAVIOR:	Learner can pull to a sitting position from lying on his back with little or no help.
MATERIAL:	Balloon on a string, or a favorite toy on a string or elastic strip.
PROCEDURE:	The facilitator will place the learner on his back with his knees bent and feet held on the floor by the facilitator's crossed legs. The facilitator will sit facing the learner in the tailor position, or pillow may be placed on the learner's feet to hold them down. The facilitator will dangle the balloon above the learner's knees and ask him to pull up and bat the balloon. It is important to hold the balloon in a position within the learner's easy reach, especially at first. The facilitator will gradually increase the distance and height of the balloon so that the learner eventually has to straighten and raise his arms to shoulder level and above to bat the balloon.
TERMINAL BEHAVIOR:	Learner will be able to hold an object, straighten his arms, and lift the object to and above shoulder level while sitting or standing with a straight back.

UNIT:	I 15 / Fine Motor
EPISODE:	E / Hand One, Two, Three Objects in a Row
PURPOSE:	Learner learns to let go of one object in order to reach for another and develops problem-solving strategy.
ENTRY BEHAVIOR:	Learner can reach and grasp, and can hold onto two objects at a time.
MATERIAL:	Several sets of three objects each. Some sets should have three things that are the same, such as three blocks. Other sets should be made up of three different items, such as a toothbrush, a bracelet, and a sponge. For a learner with visual impairments, items having noises, three the same, three discriminably different, should be used.
PROCEDURE:	Have two or three sets of objects ready. Hand one of the objects from the set having the same things in it to the learner. When he grasps this, hand him the second item for grasping. Then hold out the third object from the same set. If the learner does not drop one of the two objects he is holding, or if he does not seem to be trying to figure out a way to get all three objects (for example, by transferring one of them under his arm), put the third object from the set of similar objects down and ask the learner to give you the first two objects. Hand the learner the object or toy which you guess would be the least attractive to him first. After he grasps this, hand him the second most attractive object for grasping. Finally offer him the most attractive object or toy of the set. Each time you offer an object encourage him to grasp it. Help the learner to figure out a way to solve the problem of getting all three objects, or at least help the learner to understand that he can reach for a third object if he drops the second one or transfers it to his other hand. You can do this by easing one object out of his hand and replacing it with the third item.
	Return to using a set of three similar objects when the learner tires of the three different ones. Always praise the learner for picking up the third object no matter what the process. As he becomes better at dropping or transferring to reach for the third object, help him to figure out a way of holding all three objects in his hands or arms. Do not forget to accept and praise whatever strategy he develops for solving this problem.
TERMINAL BEHAVIOR:	Learner can hold two objects, one in each hand, and when third object is presented learner either immediately drops one of the two objects he is holding, reaching for the third object, or solves the problem by holding onto it in some way (tucking it under his arm, grasping two objects in one hand, etc.) to successfully grasp the third object.

UNIT:	I 15 / Fine Motor
EPISODE:	F / Clapping Two Objects Together
PURPOSE:	Learner explores more than one toy at a time, relates two objects together, and develops eye-hand coordination.
ENTRY BEHAVIOR:	Learner can reach and grasp and bring both hands together at the midline of his body.
MATERIAL:	Pairs of objects that are attractive to the learner, that can be easily held, and that make noise when banged together. Blocks, spoons, rattles, and small pots are some suggestions. Pairs of toys or two different toys may be used.
PROCEDURE:	Place the learner in a relaxed position (see Learning Episode I 22C). When the learner is positioned properly, the facilitator can present one toy for the learner to grasp. A second toy should be presented after the first is grasped. The learner may drop the first toy and only pay attention to the second toy. The facilitator can then demonstrate holding on to two different toys and clapping them together. The facilitator should encourage the learner to imitate the clapping action through verbal direction or manual guidance.
	The learner may begin relating two objects together by banging a toy on a tray or another toy. Ultimately the learner realizes he can hold two objects, one in each hand, and bring these objects together to bang.
	If the learner seems to use one hand much more than the other, the learner should be encouraged to use the non-preferred hand to come to the middle on an equal basis with the preferred hand. Learning Episode I22M may encourage the learner to bring both hands together symmetrically.
TERMINAL BEHAVIOR:	Learner purposefully brings one toy to another or bangs toys together, using equal motions of both hands.

UNIT:	I 15 / Fine Motor
EPISODE:	G / Poking Bubbles and Spaces
PURPOSE:	Learner increases eye-hand coordination and learns effective use of forefinger. Learner also learns cause and effect relationships and develops a sense of mastery.
ENTRY BEHAVIOR:	Learner has begun to use thumb and first fingers of hand to pick up objects.
MATERIAL:	Commercially available liquid for blowing bubbles through a wand.
PROCEDURE:	As the learner is lying on his back or sitting upright, blow bubbles through a wand in front of him so that the bubbles fall within his reach. Encourage the learner to poke at the bubbles, show him how to do it by demonstrating and offering manual guidance, and describe the actions that occur. Show him how pleased you are if he manages to reach out and touch, and therefore break, any bubble. Help the learner to isolate his forefinger for poking by placing your hand over his and curling his fingers and thumb, excepting the forefinger, into a loose fist. Then blow the bubbles and encourage the learner to reach, keeping your hand lightly around his and following his lead.

Variation

MATERIAL:	Small bottle with raisin or other edible inside; toy telephone.
PROCEDURE:	These are items that will also encourage the isolation of the forefinger and further development of fine motor skills. Imitative games using the telephone for "dialing," and inserting snack food into small bottles or containers will encourage poking and other forefinger use.
TERMINAL BEHAVIOR:	Learner points with forefinger and accurately touches bubbles within his reach, or pokes and explores holes and other small openings.

UNIT:	I 15 / Fine Motor
EPISODE:	H / Scribbling
PURPOSE:	Learner learns the relationship between his own actions and the resulting marks on paper, and develops eye and hand coordination and an enhanced sense of accomplishment with regard to his own products.
ENTRY BEHAVIOR:	Learner can sit with support and grasp thick crayon or marker in his hand, or will tolerate sticky substance on his hands. Learner has vision sufficient for discerning color on paper.
MATERIAL:	Thick crayons or water-based, colored "magic markers," commercially available finger paints, and paper; homemade finger paints and magazine pages; or Ivory dishwashing liquid to which a few drops of food coloring has been added and a large, smooth table top.
PROCEDURE:	Sit the learner comfortably in a relaxed position at a table and give him one or two bright colored crayons or pots of finger paints and a large piece of paper. The facilitator should sit next to the learner, close enough to be able to reach around to guide both of the learner's hands if necessary. If the learner does not scribble spontaneously, demonstrate the technique with the crayon, or dip his fingers in the finger paint and move them around. If he does scribble by himself, show him how to make lines up and down or across the paper from one side to the other. Encourage him to copy your motions by demonstration, and call attention to the results. Give the learner only as much help as he needs to hold the crayon effectively. If the learner cannot hold a crayon well enough to mark the paper, finger paints are usually the best medium to give him, although, since magic markers do not have to be pressed down in order to make a mark, they may also be easy enough. Encourage the learner to move his hands or the markers in all directions through demonstration or manual guidance of up and down, side to side, and circular strokes. Do not forget to label the colors the learner uses and the shapes he makes ("That is a red circle") and to praise him for any of his accomplishments. All papers should be displayed at the children's eye-level where adults and other children may admire them. Learning episodes involving other "art" activities can follow this one (see T17G).
TERMINAL BEHAVIOR:	Learner enjoys scribbling on paper with crayons and will do so in all directions in side to side and up and down movements. Learner enjoys smearing finger paints and will do so with his whole hand as well as his fingers, making various motions such as side to side, up and down, and around in a circle.

UNIT:	I 15 / Fine Motor
EPISODE:	I / Picking Up Small Objects
PURPOSE:	Learner will pick up small objects with thumb-finger grasp.
ENTRY BEHAVIOR:	Learner is able to reach out with a gross grasp and grasp large objects with thumb and first finger.
MATERIAL:	Small buttons; small pegs; cereals (Cheerios, Rice Chex, etc.); raisins; can or bottle.
PROCEDURE:	Learner is sitting, with support if necessary, at a table or on the floor in front of a small stool. The facilitator places one group of small objects in a row about an inch apart. Pointing to one object the facilitator says, "Look at the *button*. Give me the *button*." The facilitator's open palm, or the can or bottle, must be held at midline in front of the learner within his easy reach. The facilitator should vary the objects, using only one group of objects at a time. Of course, raisins and cereal may be eaten as a reward, using either of these as a *last* group. The facilitator will say, "Look at the raisin. Pick it up. You may eat the raisin." Be very observant and make sure the learner does not put any of the other objects in his mouth. If he moves to do so, put a hand between the learner's hand and mouth, saying, "No. Buttons are *not* for eating. Buttons do not go in your mouth. Buttons go here (indicating palm or receptacle)."
TERMINAL BEHAVIOR:	Learner will be able to use a thumb-finger grasp to pick up small objects and place them in a receptacle.

UNIT:	I 15 / Fine Motor
EPISODE:	J / Reaching with Palm Up
PURPOSE:	Learner will be able to turn hand over and receive an object that is most appropriately placed in the palm of his hand.
ENTRY BEHAVIOR:	Learner has difficulty turning his arm over (rotating his wrist) to the palm up position in order to receive objects that are offered to him.
MATERIAL:	Bits of food or other small toys or play materials that the learner desires.
PROCEDURE:	The facilitator will assume a face-to-face position with the learner. The learning facilitator will offer the learner an item that the learner desires with his hand on the opposite side to the hand which the learner is using to reach. With his other hand the learning facilitator will reach across the learner's body and grasp the learner's forearm at the point at which it joins the elbow. The facilitator will guide the learner's hand over by turning the learner's forearm in such a way that the wrist is rotated and the palm turns up with the inside of the hand toward the midline of the learner's body and the thumb on the outside of the learner's body. The item desired by the learner will then be dropped into the learner's palm.
TERMINAL BEHAVIOR:	Learner can reach his hand out with palm up in order to receive offered items.

Unit T 15 / FINE MOTOR

UNIT: T 15 / Fine Motor

EPISODE: A / Placing Pegs

PURPOSE: Learner increases eye-hand coordination and understanding of spatial relationships.

ENTRY BEHAVIOR: Learner can reach, grasp, and let go. Learner has shown interest in putting objects in and taking them out of containers.

MATERIAL: There are many commercially available peg-placing sets. Generally, for younger learners, large pegs of the same size but different colors are best. Some pegs are knob shaped and have rubber-mat boards. These are excellent and encourage use of hand pressure along with coordination. Older learners still enjoy this game but usually prefer smaller pegs with boards having holes close together so they can make designs.

PROCEDURE: There are many different games in which the learner simply places a peg in a hole. Start with a peg board that has large pegs and holes and that is easy for the learner to manage. Show him how the pegs fit into the holes, and guide his hands if necessary. At first the learner may simply remove the pegs and explore the board by poking at the holes. Allow this, and continue to place the pegs yourself or guide the learner's hands. When he is successful with the big pegs, you can move on to those peg boards that have smaller pegs and holes. You may also use the pegs and boards to encourage the older learner to select the same color peg as yours for a matching learning episode or encourage the learner to copy your peg pattern for a sorting learning episode.

TERMINAL BEHAVIOR: Learner grasps peg, rotates wrist, and places peg in hole without hesitation. Learner can remove and replace peg with ease. Older learner can select the "same" peg as the facilitator's and copy the facilitator's design.

UNIT:	T 15 / Fine Motor
EPISODE:	B / Winding Up Action Toys
PURPOSE:	Learner learns cause and effect relationships and improves finger dexterity.
ENTRY BEHAVIOR:	Learner has learned to attend to action toys until their performance stops. Learner will hand facilitator the toy to wind for repeat performance.
MATERIAL:	Commercially available toys with key action-winding mechanism. Those with the key attached are easier for the learner to handle.
PROCEDURE:	Wind-up toys are delicate and may be broken easily into small pieces so you need to closely oversee the learner's play with these toys. Learners should be discouraged from banging, throwing, or doing other things that might break the toy. To do this simply take the toy yourself and activate it out of his reach if he misuses the toy. As before, the object is for the learner to pay attention to the performance of the toy, but in this case you should concentrate on showing the learner how to get the toy to make it move again by himself. By holding his hand and moving his fingers you can show him how the toy is wound up. You can then tell him to "let the *toy* go" and encourage him to "wind up the *toy* again" when it stops moving.
TERMINAL BEHAVIOR:	Learner can wind up any wind-up action toy and, after doing so, will watch until its performance ends.

UNIT:	**T 15 / Fine Motor**
EPISODE:	**C / Stringing Beads**
PURPOSE:	Learner will use both hands to develop eye-hand coordination.
ENTRY BEHAVIOR:	Learner can grasp and release and has a pincer grasp. Learner can clasp hands at midline and transfer objects from one hand to the other. Learner has shown understanding of "in" through peg placing or other activities.
MATERIAL:	Box of macaroni with very large holes, such as rigatoni style. Shoelaces with metal or plastic tips approximately 2 feet in length or longer, or 18 to 24 inches of ordinary stiff cotton clothesline with a knot at one end. The other end should be tapered and treated with glue or shellac for 2 or 3 inches to form a "needle" or threader. Beads made from cutting bamboo or cardboard mailing tubes.
PROCEDURE:	Place the learner in a long sit or a tailor sit on the floor, or place him comfortably in a chair offering him as much support as he needs to maintain sitting balance but not so much support that he leans completely against the chair.
	The learning facilitator should demonstrate stringing the first piece of macaroni onto the shoestring by showing and describing his actions. The first piece of macaroni should be tied onto the string by making a loop around it and a knot. This will serve to prevent the macaroni strung by the learner from slipping off the string. The learner should be encouraged to hold the string in the hand having the best pincer grasp and/or in the non-preferred hand. The learner should then be encouraged to pick up the pieces of macaroni with the other hand and to pass them over the end of the string. When the piece of macaroni is passed over the end of the string it should be necessary for the learner to grasp the macaroni and the string with the preferred hand and use the non-preferred hand as the means for pulling the string through the macaroni. As the learner proceeds in mastering this task, macaroni of different shapes having smaller holes may be used for variety. Finally, as skill allows, beads with small holes may be used to make "jewelry" to wear for play.
TERMINAL BEHAVIOR:	Learner is able to string macaroni and/or beads having holes with diameters just slightly larger than the shoestring. Learner can do this without using hands as support for sitting, although he may support some of his weight on his elbows if working on a table surface.

UNIT:	T 15 / Fine Motor
EPISODE:	D / Clothes Wash and Wring
PURPOSE:	Learner will develop fine motor coordination, using both hands to accomplish a task.
ENTRY BEHAVIOR:	Learner must be able to sit or stand without using both hands for full support. Learner must be able to imitate and/or become involved in imaginary play.
MATERIAL:	Pan of water or tub of water; washcloths, baby clothes, doll clothes, socks, or other small items in need of laundering; mild soap such as Ivory Snow; clothesline and clothespins.
PROCEDURE:	The learning facilitator will place items to be laundered next to basin filled with warm water and soap suds in front of the learner. The basin should be at chest level. If the learner is to launder the items in the bathtub they should be draped over the edge of the bathtub. The facilitator should demonstrate to the child how each item to be laundered is dipped into the soapy water, rubbed together, squeezed, and finally wrung out in a twisting motion. When each item has been laundered, the basin of soapy water should be replaced with warm, clear water, or the bathtub should be refilled with clear water. Each item should be swished around in the water to be rinsed of the soap suds, and the squeezing and wringing process should be repeated with each item until each item has been rinsed. The learner may then proceed to dry the clothes, either in an automatic clothes dryer or, preferably, to hang each item on a clothesline arranged at the same "reachable" level as the learner's own towel and washcloth should be. To do this the clothesline can be strung between two chairs in the basement or bathroom area. The pinch-type clothespins with the spring are good for the learner to use if he has the strength. If the strength in the learner's fingers is not sufficient to open these clothespins, the facilitator may help the learner to place the clothespins on, although the learner may be able to remove them himself. Also, if the learner cannot manage the spring-type clothespin, other clothespins can be used. The learner can remove the clothes from the clothesline or dryer and help fold the clothes. The facilitator should employ demonstration and manual guidance to encourage toddlers in this activity. The emphasis in this activity is not on perfection as far as getting the clothes clean but on participation of the learner in the process, i.e., swishing, squeezing, wringing, and rubbing with both hands.
TERMINAL BEHAVIOR:	Learner is able to participate with the learning facilitator's guidance and perform all the motions necessary to launder and to dry clothing.

UNIT:	T 15 / Fine Motor
EPISODE:	E / Stacking Hands
PURPOSE:	Learner will use both hands equally in play.
ENTRY BEHAVIOR:	Learner can open hands and straighten arms.
MATERIAL:	None.
PROCEDURE:	The facilitator and learner sit facing each other at a narrow table or side-sit facing each other on a bench, a sofa, or the floor. The facilitator places his right hand flat on the table, palm down, and says to the learner, touching the preferred hand, "Open your *right* hand and put it on top of mine." The facilitator guides the learner's hand if necessary. The facilitator says, "Now, I put my left hand on top of yours" and does so. Then he says to the learner, "Put your *left* hand on top of mine" and guides it into place. When the learner has done this, the facilitator says, "Now the fun begins! I will pull my *bottom* hand out and put in on top," and proceeds by doing this. Then the facilitator says, "You pull your bottom hand out and put it on top," and guides the learner as needed. "Now I pull my hand out," etc. The facilitator and learner will continue pulling their bottom hands out one by one and putting each on top slowly until the procedure has been learned. Then the speed can be increased, going faster and faster until either facilitator or learner pulls the wrong hand out. This activity can be repeated as many times as the learner wants.
TERMINAL BEHAVIOR:	Learner spontaneously uses both his hands in manual activities.

UNIT:	**T 15 / Fine Motor**
EPISODE:	**F / Rolling Ball into Box**

PURPOSE: Learner will develop eye-hand coordination, trying to roll a ball into holes with accuracy by focusing on the target, holding the ball in hand, and rolling in the palms-up position.

ENTRY BEHAVIOR: Learner will be able to grasp ball and focus on a target. Learner can locomote.

MATERIAL: Sturdy, corrugated cardboard carton, approximately 20″×6″ deep, modified as illustrated below.
Construction:

1. Cut top completely out of carton.
2. Cut center of bottom out leaving at least a 2″ frame for strength.
3. Glue any loose areas, particularly on the bottom, which will be the top of completed box.
4. Cut square holes 1″, 2″, and 3″ in size in the bottom of the front edge (top of the original box), as shown in diagram.
5. Cover with contact paper or paint a bright color. Be sure to cut contact paper ½″ larger at openings to be folded over to strengthen the edges. If box is to be painted, strengthen the edges of the openings with tape.

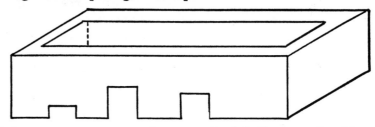

Paint or contact paper; glue; tape; Jack ball, or small rubber ball 1″–2″ in diameter.

PROCEDURE: The facilitator will set box against a wall. Using a Jack ball, the learner will kneel on one or both knees a few feet in front of the box and roll the ball forward into the largest hole. The learner will move to the box, retrieve the ball, and return to his place. When the learner is proficient, he may try the next larger hole. The learner's position away from the box should be modeled by the facilitator: close at first, and then a greater distance away as the learner is successful.

When the learner no longer has difficulty rolling the large ball into the holes, large marbles may be introduced, with the goal of finally rolling the marbles into the smallest hole.

To make this a game, several learners may take turns and, if meaningful, a score may be given each time a ball is rolled into a hole. Larger scores may even be given for rolling the ball into smaller holes.

TERMINAL BEHAVIOR: Learner is able to roll ball into small holes, holding hands in the palms-up position.

UNIT:	T 15 / Fine Motor
EPISODE:	G / Precision Placement
PURPOSE:	The learner develops precise eye-hand coordination and perception of horizontal and vertical.
ENTRY BEHAVIOR:	Learner is able to do peg-placing and simple shape-sorting activities, i.e., round object in round hole, square object in square hole.
MATERIAL:	Coffee cans with plastic lids and slits cut in plastic lids; checkers or tokens to fit slits; other "piggy-bank" types of toys with openings large enough for the learner to see easily.
PROCEDURE:	Present the learner with the tokens to be placed in the coffee can or other receptacle. Hold the receptacle in such a way that the slit is parallel to the ground and horizontal to the learner's position. After the learner has inserted the chips, encourage him to lift the plastic lid off of the jar or the can and dump out the chips. Then turn the can in such a way that the lid is parallel to the floor with the slit in a vertical position to the learner's midline. Repeat the learning episode. After the learner has successfully added all the chips to the receptacle, encourage him again to take off the lid and dump out the chips. Then hold the can in such a way that the lid is perpendicular to the floor with the slit in a horizontal position, and finally repeat the activity a fourth time in such a way that the lid is perpendicular to the floor with the slit in a vertical position. This episode may be repeated so that the learner inserts the chips or the checkers into the slit in many visual planes while the slit is held in both vertical and horizontal positions.
TERMINAL BEHAVIOR:	Learner will be able to adjust his fine motor movements and his visual perception to match the position of the slit as he moves the chip toward the slit so that when the chip makes contact it is in correct alignment and slips easily through the opening.

Unit I 16 / LANGUAGE

Expressive language includes all attempts by the learner to communicate with the learning facilitator. These include gestures and sounds as well as real words. Even before the learner is forming words he generally babbles and makes other baby noises. If the learning facilitator encourages "conversations" by repeating the learner's babbling sounds and then encouraging the learner to modify these sounds, the learner will become more responsive to vocal interchanges with the facilitator. The importance of the ability to communicate is so obvious that it need not be stressed here. The development of a mode of effective communication between the learning facilitator and the learner should be one of the paramount goals of developmental intervention.

If a learner has a deficit in the area of expressive language, a speech pathologist should be consulted. For young learners, especially those having motor difficulties, a speech pathologist and physical or occupational therapist familiar with prespeech and feeding activities that promote good oral-motor development can be of great help. Because speech is a combination of language and oral-motor control, often those learners who are able to understand what is said to them (i.e., they have adequate receptive and associative language ability) and can indicate understanding by their responses, nevertheless cannot produce vocalizations as a response to the learning facilitator. This can be extremely frustrating for the learner; in order to avoid undesirable behavioral reactions, the learning facilitator may wish to consult with a speech pathologist about alternative or parallel modes of communication.

This is also true of learners whose delay in expressive language, as well as perhaps in receptive language, is caused by a deficiency in hearing. If the hearing loss is severe enough, it is helpful for an alternate mode of communication to be taught along with vocalization and used with the learner from an early stage so that the learner's inner language can develop. It should be noted that the introduction of alternative modes of communication to very young learners, especially those with some ability to hear, is not always necessary and may be quite controversial. In these instances the advice of the speech pathologist and/or audiologist is essential. For most children many of the language learning episodes can be performed during the other activities, especially in the cognitive and gross and fine motor areas.

UNIT:	I 16 / Language
EPISODE:	A / Imitation of Speech Sounds
PURPOSE:	Learner will imitate speech sounds.
ENTRY BEHAVIOR:	Learner makes some spontaneous verbalizations (vowel sounds — "ah," "oh," grunting sounds, "raspberries").
MATERIAL:	None.
PROCEDURE:	The learner is in a quiet room which is free from distractions. The facilitator faces the learner about 12″ away from his face and makes sounds that the learner has been heard to produce (e.g., vowel sounds, grunting sounds, "raspberries") in a normal voice level. The facilitator will wait 3 to 5 seconds for the learner to vocalize and then repeat his sounds.

If the learner does not imitate the facilitator, then the facilitator should start by imitating the learner whenever he hears the learner make a sound during the day. This is especially likely to occur during bath, feeding, or roughhouse play. Once the facilitator starts imitating the learner and the "conversation" is going back and forth, the facilitator can shift to a different sound and then proceed as above.

TERMINAL BEHAVIOR: Learner will imitate sounds.

UNIT:	I 16 / Language
EPISODE:	B / Place of Articulation
PURPOSE:	Learner will become aware of the place and position of his jaw, lips, and tongue when different sounds are produced.
ENTRY BEHAVIOR:	Learner has few sounds involving different parts of the oral mechanism. Learner imitates learning facilitator's production of at least one sound.
MATERIAL:	None.
PROCEDURE:	The learning facilitator can help the learner become aware of the place where various sounds are produced and thus help him formulate the sounds in a more voluntary and spontaneous manner. The facilitator will guide the learner's hands to the places where the sound is created to feel the vibrations or airstream emitted. The facilitator can also use a mirror and point to the movements of the learner's mouth as the learner produces different sounds or words containing the indicated sounds.

For example, the learning facilitator can make the sound of "Mmmm" holding the learner's hand to his lips and nose to pick up the vibratory sensations along with hearing the sound. The facilitator can then encourage the learner to make the "Mmmm" sound and guide his hands to his own lips and nose to pick up the same sensations (i.e., one hand on his nose, one hand on his lips).

In a similar fashion the facilitator could encourage the production of other sounds. The chart shows where the learner's hands could be placed in order to best feel the sound as either he or the facilitator makes the sounds.

Sounds	Where to look	Where to place hands			
		Throat	Lips	Nose	1″ from mouth
M	Lips		X	X	
N	Tongue tip			X	X
B	Lips	X	X		
P	Lips		X		X
D	Tongue tip	X			X
T	Tongue tip	X			X
G	Tongue	X			X
K	Tongue	X			X
F	Lip and Teeth		X		X
V	Lip and Teeth	X	X		
L	Tongue tip	X			
J	Tongue and Teeth	X			
Sh	Tongue and Teeth				X
Ch	Tongue and Teeth				X
Z	Teeth	X			
S	Teeth				X
R	Tongue	X			
Th	Teeth and Tongue (as in "teeth")				X
Th	Teeth and Tongue (as in "that")	X			X

TERMINAL BEHAVIOR: Learner spontaneously uses sounds generated from all parts of the oral-motor mechanism, i.e., from the lips, through the mouth, to the throat, in the course of speaking.

UNIT:	I 16 / Language
EPISODE:	C / Imitating Gestures: "So Big," etc.
PURPOSE:	Learner learns to copy body language and to communicate with facilitator.
ENTRY BEHAVIOR:	Learner will attend to facilitator and enjoys body movement.
MATERIAL:	None.
PROCEDURE:	The point of this game is to get the learner to imitate things that you do with your body. For example, you can raise your arms up over your head and say "so big" to the learner. If the learner does not imitate you right away, you can take his arms in your hands and raise them over his head saying, "So big." There are many other gestures which you can do and teach the learner to imitate. Some of them might be rubbing your tummy and his saying, "Yum, yum," stamping your feet saying, "Stamp, stamp, stamp," etc. The idea is for the learner to first be able to see your activity as well as his own as he imitates you. Do not expect the learner to be perfect in his imitations right away, but praise him for any movement that looks at all like the one you have done. Later, as he does the gestural imitations easily, you can combine them, doing one after another, to increase his ability to follow you. Then you can also do gestures which he cannot see himself perform, such as patting his head. Learning episodes involving songs and fingerplay can follow this (see T9C, T9D, and T9E).
TERMINAL BEHAVIOR:	Learner will imitate gestures which the facilitator does first. Learner can imitate gestures that he can see himself perform, like "Pat-a-Cake," and that he cannot see himself perform, like patting the top of his head.

UNIT:	I 16 / Language
EPISODE:	D / Point and/or Name Pictures in a Book
PURPOSE:	Learner will recognize objects visually and by name. Learner will vocalize name of object.
ENTRY BEHAVIOR:	Learner will attend to pictures. Learner can hear and makes word-like sounds.
MATERIAL:	Book with stiff pages with only one bright colored familiar object to a page. You can make these by putting magazine cutouts on cardboard, punching holes in the side, and tying yarn through the holes.
PROCEDURE:	Place the learner in a relaxed position on your lap, at your side, or in front of you. Hold the book within the learner's reach where he can see and point to the pictures and turn the pages. Point to a picture. Name the object pictured and say, "See the ball." Then say, "Point to the ball" or "Touch the ball." You can also ask, "Where is the ball?" Always repeat the name of the object. If the learner vocalizes any sound, repeat after him any word or sound he makes to name the object. Then repeat the correct name of the object, e.g., "Ba. Ball." Keep a sense of excitement in your voice when repeating the learner's sounds and modeling the correct sounds to encourage the learner.
TERMINAL BEHAVIOR:	Learner can point to an object in a book when asked and vocalize a response that approximates the name of the object.

Unit T 16 / LANGUAGE

UNIT:	**T 16 / Language**
EPISODE:	**A / First Words**
PURPOSE:	Learner will begin to use common words for daily communication and interactions.
ENTRY BEHAVIOR:	Learner has indicated comprehension of single words in context and has uttered consonant-vowel and vowel-consonant combinations in sequence.
MATERIAL:	None.
PROCEDURE:	The following list of words are those which learners usually say first:

No
All gone, away
Stop
More, again, another
This, there, that, where
Give, do, make, get, throw, eat, wash, kiss
Put, up, down, sit, fall, go
Big, hot, dirty, heavy
Personal names
Any common household object
Familiar toy (truck, doll, ball, *etc.*)[1]

Use these words to emphasize activity and events during the course of daily routines and any learning episode that uses these activities or objects. The learning facilitator can heighten the learner's attention to his words through modulation of the volume of his voice and by varying its pitch and intonation. The facilitator can also add emphasis by pausing after significant phrases and repeating key words. As the learner begins to imitate single words these words can be used by the facilitator to offer models for first two- and three-word utterances, e.g., *"Give* me the *truck."*

TERMINAL BEHAVIOR: Learner is able to use the "first lexicon" words in spontaneous speech.

---

[1]From Lahey, M., and Bloom, L. 1967. Planning a first lexicon: Which words to teach first. *J. Speech Hear. Disord.* 42:340–351.

UNIT:	**T 16 / Language**
EPISODE:	**B / Tape Record Sounds, Play Back**
PURPOSE:	Learner learns to recognize his own sounds and increases his interest in making his own sounds and imitating those made by the facilitator.
ENTRY BEHAVIOR:	Learner will imitate one- or two-syllable sounds or words made by the facilitator. Learner has begun to use single words such as "Ma-ma" or "down." Learner shows understanding of representation by looking at picture books.
MATERIAL:	Cassette tape recorder and tape.
PROCEDURE:	At first, turn on the tape recorder and catch whatever sounds or words the learner happens to be saying. Play them back for the learner right away. Then say one or two words or sounds yourself into the tape recorder and play them back for the learner immediately. Repeat this game until you are sure that the learner understands that he is hearing his own sounds and your sounds. You will know this when the learner says his own sounds and then waits looking at the tape recorder or you expectantly. As the learner learns to say sounds for the tape recorder, encourage him more and more to copy your words or to say real words of his own. You can tape picture book play (Learning Episode I16D) and other sound-producing activities.
TERMINAL BEHAVIOR:	Learner repeats sounds made by the facilitator or says his own words into the tape recorder microphone. Learner then waits until tape is rewound to hear the facilitator's voice and his own.

UNIT:	T 16 / Language
EPISODE:	C / Telephone Talk
PURPOSE:	Learner's language skills, especially the use of longer sentences, are encouraged.
ENTRY BEHAVIOR:	Learner has begun to use single words and imitate sound patterns.
MATERIAL:	A toy telephone. You can buy one commercially or make one as follows: Use a milk carton, a shoebox, or any other small box; cut a round hole in the side of the box to hold the receiver; the receiver can be made from an empty toilet paper roll core (seal one end); attach the receiver to the box with yarn or string; color or paste a picture of a telephone dial on the front of the box, or cut one out and attach with a fastener.
PROCEDURE:	Show the learner how to "talk" into the telephone, using familiar words such as family names, toys, foods, body parts, clothing, or those listed in Learning Episode T16A. Also, talk about activities — doing, seeing, hearing, feeling — that the learner enjoys as well as routines or household activities you do. Encourage the learner to imitate pretend conversation on the telephone. With two telephones you can encourage back and forth talking. At times let the learner listen to a voice on the real telephone.
TERMINAL BEHAVIOR:	Learner spontaneously talks into the telephone, using longer sentences.

UNIT:	T 16 / Language
EPISODE:	D / Run, Spot, Run
PURPOSE:	Learner will be able to understand and use verbs in speech.
ENTRY BEHAVIOR:	Learner has begun to use single words to convey meaning with regularity, and is beginning to combine words.
MATERIAL:	Any and all types of actual items that can illustrate the verb to be used, e.g., a door and doorway to illustrate go and come, blocks and a large can to illustrate put and take, a small doll carriage to illustrate push and pull.
PROCEDURE:	The learning facilitator will decide on a "verb or two for the day." The facilitator will perform this action as many times throughout the day within the course of the learner's routine as is feasible. The learning facilitator will label this activity each time the activity is performed by himself or spontaneously by the learner. For example, the learning facilitator might choose the words "go" and "come." With this choice the learning facilitator could play a hide-and-seek or peek-a-boo game, with the learner using the words "go" and "come." For example, the learning facilitator could hide behind the door and appear to the learner and say, "I come." The facilitator could then exit through the door saying, "I go."
	Another example would be for the learning facilitator to assemble a number of cubes and a can, or clothespins and a bottle, and, while encouraging the learner to play with them, repeatedly use the word "put" each time the learner puts a block or clothespin into the container and "take" each time the learner takes an object from the container. Many such examples can be incorporated into the daily routine and play of the learner.
	Generalization of this skill can be enhanced by using the same words in other contexts. For example, the learning facilitator could use "put" and "take" for spooning food into and out of the learner's bowl.
TERMINAL BEHAVIOR:	Learner will use many verbs in speech spontaneously.

UNIT:	**T 16 / Language**
EPISODE:	**E / Flannel Board: Place and Label Shapes and Pictures**
PURPOSE:	Learner learns to follow directions, to recognize representations of familiar objects, to learn names of representations, and to increase eye-hand coordination.
ENTRY BEHAVIOR:	Learner can reach, grasp, reach and release with good control, or observe while the facilitator performs these actions. Learner has shown interest in looking at pictures of familiar objects.
MATERIAL:	Commercially available flannel board or one that is homemade by gluing a piece of felt to a large, heavy cardboard. Commercially available shapes and objects, or homemade stick-ons made by cutting shapes from felt or pasting pieces of felt on the back of pictures.
PROCEDURE:	Hold the learner on your lap, or sit the learner in a relaxed position, with the flannel board on a table or the floor in front of both of you. Arrange the shapes or pictures to be placed on the flannel board so that both you and the learner can reach them or see them. Place the shapes or pictures on the flannel board one by one, and label or name each one. As the learner imitates you and begins to indicate or pick out and put his own pictures or shapes on the flannel board, name and describe each of these pictures for him. Praise him for his initiative, and encourage him to continue.
	As he begins to learn the names of familiar pictures or shapes, you can begin to direct him to "pick up the dog," "put the horse on the board," "put the horse up high," etc. Or you can show him, "This is the dog. I put the dog up high," etc.
TERMINAL BEHAVIOR:	Learner selects shape or picture named and places it on flannel board, following the facilitator's directions, or watches the facilitator place it on the board.

UNIT:	**T 16 / Language**
EPISODE:	**F / Scrapbook**
PURPOSE:	A visual representation of objects a learner can identify is made.
ENTRY BEHAVIOR:	Learner is identifying and saying the names of familiar objects.
MATERIAL:	Magazines with a variety of large, brightly colored pictures of things with which the learner is familiar and which have names he can say or try to say; cardboard (cut up boxes); scissors, paste, and yarn.
PROCEDURE:	Look at pictures in magazines, helping the learner find things he can identify and name or try to name. The learner can be helped to cut out the pictures if his fine motor skill is far enough advanced. Otherwise cut the picture for the learner while he is watching. Talk about it as you do it. Pasting can be fun for both learner and facilitator. Paste the pictures into a scrapbook made of cardboard pages. Punch holes in the pages, and tie them together with yarn. Collect and make additional pages as the learner adds new words to his vocabulary. Use the book in helping the learner practice newly learned words. Always make looking at *his* book a fun thing to do.
TERMINAL BEHAVIOR:	Learner has a scrapbook of pictures representing the words in his vocabulary. The learner enjoys looking at his book and identifying the pictures.

UNIT:	T 16 / Language
EPISODE:	G / Two-Word Varieties
PURPOSE:	Learner will expand the varieties of two-word combinations to include the agent-action ("Bobby run") or action-object ("Throw ball") construction.
ENTRY BEHAVIOR:	Learner has limited expression of agent-action and action-object language constructions.
MATERIAL:	Any of the materials or behaviors that occur throughout the day in the form of routines or other learning episodes.
PROCEDURE:	In the course of the learning facilitator's action with the learner, he will consciously attempt to introduce alternatives to the learner's present agent-action or action-object speech productions, concentrating on one form until the learner shows comprehension of that form. Some suggestions are the following:

1. Adjectives+nouns (object), such as "big ball," "red ball," "cold juice," "big boy."
2. Pronouns+verbs, such as "he throws," "she kicks," "you eat."
3. Pronouns+nouns, such as "my ball," "your dress."
4. Use of negation, such as "no"+noun ("no ball").
5. Prepositions+nouns, such as "on the chair," "in the box."

The process for encouraging the learner's language output should include modeling, i.e., "Say, _____" and expansion of the learner's words. For example:

Learner — "Ball."
Facilitator — "Big ball."

| TERMINAL BEHAVIOR: | Learner uses a wide variety of two-word combinations in spontaneous speech. |

UNIT:	T 16 / Language
EPISODE:	H / "Mine," "Your what?"
PURPOSE:	Learner uses possession when referring to his own or other's object.
ENTRY BEHAVIOR:	Learner has understanding of possession indicated by use of word "mine" when retaining something of his own.
MATERIAL:	Any object used within the learner's routine or the learning episodes that is familiar, or any familiar possession of another person well known to the learner. Examples would be "Megan's doll," "Mommy's shoes."
PROCEDURE:	In the course of the learner's routines (dressing, bathing) or in the course of learning episodes, the learning facilitator could say "Whose _____ is this?" and reply "(Person's name) object." This form of the question and answer could be repeated through the course of the day in many contexts. As with other verbal exchanges which encourage expressive language on the part of the learner, it is most advisable for the learning facilitator to concentrate on one form of the expression ("Mommy's shoes," "Mommy's towel," etc.) over a period of time until the learner indicates understanding.

It is also important for the learning facilitator to use the proper names of people rather than pronouns to encourage development of this form of verbal expression. |
| **TERMINAL BEHAVIOR:** | Learner indicates understanding of questions "Whose _____ is this?" by saying "mine" if it belongs to the learner, or using the learner's own name, "Megan's." When the question refers to someone other than the learner, the learner will indicate understanding by pointing to, looking at, or handing the object according to the questioner in the course of daily interactions. |

UNIT:	**T 16 / Language**
EPISODE:	**I / Three Words Together**
PURPOSE:	Learner uses three-word combinations expressing the agent-action-object sequence, e.g., "Mommy *(agent)* throws *(action)* the ball *(object)*."
ENTRY BEHAVIOR:	Learner uses two-word agent-action ("Mommy throws") or action-object ("Throw ball") combinations.
MATERIAL:	This learning episode can be added to, and inserted within, any of the movement and/or cognitive learning episodes, as well as in any of the routines of the day. Therefore, any materials used in these learning episodes would be appropriate.
PROCEDURE:	This learning episode uses the same procedure as Learning Episode T16H, except that the three-word agent-action-object construction is used. For example, the learning facilitator would say "*(Facilitator's name)* throws the ball," or "*(Learner's name)* throws the ball." Techniques for encouraging two- and three-word expressions include modeling by repeating the phrase, accompanying the repeated phrase with the action or a gesture, and expanding the learner's own two-word combinations. This latter technique is especially useful because it utilizes language that the learner has already incorporated into his understanding and therefore can be most effective in producing additional speech.
TERMINAL BEHAVIOR:	Learner uses agent-action-object constructions in spontaneous speech.

UNIT:	T 16 / Language
EPISODE:	J / "Same As"
PURPOSE:	Learner learns the concept "Same *(object/picture)* as."
ENTRY BEHAVIOR:	Learner is able to point to and/or name familiar objects or pictures.
MATERIAL:	Shoe boxes, bags, or plastic containers can be used as sorters. Use an assortment of familiar objects or pictures, making sure to have at least two of each for the matching task, **or** use commercially available "Pick-a-pair" game.
PROCEDURE:	1. Place three to six sorting containers out so they are easily accessible to the learner. Place one object or picture in each sorter as you say the names of each. Make sure of the learner's familiarity with the objects/pictures by asking him to either point to, or name, them. 2. The facilitator demonstrates the matching activity by performing the matching task using all the objects. As each match is performed, the facilitator says and points out that the objects are the "*same.*" 3. The facilitator then begins the activity again, this time asking the learner to find an object/picture that is the "same as this." It may be necessary to have the learner first identify the object being presented, as well as to scan all of the objects in the sorter before performing the matching task. 4. With each successful match the learner is reinforced with a phrase such as "you found the same *(object/picture).*"
TERMINAL BEHAVIOR:	Given an object or picture the learner can follow a verbal instruction to find another object or picture that is the "same."

Unit I 17 / SOCIALIZATION AND IMITATION

The earliest socialization experiences of the learner are those that involve the provision of comfort and security by the learning facilitator. Activities that facilitate the attachment process between learner and facilitator also enhance the potential for developing learning and capabilities in other areas. The learner will often come to understand essential facts about his environment first through his interactions with the learning facilitator. For example, there is good reason to believe that "person permanence" precedes "object permanence." As the learner expands his horizons beyond himself to include the facilitator and other important adults in his environment, essential discriminations are made. Later, toddler learners will begin to interact with peers and thus widen their understanding of themselves and others in their environment. As the learner imitates the facilitator, and later his peers, a great deal of instrumental information is also acquired. For these reasons specific activities dealing with relationships between the learner and facilitator, as well as other peers, are included, and imitation is emphasized.

UNIT: I 17 / Socialization and Imitation

EPISODE: A / Faces

PURPOSE: Learner focuses on drawings of faces.

ENTRY BEHAVIOR: Learner's eyes react to light.

MATERIAL: Face drawn simply on a stiff paper.

PROCEDURE: When the learner is in an alert state, the facilitator talks and smiles to him with his face directly in front of the learner's face. The distance at which the facilitator stands from the learner may vary from one to several feet, since different learners begin to focus at different distances. The facilitator should try different distances until the learner's face "brightens." Very young learners seem to prefer to focus on faces rather than anything else. Thus, the facilitator may also want to draw a very simple outline face with black magic marker on white paper. This may be placed near the learner at different times and places when the learner is in different positions, (lying down, supported sitting, head held over shoulder, etc.).

TERMINAL BEHAVIOR: Learner looks at a person as the person talks to him.

UNIT:	I 17 / Socialization and Imitation
EPISODE:	B / Visual Tracking, Human Face: Up and Down, On Stomach and Back
PURPOSE:	Learner learns to recognize facilitator's face and to coordinate eyes in following.
ENTRY BEHAVIOR:	Learner can focus eyes to discriminate features of facilitator's face.
MATERIAL:	None.
PROCEDURE:	Put the learner on his back. Smile and talk to him until he focuses his eyes on your face. While continuing to talk and smile at the learner, move your face so that the learner's eyes must follow you. If he follows from side to side, move your face up and down, back and forth, and then around in a circle. You should move your face slowly enough so that the learner's eyes can always follow you, no matter which direction you move. As a variation you can repeat this game while smiling at the learner but not talking to him, which is more difficult for the learner.

Turn the learner over on his stomach, and encourage him to look at and follow your face while he is in this position. Repeat while talking and while quiet in this position, also. |
| **TERMINAL BEHAVIOR:** | Learner shows by his behavior (either quieting or becoming more excited) when facilitator's face appears. Learner can follow facilitator's face in all areas of his visual field, whether he is on his back or on his stomach. |

UNIT:	I 17 / Socialization and Imitation
EPISODE:	C / Mirror Play: Facilitator and Learner
PURPOSE:	Learner develops an understanding of self as a separate, independent person and learns the difference between real and apparent images.
ENTRY BEHAVIOR:	Learner can hold his head steady when held in an upright position, focus with eyes to discriminate his face, and follow 180° or glance from one point to another.
MATERIAL:	Wall or floor mirror large enough for the upper part of the facilitator's body and all of the learner's body to be seen.
PROCEDURE:	Pick the learner up in your arms so that he is in an upright position. Stand in front of a large mirror in such a way that both of you can be seen clearly by each other. Smile at and talk to the learner while looking at him in the mirror. Encourage him to regard the mirror images. You can point to his nose in the mirror and then touch his actual nose. Point to your nose in the mirror and then touch your own nose. You can repeat this with other body parts. Also, allow the learner to explore the situation by patting his reflection in the mirror. Encourage him to touch your reflection in the mirror and then to touch you. For fun and variety you can also make faces which show different moods and label these. For example, you can smile and say, "I'm happy," or frown and say, "I'm angry." Stick your tongue out and say, "Yuk," etc. Repeat whenever you carry the learner past a mirror.
TERMINAL BEHAVIOR:	Learner demonstrates understanding of the differences between mirror images and actual persons by behaving differently toward mirror images than to actual persons. For example, learner might point to mirror image but pat or hug actual person.

UNIT:	**I 17 / Socialization and Imitation**
EPISODE:	**D / Reach and Touch Faces**
PURPOSE:	Learner develops ability to grasp and explore with hands and eyes. Learner develops sense of self–not self and becomes familiar with others.
ENTRY BEHAVIOR:	Learner has eye contact and watches people's faces.
MATERIAL:	None.
PROCEDURE:	When learner is seated or lying down, talk to him with your face 7 to 12 inches away from his face. Let him touch and explore your face. You may have to guide his hand to your face and help him feel it. Smile at the learner and describe to him what he is doing with his hand ("You're touching my nose").

Variation

ENTRY BEHAVIOR:	Learner has eye contact and watches people's faces. Learner may be reluctant to touch facilitator's face.
MATERIAL:	Toys with faces like teddy bears, dolls, etc.; hand puppets with three-dimensional features.
PROCEDURE:	When the learner is seated or lying down in a relaxed position, present a toy with a face 7 to 12 inches from the learner's face. Encourage him to touch and explore the toy. You may have to guide his hand to the toy and help him explore it. Smile at the learner when he is exploring the toy. Describe what he is doing with the toy, or have the toy respond by pretending to talk to the learner, "This is my nose," "You're touching my nose," etc.
TERMINAL BEHAVIOR:	Learner reaches and explores face by examining and feeling.

UNIT:	**I 17 / Socialization and Imitation**
EPISODE:	**E / Peek-a-Boo with Facilitator's Face**
PURPOSE:	Learner learns to cooperate in games.
ENTRY BEHAVIOR:	Learner can focus eyes on facilitator's face.
MATERIAL:	Small cloth or other material to cover face.
PROCEDURE:	While the learner is on his back in his crib or sitting propped up comfortably, lean just close enough to him to ensure that he sees your face and cover your face with your hands. As you take your hands away and show your face say, "Peek-a-boo, I see (*learner's name*)." Use the learner's name when saying peek-a-boo and also use your own name from time to time instead of saying "you" or "I." You can change this game to make it interesting by putting a cloth over your face or by holding a picture of another person cut from a magazine over your face, etc. You can also reverse roles and cover the learner's face to snatch off the cloth. Playing this game during dressing also is fun and generalizes the situation.
TERMINAL BEHAVIOR:	Learner anticipates facilitator's revealing his face. If a cloth is used learner will snatch cloth from facilitator's face. Learner may cover own head or face with cloth or hands.

UNIT:	I 17 / Socialization and Imitation
EPISODE:	F / Ball Play: Rolling Back and Forth
PURPOSE:	Learner learns to cooperate in games and increases eye-hand coordination.
ENTRY BEHAVIOR:	Learner can sit upright without support and clasp hands together at the midline. Learner can see and track a large moving object.
MATERIAL:	Several balls that have different characteristics, for example, some may be large and smooth, some may be smaller and soft (such as the "Nerf" ball).
PROCEDURE:	Pick out one or two balls that are different in some way. Sit the learner on a smooth surface on the floor, and place yourself at a greater or closer distance away, depending on the age and skill of the learner. Roll the ball to the learner, encouraging him to push it back to you by gestures and verbal directions, "Push the ball back with two hands. Roll the ball to me."
	With your close direction and supervision, two learners can play this game with you at the same time. You can encourage peer interaction and turn taking, by alternating the learner who receives the ball and having the learners roll the ball to one another.
TERMINAL BEHAVIOR:	Learner opens arms to accept ball rolled toward him by facilitator, corrals ball, and then pushes it back in the general direction of the facilitator or other learner.

Unit T 17 /
SOCIALIZATION AND
IMITATION

UNIT: T 17 / Socialization and Imitation

EPISODE: A / Stop Activity for Change of Activity

PURPOSE: Learner adapts to changes in activities.

ENTRY BEHAVIOR: Learner continues an activity, even though he is told it is time to do something else.

MATERIAL: None.

PROCEDURE: When the learner is involved in an activity, it is sometimes necessary to change activities (for instance, to go to the store, to bed, to eat). Learners often become very involved in what they are doing and may not want to stop their activity. The facilitator can prepare the learner for a change by telling him a few minutes ahead of time that they are going to do something else. When it is time for the learner to change activities, the facilitator can tell the learner that "It is time to stop _____. Let's get ready to _____." If the learner does not stop his activity, the facilitator can then aid him by helping him put his toy away or physically removing him away from the situation.

The signal for change and the new activity should be repeated as the facilitator moves the learner.

TERMINAL BEHAVIOR: Learner stops one activity and is able to go onto another activity when directed.

UNIT:	**T 17 / Socialization and Imitation**
EPISODE:	**B / Doll Play and Imitation**
PURPOSE:	Learner learns to take the role of another.
ENTRY BEHAVIOR:	Learner will imitate facilitator's gestures and vocalizations and has begun to do simple pretend activities.
MATERIAL:	Dolls, beds and their covers, furniture, utensils, etc. Try to have dolls of different skin colors and sexes.
PROCEDURE:	Pick up a doll and, while the learner is watching, pretend to do with the doll the many activities you usually do with the learner himself. Rock the doll, feed the doll, burp the doll, change the doll, etc. After you do each one of these things with the doll, hand the doll to the learner and encourage him to imitate you by doing the same thing with the doll that you have done. As the learner begins to copy you, you can each use the doll to play many imaginary games involving themes and dialogues, such as going to bed, going to the toilet, going out to play, getting dressed. In this way you not only encourage the learner's play but also model appropriate behaviors for him.
TERMINAL BEHAVIOR:	Learner will use dolls to "play house" or perform routines, assuming another's role in his play by himself or with other learners.

Variation

MATERIAL:	Common household objects, such as sponge, mop, dust cloth, pot and spoon, etc.
PROCEDURE:	When the facilitator is cleaning or doing other household activities, he provides the learner with a similar object to the one he is using. For instance, if the facilitator is wiping the table after mealtime, he can also give the learner a sponge or washcloth to wipe off the area in front of him. Learning episodes could include dusting, vacuuming, washing dishes, folding clothes, and other household activities. If the learner does not imitate the action by himself, the facilitator can demonstrate the action a second time, then wait expectantly for the learner saying, "_____ dust," "_____ fold," etc. It is also important to talk to the learner about the activity while you are performing it. Simply describe what is happening with short phrases or sentences, such as, "Let's clean the table. You help me wipe the table. Good! You are cleaning the table."
TERMINAL BEHAVIOR:	Learner imitates familiar household activities and pretends to do them in the course of his own play.

UNIT:	**T 17 / Socialization and Imitation**
EPISODE:	**C / Activity Songs**
PURPOSE:	Learner learns to cooperate in games and to imitate language.
ENTRY BEHAVIOR:	Learner has shown willingness to interact with other learners and will imitate facilitator's gestures.
MATERIAL:	Records, record player (optional); props such as tools, clothes, brushes, spoons, etc.
PROCEDURE:	One, two, or three learners can be encouraged to sit in a circle with the facilitator who leads, demonstrates, and encourages them to participate in singing these songs and imitating his gestures. Facilitator can sit behind a learner who is first participating and guide his hands through the gestures.

One song for finger play and imitation may be sung to the tune of "Here We Go 'Round the Mulberry Bush," adding your own lines such as:

"This is the way we wash our hands"
"This is the way we eat our soup"
"This is the way we comb our hair"
"This is the way we brush our teeth"

Show the learner how to act out each new line, encouraging imitation of both gestures and words. Manual guidance can be used when necessary. You can create many other songs or purchase commercially available records for listening or use songs such as those given in Learning Episodes T9C, T9D, and T9E.

TERMINAL BEHAVIOR:	Learner will participate in activity songs by joining in singing and/or by participating in gestures.

UNIT:	T 17 / Socialization and Imitation
EPISODE:	D / "Follow the Leader": Label Activities
PURPOSE:	Learner learns to follow directions, cooperate with others, and imitate. Learner plans motor acts efficiently.
ENTRY BEHAVIOR:	Learner can imitate simple gestures of facilitator.
MATERIAL:	Natural obstacles in the environment.
PROCEDURE:	This game can be played either standing in place (as in "Simple Simon") or walking around the room or yard performing "tricks" (as in the traditional "Follow the Leader"). With this game the emphasis is on having the learner follow the verbal direction as well as the movement. Thus, you would say, "Go around the chair, cross the fuzzy rug, go through the big door." You can also switch roles with the learner by encouraging him to be the leader so that you can follow him or imitate his directions and actions.
TERMINAL BEHAVIOR:	Learner can follow gestures and movements of facilitator and other children without making errors until the group stops playing the game. Learner can follow one-part directions in routines. Learner will participate in, and plan, a variety of gross motor activities.

UNIT:	**I 17 / Socialization and Imitation**
EPISODE:	**E / "Boat" Rocking and Singing**
PURPOSE:	Learner develops cooperation with other learners and increases language skills.
ENTRY BEHAVIOR:	Learner can sit without support and with good balance.
MATERIAL:	Commercially available play steps that can be turned over to make a rocker with sitting platforms for two to four learners.
PROCEDURE:	Place the learner with one or two other learners in the play-steps "rocking boat." Encourage the learners to rock the boat back and forth; help them to do this by rocking the boat yourself. You can sing songs such as "Row, row, row your boat" and other rhythmic chants.
	The "boat" can then be tipped so that one learner is higher than the other. You can use this opportunity to teach, "Who is up high?" and "Who is down low?" Using the boat you can also teach many other prepositions such as "on," "in," "out," etc. as the learners sit *on*, get *in*, and get *out* of the boat.
TERMINAL BEHAVIOR:	Learner will sit in the boat with other learners and cooperate in rocking. Learner will attend to songs sung by the facilitator or other older learners. Learner will get *in* and *out* in response to directions.

UNIT:	T 17 / Socialization and Imitation
EPISODE:	F / Marching and Following
PURPOSE:	Learner learns to cooperate in play with other learners and to increase large muscle skills and motor planning.
ENTRY BEHAVIOR:	Learner can walk with good balance. Learner can imitate gestures and sounds of the facilitator.
MATERIAL:	Furniture in the environment, large boxes, and other things that may be used as obstacles.
PROCEDURE:	These kinds of games are similar to other rhythm games except that instead of sitting in one place the learner can follow either the facilitator or other learners around the room, overcoming obstacles, going around barriers, etc. The rhythm of the marching and following can be changed from very slow to quite fast for variety. You can describe the activities, such as "march, march, march," "tip-toe, tip-toe," "go around," etc. in the rhythm of their pace.

Variation

ENTRY BEHAVIOR:	Learner can creep or walk on even surfaces but does not like to experience increased or uneven pressure to feet or hands and knees.
MATERIAL:	Long piece of ordinary clothesline on a hard surface floor.
PROCEDURE:	Arrange a clothesline in a snake-like or other easy to follow pattern on the floor. Play "Follow the Leader," encouraging the learner to creep or walk along over the clothesline with bare hands and knees or bare feet. Reinforce the completion of following the leader by a sensory or gross motor activity that the learner enjoys or by changing roles, letting the learner be the leader.
TERMINAL BEHAVIOR:	Learner follows facilitator and/or other learners around the room or yard without avoiding any surfaces and with good motor planning, imitating their gestures and behaviors until the game is terminated.

UNIT:	T 17 / Socialization and Imitation

EPISODE: G / Cooperative Scribble

PURPOSE: This learning episode facilitates interpersonal interaction among the learners. The learner cooperates with others and exercises patience in waiting for his turn at an activity.

ENTRY BEHAVIOR: Sufficient gross/fine motor control to grasp chalk or magic marker and make a mark or touch finger paint, plus the ability to understand instructions.

MATERIAL: Chalkboard and chalk, or large sheet of paper and magic markers, finger paints, etc.

PROCEDURE: Cooperative Scribble can be done in several ways. You could have one learner specify something for the group to draw. For example, he might say, "Let's all draw a man." Then he goes to the chalkboard and begins the drawing, perhaps by drawing a face. He can choose a second learner to go to the board and add something to the face (e.g., the eyes). The game continues until all learners have made their contributions and the drawing is complete.

Still another way is to have the group make a drawing without planning in advance what the final creation will look like. Have one learner go to the chalkboard or use paper and draw or scribble anything he wishes. The other learners take turns adding to his drawing. When the drawing is completed, encourage the learners to talk about what they have drawn and allow each one to say what the drawing looks like to him.

TERMINAL BEHAVIOR: Learner is able to take turns adding to the group "picture."

Unit I 18 / SELF-HELP

As the learner gains developmental competency, it is natural that he will begin doing things for himself. For example, it is difficult to stop a sitting learner from grabbing the food or the spoon in the process of feeding. Obviously, even though it may not "facilitate" the feeding process itself, it certainly does facilitate the drive toward independence and a positive self-image to encourage this kind of behavior on the part of the learner. Although at first it may be more difficult (and more time consuming) for the learning facilitator to encourage the beginning attempts of the learner at self-care activities, in the long run it not only will make it easier for the learning facilitator but also will enhance the self-image and feelings of independence of the learner. For the learners with deficiency in fine and gross motor skills, special efforts may be made to develop self-help skills. The learning episodes in Unit I 22 may be helpful in relaxing the learner and thereby enabling the facilitator to promote learning in these areas.

For the learner with developmental difficulty in the area of cognitive skills, special help in the areas of acquisition of self-help skills should be given. In this way learners who are slower in the acquisition of new abilities may be helped toward independence and their self-concept may be enhanced. Special programs for the stepwise teaching of self-help skills are available to enable the facilitator to teach even very slow learners. These include: Baker, B., Brightman, A., Heifitz, L., and Murphey, D. 1976. *Steps to Independence: A Skills Training Series for Children with Special Needs.* Research Press, Champaign, Ill.; and Bachrach, A., Mosley, A., Swindle, F., and Wood, M. 1978. *Developmental Therapy for Young Children with Autistic Characteristics.* University Park Press, Baltimore.

UNIT:	I 18 / Self-Help
EPISODE:	A / Finger Feeding
PURPOSE:	Learner gains independence by learning to feed himself some foods.
ENTRY BEHAVIOR:	Learner can reach accurately and grasp small bits of food with thumb and first finger, or can reach, grasp, and hold onto larger pieces of food and bite off chunks.
MATERIAL:	Chewable foods cut into small pieces, such as cheese, banana, hot dog. Large pieces of foods such as Zweiback or other food that, when bitten on, can be easily chewed or softened in the mouth.
PROCEDURE:	Sit the learner in a high chair, or at a feeding table, so that he is properly supported and relaxed (to facilitate see Learning Episode I22H). If you are using small pieces of food, place several of them on the tray or table in front of the learner. It is not necessary to use a plate at first since, if you do, the learner is most likely to pick it up and dump his food off anyhow. It is not likely that the learner will need much teaching or encouragement to pick up and eat the small pieces of food because he will tend to put many things in his

mouth anyhow. What you may need to do is encourage him to persist at practicing picking up very small bits. With larger pieces of food which he can hold in his hand, you need only to watch for those pieces that he may drop in order to point them out so he can pick them up and eat them.

TERMINAL BEHAVIOR: Learner is able to feed himself some foods (finger feeding).

UNIT:	I 18 / Self-Help
EPISODE:	B / Cup Holding
PURPOSE:	Learner becomes more independent by becoming able to give himself a drink.
ENTRY BEHAVIOR:	Learner can grasp cup-size object at the midline with both hands and bring it to his mouth. Learner can drink from cup held by facilitator.
MATERIAL:	Wide based, clear plastic cup without handles. Half moon shape 2″1″ may be cut from the edge of the cup to leave room for the learner's nose and allow the facilitator to see the liquid in the cup.
PROCEDURE:	Place only enough liquid in the cup to cover the bottom of it. Show the learner the liquid in the cup to cover the bottom of it. Show the learner the liquid in the cup, and hand him the cup to hold with the optional cut-out at the top. Guiding it with your hands, help him tip it up to his mouth (you will be able to see the liquid through the cutout). When the learner can drink this small amount of liquid without spilling it, you can begin to gradually add more and more and to guide him less and less.
TERMINAL BEHAVIOR:	Learner can drink liquid from half-filled cup without spilling any.

Unit T 18 / SELF-HELP

UNIT:

T 18 / Self-Help

EPISODE:

A / Clothing Skills

PURPOSE:

Learner learns skills necessary for dressing and undressing and develops independence.

ENTRY BEHAVIOR:

Learner can grasp clothes over parts of body with hands and release. Learner has shown interest in imitating facilitator.

MATERIAL:

Learner's own clothes. Additional grown up sized gloves, hats, socks, etc. Commercially available or homemade zipper frames, button frames, snap frames, tying shoes.

PROCEDURE:

While you are changing or undressing the learner, encourage him to take off the clothes he is wearing that he can reach. This might include shoes and socks, hats, mittens, and even coats after they are unbuttoned or unzipped. Besides this ongoing experience, you can also give the learner grown-up sized shoes to slip on, hats to wear, large gloves to pull on and pull off his hands, heavy buttons or zippers in frames, or on a jacket slipped over the back of a chair to slide up and down, etc. Show the learner how you do these things yourself by slipping your feet in and out of shoes, hands in and out of gloves, etc., and then do the same thing with the learner's hands and feet. Encourage him to do the same thing for himself and praise him for any attempts.

TERMINAL BEHAVIOR:

Learner can remove gloves, hats, socks, and clothing that does not have fasteners. Learner can put on socks, pants, hat, and shoes, needing minor adjustments. (Putting on sweaters and shirts may not be accomplished for some time.)

UNIT:	**T 18 / Self-Help**
EPISODE:	**B / Taking Turns Sharing Clothes**
PURPOSE:	Learner learns to put on clothes and to use them for pretend games and role playing.
ENTRY BEHAVIOR:	Learner can pull on socks, mittens, hats, etc.
MATERIAL:	Articles of clothing which fit both the facilitator and the learner, including bracelets, hats, shoes, shawls, necklaces, etc.
PROCEDURE:	This game is similar to Clothing Skills (Learning Episode T18A), except here the emphasis is on sharing and identification. Get together several articles of clothing which you and the learner can each wear. Show the learner how you can put on the clothes, and "wear" them, modeling each as you do so. Then either take your selected article of clothing off and hand it to the learner to put on, or give him another article like it. Then you both can "show off your finery" or play whatever pretend game you create together to model the clothes you both have put on.
TERMINAL BEHAVIOR:	Learner imitates facilitator in putting on articles of clothing and then proceeds to role play spontaneously with them.

UNIT:	**T 18 / Self-Help**
EPISODE:	**C / Good Grooming Merry-Go-Round**
PURPOSE:	Learner develops good grooming skills and gains a more positive self-image by learning to take pride in his appearance. He learns the words for various articles used in good grooming.
ENTRY BEHAVIOR:	Learner has some labeling ability and self-help skills.
MATERIAL:	Each learner needs a cigar box filled with items to be used for personal grooming (e.g., comb, brush, mirror, toothbrush, toothpaste, Kleenex, washcloth, soap, nail file), and small index cards with pictures of each of the above items on them. The cards can then be fastened to the child's "pony rider." A merry-go-round made out of heavy construction paper. The child riding each "pony" can hold a set of pictures identical to the grooming items contained in the cigar box. Below is a drawing of a "merry-go-round" you might make:

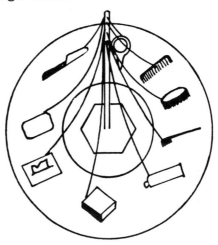

For example: A lazy-susan could be used for a base and then cover it with construction paper. Streamers could be attached to a center fixed pole or be part of the lazy-susan base.

PROCEDURE:	Place each learner's personal grooming kit in front of him. Place the good grooming "merry-go-round" in the center of the group, and allow each learner to have a turn spinning the "ponies" and naming the item held by one "pony rider." The learner is then to select from his kit the item pictured. He can demonstrate for the others how this item should be used. Encourage him to verbally describe the actions as he performs them. Try to get the learners to associate the picture with the real-life item. As he finishes using one item, allow another learner to have a turn as the "pony rider."

This game may be extended to the home situation by helping the learner or his parents make a self-help chart for the wall at home. In one column list all of the various grooming articles (you may wish to add others to the ones suggested here). Beside each word attach a drawing of the item. Make squares to represent the days on which the learner can glue a star when he uses that item in his personal grooming. Help him to decide what special prize he can earn by acquiring a predetermined number of paper stars.

Some facilitators may feel that the "merry-go-round" is somewhat gimmicky. If so, omit this, and just provide the learners with the personal grooming kits. You can request that the learner find various items in his kit and demonstrate how they are used. Then continue as described above.

TERMINAL BEHAVIOR:

Each learner takes greater pride in his own personal appearance and feels good about being well-groomed. He can recognize the picture of a particular good grooming article by selecting from his own kit the one indicated on the merry-go-round index card; he can demonstrate the appropriate use for each article of personal grooming. The learner may keep a home good-grooming chart.

Unit T 19 / SOCIAL COOPERATION — COOKING

Cooking projects provide numerous learning opportunities. The following unit covers four interrelated areas with emphasis on the first two: mathematical learnings, language arts, science, and sensory explorations. The learner is exposed to math while cooking, learning about quantity, weight, and measure. Cooking incorporates language arts as the child learns new cooking vocabulary words related to ingredients, equipment, cooking procedures, cooking smells, sounds, textures, and colors. The facilitator encourages the learner to describe what he is doing while cooking and to use recall in later telling about the cooking experience. Prereading readiness skills are further refined in learning to follow and interpret a recipe chart in a given sequence. The learner is learning that words and pictures on a chart stand for certain things. Cooking involves aspects of science, interrelating changing seasons and holidays with growing things and their sources. The learner observes how food forms change when combined, heated, or cooled. Sensory experiences are vital, informing the learner about different cooking smells, tastes, textures, sounds, and colors. The learner first explores the properties of a single item; then he proceeds to compare two or three contrasting items and verbalizes about these sensory impressions (such as comparing different spices).

With this unit start with easy recipes to ensure success. Then slowly proceed to more complex ones. The harder recipes entail more steps, more ingredients, and more complex motor skills in handling the kitchen equipment and ingredients. Also, heat and sharp knives are used later. Cooking should offer enjoyment for its own sake. The finished product takes a backseat to the active process of blending, tasting, noting food changes, cleaning up, and so forth.

The learner can be surrounded by learning opportunities as long as the facilitator's attitude is inquisitive, open, and allows for trial-and-error plus possible cooking failures.

UNIT:	T 19 / Social Cooperation — Cooking
EPISODE:	A / Instant Pudding and Icing (Initial, easy toddler cooking activities that exclude the use of hard and sharp utensils)
PURPOSE:	Learner learns to follow and interpret a recipe, and to follow directions in a specific sequence (through recipe chart). He begins to learn about measure, quantity, and weight. He shares and takes turns.
ENTRY BEHAVIOR:	Learner is interested in cooking, has at least beginning ability to work cooperatively with other learners and a facilitator, and can adhere to facilitator-established safety precautions.
MATERIAL:	Equipment: measuring spoons, knives, plastic stirring spoons, bowls of different sizes, graduated measuring cups, a timer, several pans and cookie sheets, small paper cups.

Ingredients for basic white icing: soft butter, powdered sugar, milk, vanilla, food coloring, graham crackers or vanilla wafers.

Ingredients for pudding: instant pudding, milk.

Recipe chart: white poster paper, magazine pictures or labels from actual packages or magic marker line drawings of ingredients used. (Chart may be put on posterboard or a chalkboard.)

PROCEDURE:

These first simple cooking experiments involve no hard or sharp kitchen utensils. Only a few ingredients are needed, the cooking procedure is limited to one or two steps, exact measurements are not vital, the cooks work together, and their cooking process leads to a readily made product. The learner's first cooking activity should be successful. The facilitator should plan to repeat the same recipes with the children so that they can repeat familiar steps, yet try out new and more challenging variations to the original recipe. The facilitator needs to be well organized and familiar with a new recipe before presenting it to the children. He must be sure the equipment and ingredients needed are available. The facilitator initially might premeasure all ingredients, and only have the learners do the combining, stirring, spreading, and eating. The next time he might premeasure ingredients into different bowls, but have the learners remeasure each ingredient and combine them. As the learners become more adept and experienced with cooking, they can look at a recipe chart, decide what ingredient will be needed, walk to a nearby market to purchase those items, and measure more precise amounts. In concluding a cooking activity, the learners might discuss using the recipe chart, what ingredients were used, how they did it, what came first, what came next, and so on. In other words, they verbalize the sequential steps involved. At the end of a cooking activity, the facilitator might talk about each "chef's" contribution.

Instant pudding: With *all* cooking activities, before the "doing" begins the facilitator helps the learners interpret and talk about the pictured recipe chart (ingredients, steps involved, etc.). The facilitator places the ingredients and equipment beneath the chart so that the learners can relate and talk about these actual ingredients which correspond to their pictured representations. The ingredients are measured, combined, and stirred as stated on the recipe chart. The learners take turns stirring the pudding mixture. Have the learners count their stirs. Encourage the learners to talk about what they are using (ingredients, measurements) and what they are doing as they are cooking. Ask the learners how cooking experience relates to their cooking ventures (or their mother's) at home.

One learner pours the milk into the measuring cup 3½ times. Pour milk into a smaller, more manageable pitcher for preschoolers to handle.

Another learner pours the measured milk into the mix. All take turns stirring. Learners should feel, smell, taste, and talk about what they are doing. Have them closely observe and describe what happens to the pudding as it is mixed into the milk liquid. Have them count the children who need to be served, and dole out one Dixie cup and spoon for each one. Encourage prediction by asking the learners how much pudding should be spooned into

each one of the cups. The cooking project should be planned so that it is completed and eaten before the end of the day. Snack time offers a good time for eating the pudding. Cooking projects should offer concrete, interesting, and challenging experiences to the learner which are enjoyed for their own sake. The learner will be exposed almost effortlessly to a wide variety of learning experiences in this more informal way.

Icing: Use the same procedure followed for the pudding recipe. The facilitator initially premeasures the sugar and butter, and the learners sift the sugar and blend it with the other items. Another time the children do the measuring. Give each "chef" a small Dixie cup of icing and have him take a knife and spread it on graham crackers (or vanilla wafers). On a later occasion the learner might experiment with food coloring, mixing up his own colored icing in a cup and spreading it on a sweet cracker. Sprinkles or Christmas decorations can be added, or different flavors can be substituted, such as sweet cocoa powder. Try peanut butter icing, using ¼ cup of chunky peanut butter and ¼ cup of milk in place of the butter, cream, and vanilla.

White Icing

Sift:

3 🥛 🥛 🥛   Powdered Sugar

Stir and Stir!

Add:

3 🥄🥄🥄 tablespoons Cream

1½ 🥄🥄 teaspoons vanilla

Stir!

Variations

1. Learners repeat the pudding project, but first walk to the grocery store to buy the ingredients and to select the flavor desired.
2. Modify the original pudding recipe by using bananas, miniature marshmallows, or chocolate chips, crushed peppermint candy, or raisins. Have the learners make whipped cream and heap it over the pudding. Have learners experiment with food coloring.
3. After learners have prepared instant pudding, they can try cooked pudding, custard, tapioca.
4. Try Floating Island — a *soft* custard pudding with floating meringue on top. Try a *hard*, steamed pudding.

TERMINAL BEHAVIOR:

Learner can understand, follow, and interpret a simple pictorial recipe. He has beginning comprehension of measures, quantities, and weight. He can recall and discuss at least some of the steps involved in preparing the pudding and icing; particularly, he makes the connection between the ingredients he worked with and the product he ate which he shares with others.

UNIT:	T 19 / Social Cooperation — Cooking
EPISODE:	B / Green Salad (Intended for use in late summer and is one of the year's first cooking experiences)
PURPOSE:	Learner learns about following and interpreting a simple recipe, following the directions in a specific sequence. He is introduced to different sorts of salad vegetables and possibly learns where they come from. The learner gains more experience with quantitative measurements.
ENTRY BEHAVIOR:	If learner is to use a sharp knife, he must have had previous safe and successful experience with using one.
MATERIAL:	Equipment: small bowl for salad dressing, large salad bowl, chopping board, enough vegetable peelers, sharp paring knives, table knives, large salad spoon and fork, tasting spoons, Dixie cups and forks, gathering baskets, vegetable scrubbing brushes. Ingredients: salad greens (such as iceberg, Bibb, or Boston lettuce, raw vegetables (such as celery, radishes, cucumbers, tomatoes, carrots,) olive oil, wine vinegar, salt and pepper. Recipe chart: white poster paper; magazine pictures or magic marker line drawings of ingredients used. (Chart may be put on posterboard or a chalkboard.)
PROCEDURE:	This activity truly would be more enriching if the learners could select the salad makings from someone's garden or farm. If a salad-gathering trip is impossible for the class, the facilitator should supply an array of different vegetables. The recipe chart is on the following pages. If the garden greens are gathered, refrigerate them that day and plan to make the salad the following day. All learners wash their hands. They look at the chart as you help them interpret the pictures and salad procedures to them, interpreting the pictures by referring to the real vegetables and equipment. Better exploration and discussion result if the group remains small. Make certain that each learner has an important role in the salad-making project, such as washing the lettuce, scraping the carrots, etc. There are a lot of things to talk about while making the salad. Have the learners look at the vegetables' insides while they are peeling them. Have them feel and taste each different one — can they identify each vegetable by name? Talk about how the vegetables feel, different or alike. For example, the tomato feels smooth while the carrot feels ridged. Have the learners taste and talk about vegetable sounds — which ones sound crunchy and which ones sound squishy? What are other ways to describe their sounds? Can the learners find and name a vegetable that feels stringy in the mouth (celery)? Can the learners find and name two vegetables that have the same color? If so, are these two vegetables also alike in form, texture, and taste? Talk about how some vegetables come from the *root* of the plant, such as carrots. We eat the *leaf* part of some vegetables, such as lettuce. We eat the *seed* part of other vegetables, such as peas. We eat the *stem* part of some vegetables, such as celery.

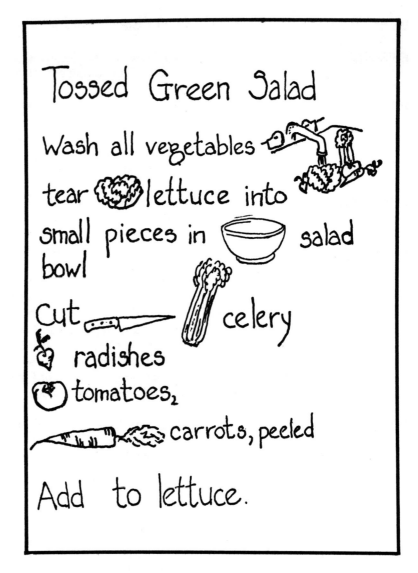

Tossed Green Salad

Wash all vegetables

tear lettuce into

small pieces in salad bowl

Cut celery

radishes

tomatoes,

carrots, peeled

Add to lettuce.

As the learners make the dressing, have them taste and correct for the right amount of seasoning. Have the learners take turns in tossing the salad. The tossing part, as with the lettuce tearing, is done with the hands. The salad is tossed with the other vegetables and the dressing. The salad can be eaten at snack time.

Variations

1. Cook the same salad vegetables (excluding the lettuce), and talk about how these same vegetables look and feel different when cooked (tomato, celery, carrot).
2. Grow some vegetables in an indoor window box or outside garden.
3. Use different vegetables and repeat the salad-making project (cabbage, raw peas, cucumbers, avocados). Use vegetables and make a gelatin-type salad.
4. *Vegetable feel box*: Put a vegetable such as a carrot, in a box. Have the learner close his eyes, feel the vegetable, and try to name it (learner must obtain clues from the form and texture of the vegetable).

Mix in small bowl:
8 ⟋⟋⟋⟋⟋⟋⟋⟋ tablespoons COOKING OIL
4 ⟋⟋⟋⟋ tablespoons VINEGAR

SALT PEPPER

Add to salad.

Toss.

TERMINAL BEHAVIOR:

Learner can understand, interpret, and follow in sequence simple directions indicated by the pictorial recipe chart. He can work cooperatively and take turns with other learners. He knows the names of the vegetables and other ingredients used and has tasted even the ones new to him. He has beginning awareness that different parts of various vegetables are eaten and may have beginning awareness of where our salad makings come from (a garden, a farm, etc.). He has beginning comprehension of how to use quantitative measurements.

UNIT:	T 19 / Social Cooperation — Cooking
EPISODE:	C / Applesauce (Fall cooking, using heat and sharp utensils)
PURPOSE:	Learner interprets a recipe and follows its directions in a specific sequence, and gains further experience with measurements and quantities. He gains a general awareness of foods that are harvested in the fall.
ENTRY BEHAVIOR:	Learners should have previous experiences in cooking, following a recipe chart and making a food product without using heat and sharp utensils.
MATERIAL:	Equipment for a small group (6–8 learners): 2 or 3 vegetable peelers, kettle with cover or electric frying pan, graduated measuring cups and measuring spoons, 2–3 large stirring/tasting spoons, small paper cups and (enough for all) plastic spoons, hotplate or kitchen or electric frying pan, colander (or sieve). If a kitchen is unavailable in your preschool, secure a small wheelcart which is appropriate to the learner's height. Put a hotplate on the top shelf and do the cooking there. Use the lower shelf for bowls and other kitchen equipment.

Ingredients: 8 medium apples, sugar, cinnamon.

Recipe chart: white poster paper, magazine pictures or magic marker line drawings of ingredients used. (Chart may be put on posterboard or a chalkboard.)

PROCEDURE:

The recipe chart for this episode appears on the next page.

An ideal way to initiate this project would be to let learners pick the apples from an apple orchard. In any case, before the children make applesauce, the raw apples should be examined, tasted, and talked about. Serve raw apple slices at snack time and talk about the apple's shape, the exterior and interior colors, the exterior and interior textures, how the apple smells and tastes, and how the apple sounds while eating it (crunchy, etc.).

Talk about the recipe chart with the "chefs," and help them interpret the picture symbols (faucet, washing, apples, cups, measuring, colander, etc.). Ask them what ingredients are needed. What equipment is needed? How many apples are needed according to the recipe? Help them count the apples if necessary. Do not forget to use left-to-right progression while interpreting, and talk in sequential terms as to what step comes first, what comes next, and so on. Have the "chefs" locate the real ingredients and kitchen utensils that are pictured.

The learners wash the apples. Then each peels an apple, using a vegetable peeler. The facilitator quarters the apples, using a sharp knife. The apples are combined with some water in a covered pot and put on a hotplate. "Simmer" probably is a new word to the "chefs." Talk about what it means and, perhaps, look it up in a dictionary. The simmering process lasts 10 minutes, so if the facilitator has a timer or a large clock, the "chefs" might time the 10 minutes. Perhaps the learners can think of other ways of timing. There are different things to be learned, such as how the apples change colors while cooking. Texturewise, the apples change

Applesauce 1 quart

Wash and peel

8 apples

Put in covered pot with water

Simmer 10 minutes

Add: Cinnamon

Simmer 10 minutes more

Press through colander

from crunchy to soft, *but* let the "chefs" discover this themselves through tasting, feeling, smelling. Can they hear the simmering, bubbling sounds? Can they smell the apples? After the cinnamon and sugar are added, do these smells change a bit? After 10 minutes, have one learner measure the sugar and poor it in the pot. Have another learner stir the brew while a third learner adds the cinnamon. Cook for 10 minutes more (reset timer).

Put the colander on a table at a good working level for the chefs. The apples are hot and precaution is important! Spoon a few hot apple slices in the colander, but be sure to give the learners help if needed, or if a question of safety enters. Now ask how the apples have changed, formwise, texturewise, and tastewise.

Cool some sauce on a spoon, and have the learners carefully taste to make sure the applesauce it sweet enough and that the cinnamon flavor comes through. The refrigerated applesauce can be eaten at snack time, perhaps with a raw or dried apple slice for contrast. Or the children might compare their homemade applesauce with canned applesauce — do the two taste alike or different? Is one spicier, sweeter? Is one lumpier, runnier, chunkier?

At story time, the facilitator asks the learners to verbalize about their cooking venture in proper sequence.

Variations

1. Other fall cooking projects might involve baked acorn squash, roasted chestnuts, or pumpkin pie.
2. Further challenge can be added by using the homemade applesauce in a more intricate baking recipe such as applesauce pie, applesauce bread, applesauce cake, or applesauce cookies.
3. Investigate other cooking projects that use the apple. Start with something simple and slowly vary and increase its complexity (apple salad, baked apple, apple pie, apple brown betty).

TERMINAL BEHAVIOR:

Learner can interpret and follow the directions, using a pictorial recipe chart. The learner has added new words related to cooking to his vocabulary (simmering, colander, etc.) and understands the concepts behind quantitative measurements and timing in cooking. He can take turns and share his product.

T 19 / Social Cooperation — Cooking

EPISODE: **D / People Cookies** (Winter and holiday cooking activity, using heat and sharp utensils)

PURPOSE: Learner learns about following and interpreting rather complex recipe, following directions in a specific sequence. He gains further experience related to measurements, quantities, time, cooperation, and sharing.

ENTRY BEHAVIOR: Learner has had some previous experience in rolling and molding representational shapes with play dough, and in learning how to work safely with sharp cooking implements and heat. The learner has had experience in icing and decorating cookies from a "mix" or cookie dough prepared ahead by the facilitator.

MATERIAL: Equipment: several mixing bowls, graduated measuring cups and spoons, 3–6 large stirring/tasting spoons, 2 spatulas, several baking sheets, oven.
                              Ingredients: *Speedy Recipe* — one gingerbread package mix, ¼ cup lukewarm water.
                              Basic recipe: butter, sugar, dark molasses, flour, salt, soda, ginger, nutmeg, raisins, redhots, gumdrops.
                              Recipe chart: white poster paper; magazine pictures or magic marker line drawings of ingredients used. (Chart may be put on posterboard or a chalkboard.)

PROCEDURE: If the learners are making the cookie recipe from scratch, plan for a 2-day project. The first day is used for making and refrigerating the batter. On the second day the cookie people are formed, decorated, and baked. The recipe chart is on the following pages. Have the children follow the same easy progression of steps as used in Learning Episodes T19A and T19B.
                              This recipe is quite long and requires 10 ingredients. If you wish to simplify the activity, refer to Variations below. Stimulate sensory and motor exploration as well as verbalization. Initially, and throughout the baking project have the learners interpret, refer to, and follow the recipe chart. Since many different spices are used, have the learners smell, taste, and compare the cinnamon, ginger, nutmeg, and allspice before they are mixed into the flour. After dry ingredients are combined with the molasses mixture, can the learners pick out the different spice smells? Can they taste the dough's spiciness? Give the learner a small ball of refrigerated dough, and have him make at least two people cookies.
                              In forming the cookies, talk about ways in which they might form a gingerbread person (without using a rolling pin). You might ask them how they make people from clay. Give each learner a small ball of dough and suggest that they make boys, or girls, mommies, daddies, etc., by pinching out legs, head, and arms, etc. Encourage individual ideas and creativity by talking about how no two cookie people should look exactly alike. Have learners look over the available decorations (redhots, raisins, gumdrops). These can be used in all kinds of ways, such as for eyes, nose, mouth, buttons, ears, hat, shoes. The learners might want to

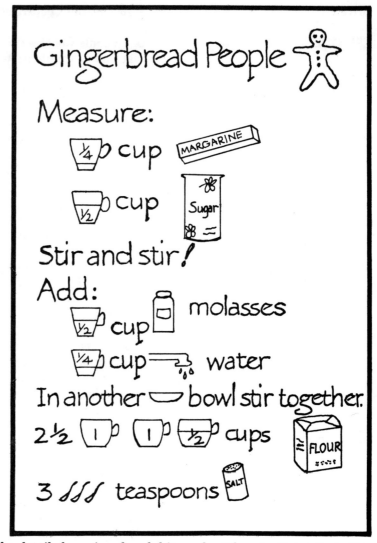

Gingerbread People

Measure:

¼ cup MARGARINE

½ cup Sugar

Stir and stir!

Add:

½ cup molasses

¼ cup water

In another bowl stir together.

2½ 1 1 ½ cups FLOUR

3 ♪♪♪ teaspoons SALT

make details by using dough bits or by "drawing" details in the dough form. Also, suggest that the gingerbread boy's legs might be running, walking, or jumping, etc. The arms could be waving, placed on the hips, etc. The head could be tilted at all kinds of angles, too. Each learner should have the opportunity to make two or three gingerbread people, and encourage that each one be different.

Now bake the cookies. Talk about the baking smells and encourage the learners to describe them. Open the oven door a crack so that the learners can see if the cookie people look the same or different. This project would be best if timed to coincide with a holiday (Christmas) party given on that day or the next day. Or the learners can decorate cardboard "house" boxes for their cookie people and give them as gifts. Be sure that there are one or two cookie people for *all* the participants. Also, if the cookies are brought home from a facility, have enough extras so that the learners can sample a cookie at snack time, have them talk about the detailed differences between their cookie people, the cookies' texture, flavor, etc. At group time, read the story "The Gingerbread Boy." Have the bakers retell in proper sequence how they made the dough, the specific ingredients used, measures used.

3 🥄🥄🥄 Ginger
2 🥄🥄 SODA
2 🥄🥄 NUT-MEG
pinch of ALL-SPICE

Stir everything together
Chill dough 2-3 hours
Put on greased cooking sheet

Decorate

Bake at 375° for 10 minutes

Variations

1. There are many ways to modify the activity of making ginger-bread people. The teacher can prepare the dough in advance. The children can make the cookie dough from a simpler recipe, using packaged gingerbread mix. The bakers can roll out the dough, cutting people forms with a cookie cutter. The baked people cookies can be frosted and decorated.
2. Use the gingerbread dough and have the bakers pinch out different animals forms. Perhaps an Animal Christmas Tree can be made, using the baked and decorated animals.

TERMINAL BEHAVIOR:

Learner is beginning to interpret and follow in sequence directions from a more complex pictorial recipe chart. He has added to his cooking vocabulary and has more understanding of the ingredients used and processes involved in making cookies.

UNIT:	T 19 / Social Cooperation — Cooking

EPISODE:	E / Ice Cream Making (In an old-fashioned freezer)

PURPOSE: Learner follows and interprets a recipe, and gains further experience with measurements, quantities, and time. He learns persistence and cooperation.

ENTRY BEHAVIOR: Learner has sufficient motor coordination and control to participate in cranking and egg beating. He has had sufficient cooking experience to be able to work safely around heat and with sharp utensils.

This activity will be more rewarding if learners have visited a dairy farm, or have done various things with dairy products (whipping cream, making butter, making different flavored milk drinks).

MATERIAL: Equipment: hand-crank ice cream freezer, several mixing bowls, graduated measuring cups and spoons, sauce pan, 3–6 large stirring/tasting spoons, hotplate or stove, eggbeater, Dixie cups and plastic spoons or cones. If the facilitator cannot obtain the crank freezer, make the refrigerated freezer kind, which calls for some modifications in the following recipe.

Ingredients: sugar, salt, milk, egg yolks, vanilla, whipping cream, rock salt, crushed ice.

Recipe chart: white poster paper, magazine pictures or magic marker line drawings of ingredients used. (Chart may be put on posterboard or a chalkboard.)

PROCEDURE: The facilitator first should familiarize himself with the operation of a crank freezer in order to anticipate possible problems that might arise.

This activity is different from previous ones in that it requires both cooking *and* freezing. The freezing procedure should be new to the learners and offer all sorts of learning possibilities. New motor skills are required in using the eggbeater and cranking. The learners will enjoy cranking for a bit, but since 20 minutes of constant cranking is required, help from the facilitator is a MUST.

The learners will be curious about the freezer's operation and the fact that it employs both crushed ice and rock salt. The learners will probably ask many "whys," offering a splendid opportunity for the facilitator later to set up scientific projects with the learners. For instance, why use salt? (Ice helps the ice cream to freeze, and rock salt makes the ice melt more slowly.) Let the children find the answers to their questions! With the ice cream project the facilitator encourages learners to taste and feel the salt and ice. Do the learners think that the custard mixture will become salty, too? Have the learners taste a few times throughout to check out taste change. More important, during the cranking process have them look at how the custard mixture is changing from a liquid to a frozen consistency. Have them taste the mixture. Does it feel any different now? (Thicker, colder, less runny.) After the cranking part is over, the mixture needs to freeze for another hour. After the hour, spoon the ice cream into small Dixie cups or into ice cream cones. Serve at snack time — maybe have

them eat outdoors. Ask what happens after awhile to the ice cream in the dish or cone. Does it melt? Could it be refrozen? (It is thought unwise to eat refrozen ice cream because of rapid growth of bacteria in melted ice cream and its effect on digestion, even in a refrozen state.) As the ice cream is eaten, talk about how the ice cream might be flavored differently. Make ice cream on another occasion to try out these "flavor" ideas. Invite another class to share the treat. During the eating, talk about the ice cream making story — how was it made stepwise, what ingredients were used, what equipment was used.

TERMINAL BEHAVIOR:

Learner is better able to interpret and follow in sequence the directions indicated by the recipe chart. He has added new words to his cooking vocabulary (fold, whip, eggbeater, hand-crank ice cream freezer, rock salt). He has observed and discussed the changing forms of the ice cream — from liquid to frozen and then to liquid again. He has learned about the properties of rock salt and crushed ice through tasting, feeling, and talking about both. He has gained new persistence and motor skills through using the eggbeater and hand-crank ice cream freezer.

Unit T 20 / CULTURAL SHARING — COOKING

Food relates to family and home life and is closely linked with parental love. The primary purpose throughout the four learning episodes that follow is to focus upon the child's emotional-social development and to relate this to his home environment.

A group setting offers opportunities for learners to try out and identify with grown-up roles that relate to the home (such as cooking activities). A child's self-confidence and initiative increases as he masters new cooking skills and procedures. He feels important and of value in accomplishing a given cooking task (such as sifting and measuring, taking the cookies carefully out of the oven, etc.).

A child from a different ethnic group can develop more self-pride and confidence as his culture's food patterns are shared with the rest of the group. This child feels very proud that the group is not only using his mother's recipe, but that *his* mother can actually help with the activity.

New social skills are developed as each child learns to work cooperatively in a cooking team. The children learn about taking turns, sharing, and trying out each other's ideas. The group can share pride regarding overall accomplishments — *"We* made these cookies together!"

The final focal point centers upon creating a bridge between the child's home and his group. This unit offers the learning facilitator an excellent opportunity to incorporate the parents' many varied skills, backgrounds, and learnings into the group setting. The parent from a particular ethnic group can share a part of his or her cultural heritage through cooking projects. Parents are encouraged to suggest recipe ideas and actively help with the food project.

UNIT:	T 20 / Cultural Sharing — Cooking
EPISODE:	A / Soul Cooking
PURPOSE:	For the learner who is a member of an ethnic group this episode develops feelings of the adequacy of his culture and fosters social acceptance by his peers. Each learner gains understanding and appreciation of other cultures, regardless of background. The learners have first-hand opportunities to try out and identify with adult roles in the family. Through parent participation the gap between home and group setting is bridged.
ENTRY BEHAVIOR:	Learner has previous experience with cooking ventures and can adhere to the established cooking safety rules.
MATERIAL:	See Unit T 19, "Social Cooperation — Cooking" for a list of basic kitchen equipment and recipe chart materials needed. Ingredients (for hoe cakes and collard greens with hog jowl): yellow cornmeal, salt, soda, buttermilk, bacon grease; Collard greens; salt pork *or* ham hock *or* fresh hog jowl, sugar, salt.

PROCEDURE:

Use the following cooking activities only if they correspond to one or more of your learner's cultural backgrounds. Other ethnic groups and geographic areas might be relevant to your particular learning situation; if so, substitute other groups (Puerto Rican, Italian, Jewish, Japanese, specific Native American tribes). In all four cooking examples, use a recipe chart and the same cooking and follow-up procedures as outlined in Unit T 19, "Social Cooperation — Cooking." These details have been omitted in the following activities.

Incorporate ideas and participation from a learner's mother who represents the Black group. This activity represents a cultural exchange among mothers as well as learners, so also incorporate help from one or two interested mothers who do *not* represent this group.

Perhaps one groups of learners can prepare the hoe cake while another group makes the greens. Otherwise, start the learners with the hoe cake recipe, and at the same time start cooking the hog jowl by putting it in a potful of boiling water. If you find that two cooking activities are too much for one day, select only one.

Hoe Cakes

On a recipe chart, print and use pictures to represent cooking equipment, ingredients, and procedures.

1½–2 cups yellow cornmeal
1 teaspoon salt
½ teaspoon soda
1 cup buttermilk
3 tablespoons bacon grease

Mix everything together; pour into *hot*, greased skillet. Bake at 350 degrees for 25 minutes.

Hoe cake should be served hot in wedges. Time the collard green recipe so that both can be tasted together at snack time. Hoe cake is good when served with maple syrup or with honey poured over it. In Soul Cooking, hot pot likker frequently is poured over the hoe cake. Pot likker is the liquid from the cooked collard greens and is rich in nutrients. Some people add 1 tablespoon of vinegar to this liquid.

During the cooking and eating periods, refer to Unit T 19 for ways in which learners might use their senses and language in exploring foods properties (and their form changes).

The learners might want to guess and find out where "hoe cake" got its name. Perhaps at storytime, and as a follow-up to the cooking, bring in a hoe. The hoe cake name originated a long time ago when black slaves who worked in the cotton fields would cook their cakes on the hot, flat, metal part of their hoes at lunchtime.

Collard Greens with Hog Jowl

1 pound salt pork, ham hock, or fresh hog jowl
4 pounds of collard greens
pinch of salt and sugar
water to cover

Boil the meat while cleaning the greens. Separate each leaf from its stalk and wash the leaf. Fold a leaf in half, roll it up, and then cut strips in it with a scissors. Put the greens in a pot full of water, and cook on high for 15 minutes, stirring. Remove from heat, and cool, still stirring.

Different greens can be substituted, such as turnip or beet greens, mixed with their chopped up roots. Also, you might try kale or mustard greens combined with turnip greens.

As the learners sample the greens, have them talk about the uncooked and cooked greens. How are they different when cooked? How do they change in color, texture, form? Can the learners smell, taste, and describe the seasoned meat's flavor (salty, sour, sweet, etc.)? Have the learners ever eaten anything that tastes like collard greens (such as spinach, beet tops)?

The facilitator might terminate the Soul Cooking project by having each learner take an uncooked collard leaf home and a mimeographed recipe sheet of what they made, thus encouraging each parent to repeat these cooking experiences while enlisting help from their child. The paper also might outline why the class is preparing soul foods (reasons such as sharing and learning about the different cultural backgrounds).

TERMINAL BEHAVIOR: Learner has participated in the preparing and eating of hoe cake, collard greens, and hog jowl and is aware of the background or history of soul cooking.

UNIT:	T 20 / Cultural Sharing — Cooking
EPISODE:	B / Chinese Cooking
PURPOSE:	Same as Learning Episode T20A.
ENTRY BEHAVIOR:	Same as Learning Episode T20A.
MATERIAL:	Basic cooking equipment.

MATERIAL: (continued) Ingredients: Chinese cabbage, bamboo shoots, snowpeas, water chestnuts, carrots, cucumbers, oil, chicken stock, sugar, soy sauce.

Recipe chart.

PROCEDURE: Use ideas and help from a learner's parent who represents the Chinese group. Also include one or two mothers who are not members of this group.

This activity will be a richer experience if the learners can walk to a Chinese market and select the vegetables. Such a market has many products, most of which are unfamiliar to non-Chinese children. Use the marketman's or the Chinese parent's help in selecting and investigating the vegetables that are needed for the following recipe. The marketman might encourage the learners to feel and talk about the different vegetables' shapes and textures, to note their colors, and to say the vegetables name (Chinese cabbage, bamboo shoots, peapods, water chestnuts).

After the vegetables are selected, plan to make the vegetable dish the following day. Do not forget to make and use a recipe chart. Before starting the recipe, review the preceding day's trip at the Chinese market, and talk about the names of the Chinese vegetables (have these real vegetables nearby).

In making this vegetable dish, the learners work on different tasks, such as peeling cucumbers and carrots, slicing cucumbers, cubing cabbage, and measuring the liquid seasoning.

Chinese Mixed Vegetables

1 small Chinese cabbage, cut in ½ inch cubes and parboiled
2 10–12 oz cans bamboo shoots, drained
1 package frozen peapods, thawed
24 water chestnuts
8 carrots
4 cucumbers
12 tablespoons oil
2 cups chicken stock
4 teaspoons sugar
8 teaspoons soy sauce

Parboil cabbage. Shred carrots fine by using a vegetable peeler. Peel and slice the cucumbers. Heat the oil in a skillet. Add the remaining vegetables, stirfrying 2 minutes. Add the chicken stock, sugar, and soy sauce. Cover and simmer 4 minutes.

As the learners are cutting, shredding, and peeling, talk about the different vegetables. How is Chinese cabbage like or different from other cabbage? (Perhaps have regular cabbage available and compare the two.) Does Chinese cabbage taste, feel, look, or smell differently? Have the learners use sensory explorations with the bamboo shoots, peapods, and water chestnuts. In each case, pose questions that encourage the learners to talk about their sensory impressions.

After the vegetables have cooked, eat them in Dixie cups at snack time. Can the learners pick out the different vegetables and name them? Do these cooked vegetables look, taste, or feel any different now? Talk about the crunchiness of Chinese vegetables. Have the Chinese mother show how chopsticks are used in eating. If possible, have chopsticks for each learner so that he can try them. It is quite difficult to operate the sticks, and most young learners' fine motor control and coordination are not sufficiently refined to enable them to use the chopsticks with facility.

As in Learning Episode T20A, the facilitator has each learner take home a mimeographed recipe sheet, explaining the Chinese Cooking project (Chinese vegetables used and procedure details). The parents can be encouraged to repeat this recipe at home and to reinforce language development by talking with their child about the names of the different Chinese vegetables.

Also the mothers might be introduced to some new vegetables and incorporate them in their home cooking.

TERMINAL BEHAVIOR: Learner has participated in the preparing and eating of Chinese mixed vegetables and is aware of the origin of the dish.

UNIT:	T 20 / Cultural Sharing — Cooking
EPISODE:	C / Chicano (Mexican) Food
PURPOSE:	Same as Learning Episode T20A.
ENTRY BEHAVIOR:	Same as Learning Episode T20A.

MATERIAL:	Basic cooking equipment.
	    Ingredients: avocados, lemon juice or wine vinegar, garlic salt, chili powder, chopped green chiles or Salsa Jalapeño, mayonnaise.
	    Recipe chart.

PROCEDURE:	Ideas and help from Chicano (Mexican) and non-Chicano mothers are important. This recipe for guacamole dip is only an example and it is understood that avocados in many regions may be either unavailable or too expensive. Therefore, substitute any other specialty that might better match your budget and product availability (such as refried beans, chile, sopaipillas, tacos).

Guacamole *(gwah-ka-mo-lay)*

2 very large, ripe avocados
4 teaspoons lemon juice or wine vinegar
1 teaspoon garlic salt
1 teaspoon chili powder or chopped green chiles or Salsa Jalapeño
4 tablespoons mayonnaise

With a regular table knife, cut the avocados in half and remove the seeds, Pry off the shells, using the back of the teaspoon. *Immediately* sprinkle the avocados with lemon juice or vinegar so they won't darken. Mash the avocados until smooth in a bowl, using a fork. Add the remaining ingredients and mix well. Makes 3 cups.

The learners can repeat this dip throughout the year and vary the basic recipe by adding peanuts, bacon bits, pomegranate seeds, or diced tomato.

The avocado is a good vegetable to explore, and many learners probably will not be familiar with it. Have them examine the avocado's outer shell and contrast this with the inner part — how are both parts different in feel and appearance? Talk about the avocado's greenness. Is the outer part as green as the inside part? Are they both the same shade of green? How does the inside part feel in the mouth (slimy, soft, mush, icky). Talk about how the avocado tastes. Examine the seeds, and talk about them in terms of size, color, shape, and texture. If possible, cut open a seed and examine its insides. As a follow-up activity, put the seed in a glass of water and see what happens.

After the avocados have been mashed, how have they changed? Do the mashed avocados taste differently? After adding the spices, taste again and ask the learners if the mashed avocados taste the same as before. If not, what added ingredients can their tongues pick out?

Serve the guacamole at snack time. Let each learner use a knife to spread some on a tortilla chip or cracker (divide the dip between several small bowls).

Have the learners take the guacamole recipe home and perhaps a Dixie cup of guacamole for his parents to sample.

TERMINAL BEHAVIOR: Learner has participated in the preparing and eating of a Chicano (Mexican) dish and is aware of the background of the dish.

UNIT:	T 20 / Cultural Sharing — Cooking
EPISODE:	D / Native American Cooking
PURPOSE:	Same as Learning Episode T20A.
ENTRY BEHAVIOR:	Same as Learning Episode T20A.

MATERIAL:	Basic cooking equipment.
	    Ingredients: boysenberries, sugar, flour, lemon peel.
	    Recipe chart.

PROCEDURE:	Use the ideas and active participation of a parent representing the Native American. Also include one or two mothers who are not members of this group. The original Native American way to make Wo-Japi is included here, because your region might contain wild chokecherries. Otherwise, follow the "White Man's" version, which uses canned or frozen boysenberries.

Original Wo-Japi

Mash the ripe wild chokecherries. If you want to preserve them, as the Native Americans once did, form them into small cakes and let dry. Then when you are ready to use the berries, soak them in water until soft. Then mash them with a stone mallet. Combine the berries in a pot of water with 2 tablespoons of flour and 2 cups of sugar. Slowly boil for 15 minutes. Serve cold.

White Man's Wo-Japi

1 can or package of frozen boysenberries
2 cups of sugar
2 tablespoons flour
½ cup cold water
lemon peel, grated

Cook the boysenberries in water. Add the sugar. Mix until smooth ½ cup of cold water and 2 tablespoons of flour, and add this to the berry mixture. Add grated lemon peel and slowly boil about 15 minutes. Chill and eat. Wo-Japi also is good when topped with whipped cream.

The boysenberry might be a new fruit to many of the learners. Talk about the boysenberry in terms of color, size, texture, form, and taste. Have the learners compare the boysenberry's characteristics with other berries available in your area, such as the blueberry, strawberry, raspberry, logenberry. Do boysenberries taste differently when cooked? Also talk about how a long time ago Native Americans stored wild berries by drying the mashed berries and forming them into cakes. The Native Americans gathered and stored many other kinds of food (such as dried beef or elk-meat jerky, corn, nuts, beans). They had to hunt and fish to get their meat, using bow and arrow and sharp spears. Post any pictures dealing with Native American food patterns, as well as with other elements of their heritage.

Eat the Wo-Japi in a homemade wigwam, or make a "pow-wow" circle on the floor. Have the learner take a mimeographed Wo-Japi recipe home.

Variations:

1. Each time that the learners prepare an ethnic dish, place products and boxes on the kitchen shelves that relate to the cook-

ing ingredients: for collard greens use strips of green tissue paper, for the hoe cake use yellow building blocks. Use the empty cans and boxes from the frozen peapods, bamboo shoots, boysenberries, taco chips. Put chopsticks on the dining table.

In the play kitchen, put equipment that the learners are using in actual cooking (measuring cups, measuring spoons). In this area encourage pretend cooking by putting cornmeal in a shallow pan with spoons, sifters, funnels, etc.

Make clothes available that correspond to the different cultures, such as kimonos, fans, bright shawls, colored skirts, lace for mantilla, wide-brimmed sombreros, Indian headbands with feathers, beaded necklaces.

2. Talk about other interesting customs within each ethnic group, such as their dress, crafts, music, holidays, language. For example, with the Chicano (Mexican) group use maracas, castanets, bongo drums, rhythm sticks. Listen to Chicano (Mexican) music. Teach the learners some simple words such as *buenas dias, adios, gracias.*

    Ideally, the Black, Chinese, or Native American parents (or visitors) will introduce these other cultural sidelines.

3. Make Native American instruments: Make Native American drums from oatmeal boxes or coffee cans with lids. Make rattles from empty juice cans; fill with dried beans, push a tongue depressor through the cardboard sides, and decorate.

4. Display corresponding ethnic pictures that show examples of clothes, family homes and members, games, music, art, special foods, and transportation. Talk and refer to these pictures at different times. Also, read picture books to the group.

TERMINAL BEHAVIOR: Learner has participated in the making of Wo-Japi and is acquainted with the cultural background of the dish.

Here are sources of further recipes:

Brown, Marion. 1950. *Southern Cook Book.* Westminster, Philadelphia.
Crocker, Betty. 1961. *Betty Crocker Cookbook.* McGraw-Hill Book Co., New York.
Verta, Mae. 1970. *Vibration Cooking.* Doubleday, Garden City, N.Y.
Zelayeta, Elena. 1958. *Elena's Secrets of Mexican Cooking.* Prentice-Hall, Englewood Cliffs, N.J.

Unit T 21 / CULTURAL SHARING — FESTIVALS

A study of holidays might be called a study of humanity. People everywhere unite to share common seasonal festivals. The winter's end also signifies the beginning of longer, sunnier days. The winter season presents a joyful, festive time, and people everywhere share renewed happiness and goodwill toward one another. Hanukkah, Christmas in Mexico, and Christmas in America all emulate this spirit. Their respective holiday music, holiday lights, and holiday traditions express this worldwide goodwill, hope, faith, and joyfulness.

UNIT:	**T 21 / Cultural Sharing — Festivals**
EPISODE:	**A / Let's Have a Party**
PURPOSE:	Learner gains experience in planning and carrying out a group activity that is fun for learners, facilitator, and parents.
ENTRY BEHAVIOR:	None.
MATERIAL:	Materials needed to make party invitations and name tags; ingredients needed to prepare and serve refreshments; decorations for the classroom; equipment needed to play the party games (e.g., a handkerchief for "Drop the Handkerchief," index cards with printed words for "Find the Same Word," a cardboard target and darts for "Hit the Number Target").
PROCEDURE:	A party is good on any occasion. You might plan one for Valentine's Day, Halloween, Christmas, or any other time. Use the appropriate decorations and activities for the particular occasion. Have the group of party planners decide who they want to invite. The guest list might include the teachers, parents, brothers and sisters, and friends. After the group had decided who to invite, help them to prepare the invitations and send them out. You could make them out of paper, cloth, or a variety of other materials. The learners might want to make special mailboxes in the classroom where they can mail invitations to you and the other learners. One person might be selected to act as the mailman and deliver the invitations to the guests. If you decide to mail invitations to parents or friends outside the classroom, you could plan a trip to the post office. Make this a learning experience by talking about the trip

beforehand, by arranging for some post office official to speak to the group, and by pointing out things of interest to the learners while you are on the trip.

Now is also the time to plan the refreshments. What kind will you have? Where will you get them? Who will make them? Who will serve them? It is up to the learners to answer all these questions. First, they must decide what they want to serve. This will depend upon the occasion and the type of party. Probably a drink and cookies will be enough. Maybe you can get the parents to bring in some goodies. More elaborate refreshments will call for more planning and more parental involvement. The learners should help buy the food. You can plan a field trip to the store and have the learners select the ingredients, pay for them, and take them back to the classroom. There, they can work together to prepare the refreshments and plan how to serve them. They will have to select three or four learners to serve the refreshments at the party. You will need glasses, silverware, and napkins.

Decorations — do you want to decorate the room? You will have to plan what kind of decorations you want for the table, walls, and ceiling. Will there be flowers? Have a few learners volunteer to serve on a committee to make and put up the decorations. You will also need a cleanup committee. Let the learners decide what kind of clothes they will wear to the party. They might like to make special costumes, as an art activity. Be sure to comment on their appearance at the party.

Now that everyone is at the party, what happens next? First, the guests must be introduced. You can have one learner pass out name tags at the door. You might have the learners make special name tags. Have each learner introduce his own guests. The learners might sing "Getting To Know You." What kind of entertainment do you want at the party? There can be games, music, skits, and a variety of other activities. You might arrange for the adults and learners to take turns presenting a skit or song they have prepared. Each group might want to act out a story or nursery rhyme, perform a dance, put on a puppet show, or sing a song.

Some group games you might want to play are, "Drop the Handkerchief," "Tag," "Pin the Tail on the Donkey," "Hide and Seek," and so on. "Find the Same Word" is played as follows: On small index cards print the names of various objects in the room. Make a duplicate set of cards, and attach them to the objects they represent. Distribute the first set of cards to various learners and have them collect the cards of the other set from the objects to which they are attached. They are to find the word on an object that is the same as the word on their index card. The game will help the learners recognize words, a necessary prereading skill.

Another game is "Number Target." Make a large target out of heavy cardboard. Draw several concentric circles, and write a large numeral on each one. Provide the learners with individual darts (perhaps with rubber tips that will attach themselves readily to the cardboard), and allow them to take turns throwing the darts. Add up the number of points earned by each learner on a particular turn. You might give a prize to the winner. There are many other games you might play. When the guests seem tired, or when you feel it is appropriate, break up the party and put the cleanup committee to work.

TERMINAL BEHAVIOR: Learner is able to help plan and carry out the party activities.

UNIT:	**T 21 / Cultural Sharing — Festivals**
EPISODE:	**B / Hanukkah or Chanukah**
PURPOSE:	Learner is introduced to some of the traditional customs used by the Jewish people in celebrating their Winter Festival — Hanukkah or Chanukah.
ENTRY BEHAVIOR:	Ability to hear, see, and participate in the activities.
MATERIAL:	Small toys familiar to the children; blue and white wrapping paper; a nine-branched menorah and nine candles (if possible borrow one from a temple, otherwise, make one from wire and clay); a real or homemade clay dreidl.
PROCEDURE:	A short background of this Jewish holiday is given below, followed by several different activities that relate to Hanukkah.

A long, long, long time ago, the Jewish people fought the Syrian-Greeks, and won and regained their Holy Temple in Jerusalem. Hanukkah is usually around Christmas time and is called the Festival of Lights, referring to the time when the Holy Temple was restored a long time ago. After the Jewish soldiers cleared the Temple, they searched high and low for some oil to light the holy lamps. They found a tiny amount of lamp oil, hardly enough to furnish one day of light. They lit the holy lamp and it burnt miraculously for eight days until a larger oil supply could be secured. Therefore, Hanukkah begins on the 24th day of the Hebrew month, falling around Christmas time, and continues for eight consecutive days. It is a happy festival, giving thanks for the survival of Judaism. |
| **Activity I** (The Lighting of the Menorah) | With the preschoolers, visit a nearby temple if possible. Borrow a menorah from the temple. The menorah is a nine-branched candlestick and looks like this: |

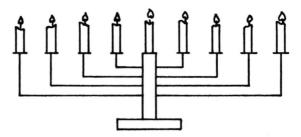

You can make one out of a coathanger wire and clay that hardens. Put the menorah on a classroom table, and at group time, starting on the first Hanukkah day, have a learner light the first candle. The ninth candle remains lighted throughout the eight days and is the extra one from which the other eight are lighted. On each of the remaining seven days a new candle is lighted by a different learner. Of course, the facilitator must extinguish these candles at the end of each day, or even before, if fire hazards seem likely. Sing Hanukkah songs following the lighting of the new candles (refer to "My Dreidl"). Here is a Hanukkah song which uses the tune to "Ten Little Indians."

The Hanukkah Song
One little, 2 little, 3 little candles,
4 little, 5 little, 6 little candles,
7 little, 8 little, Hanukkah candles,
In my menorah.

Activity II (The Dreidl)

A long, long time ago, the Jewish people were not allowed to pray together. As a result, they met, pretending to be playing with a top, or dreidl.

The dreidl is a Far Eastern name for this special four-sided top, usually made out of wood, lead, tin, or plastic. Four Hebrew letters are engraved on each of the sides (Nun, Gimel, Hay, Shin), and they stand for four Hebrew words that say, "A great miracle happened there." This refers to when the Jewish soldiers fought and victoriously recovered their Holy Temple in Jerusalem.

At Hanukkah the dreidl offers all kinds of challenging spinning games, providing fun for the entire family. It would be fun to present this dreidl to the learners. A learner with a Jewish background might show the other learners some of the games. Also, provide the other learners with opportunities to make their own dreidls. Use homemade or commercial modeling clay that hardens. Secure lollipop sticks or stiff cotton swabs with the cotton removed. Show the learners how they might mold a form around the stick. Talk about how a dreidl can be different sizes, colors, and shapes. This provides the learner with a chance to experiment with balancing ideas — the better centered and more perpendicular the stick is to the clay mass, the better the top should spin. But let the learners try out these top ideas and, through experimenting, establish their own ideas as to why some of the tops spin better.

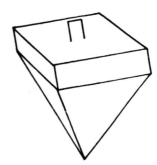

The song on the next page, "My Dreidl," can be sung, and the learners might pretend that they are tops and spin and spin until they fall to the ground. Additional verses are given below:

It has a lovely body, with legs so short and thin;
And when it is all tired, It drops and then I win.
O dreidl, dreidl, dreidl; It drops and then I win.

My dreidl, always playful, It loves to dance and spin,
A happy game of dreidl, come play, now let's begin.
O dreidl, dreidl, dreidl, It loves to dance and spin,
O dreidl, dreidl, dreidl, Come play, now let's begin.

S.S. Crossman and S.E. Goldfarb
Arranged by C. McGraw

lively

I have a little drei-dl I made it out of clay; and
when it's dry and read-y, Then drei-dl I shall play—
drei-dl, drei-dl, drei-dl, I made it out of clay;
drei-dl, drei-dl, drei-dl, Now drei-dl I shall play.

Activity III (What's Inside?)

On each of the eight Hanukkah evenings, gifts are exchanged between family and friends. These gifts are wrapped in blue and white paper which represents the colors of the Jewish flag.

Select familiar toys and materials that are of different shapes, sizes, and texture (soft/hard). Wrap these in blue and white paper. On one of the eight Hanukkah days, play this game. Spread the wrapped toys on a low table. Have the learners take turns selecting a wrapped item and guessing what might be inside. The learner must use many of his senses in finding out information about the concealed object (feeling, sharing, looking at shape, smelling). When the learner thinks he knows the contents, he can unwrap the gift and verify his guess. The facilitator should verbalize the different ways in which the learners find their clues, i.e., some might use touch and sight exclusively, some might shake the wrapped toy, using hearing, etc.

Activity IV (Making Latkes — Potato Pancakes)

Latkes is a traditional Hanukkah food. Here is a recipe that could be prepared in your learning environment:

> Latkes
> 2 cups finely grated raw potato
> ¼ cup milk
> 2 eggs, well beaten
> 2 tablespoons flour
> 1 tablespoon grated onion
> 1 teaspoon salt
> Dash of pepper

Mix all ingredients and drop by tablespoonfuls onto a well-greased skillet. Bake about 3 minutes on each side or until brown. Latkes is good served with applesauce. Yield: 12 pancakes.

Variation

The song "Joyous Chanukah":

TERMINAL BEHAVIOR:

Learner is more aware of Hanukkah and its accompanying traditions (the menorah, Hanukkah songs, the dreidl, Hanukkah gifts, and potato pancakes or latkes). He has a beginning awareness of and respect for the winter festivals of different people; he knows that everyone does not celebrate Christmas.

UNIT:	**T 21 / Cultural Sharing — Festivals**
EPISODE:	**C / Christmas in Mexico**
PURPOSE:	Learners become acquainted with the ways of celebrating Christmas in Mexico.
ENTRY BEHAVIOR:	Ability to hear and understand the oral stories and to see and appreciate the pictures.
PROCEDURE:	First, some of the meanings and traditional customs which accompany this special event in Mexico are presented. In Mexico Christmas starts on December 16, with the posadas (poh-sah'-dahs) or processions. These posadas are held for nine nights preceding Christmas and honor the difficulty that Mary and Joseph encountered when seeking shelter on their journey from Nazareth to Bethlehem. They looked for shelter during these eight days and, finally, on the ninth, found lodging in a stable. This was Christmas Eve, when the Christ child was born. Posadas are both religious and festive and mainly involve the extended family.

The posada is held at different families' households on each of the nights. Each family begins to prepare for the posadas in early December, decorating the house with colored paper lanterns, Spanish moss, and evergreen branches. A tiny altar is set up in the corner of the parlor or living room, and on this altar is placed the Holy Family looking at an empty manger. On the eve of December 16, the whole family gathers in this room, recites the rosary, and sings to the Holy Child and Virgin. Then a procession starts, led by two children carrying images of the Virgin and Joseph. The adults follow, each holding a lighted candle. The family marches through the different rooms of the house and onto the patio. Then they slowly return to the now-closed doors of the parlor. Those outside sing, asking for shelter, and those in the parlor reply and represent the innkeeper (usually those inside include the hostess and a few others). Finally, the parlor doors open and all enter and kneel before the altar, singing joyous hymns.

The festive part begins with the lighting of the patio lanterns. Fireworks, dancing, laughing, talking, and eating follow. Small toys are filled with candy and passed out to the children. The piñata is brought out and hung on a rope extending from two trees on the patio. The piñata is a clay pot, covered with papier mâché and decorated with colored paper. Its shape might be plain, round, or a fancy fairy, bird, fruit, or a clown. The children are blindfolded and take turns trying to crack it open with a long stick. A grown-up lowers and raises the piñata by its rope, making the breaking process harder. When the piñata finally breaks, delighted children scramble to gather its contents.

There is a different piñata for each posada night. On Christmas Eve a more serious posada follows the Midnight Mass, and a wax Christ figure is placed in the manger. The final piñata is cracked and a huge feast follows, which might include roasted suckling pig, chicken, turkey, pasta, soup, salads, and buñelos (thick, fluffy fried cakes). In Mexico the children receive gifts on the Twelfth Night after Christmas. They line up their shoes in the front of the manger or under the Christmas tree, and gifts are put inside them. Use the following Mexican Christmas activities only if your young learners include some Chicano (Mexican) children.

Activity I (Nine Days to Christmas)

MATERIAL:

Hall, Marie. 1959. *Nine Days to Christmas.* Viking Press, New York.

PROCEDURE:

Read this marvelous picture book story. We see and share the magic and excitement that 5-year-old Ceci feels over her first posada. She is allowed to choose her very first piñata at the Mexican market.

Encourage the learners to talk about her excitement. Show the learners a real piñata so that they can better understand what the piñata pictures represent in the book. Talk about what it is made of (clay, paper, etc.). Talk about the different sizes, shapes, and colors of piñatas as shown on pages 6, 7, 26, and 35. What kinds of goodies is Ceci putting in her star piñata? What other kinds of things might she fill it with?

Do the learners see snow, Christmas trees, or a Santa Claus in any of the pictures? You might point out that piñatas, lanterns, etc., are ways of celebrating Noël in Mexico, and that they have no snow because of warm weather. Talk about how Ceci's star piñata is hung between two trees above the patio (p. 36). Talk about the first part of the posada which is religious (pp. 38–41). Do the learners know what the two leading children are carrying? Talk about the knocking on the inn door, but only to the extent of the interest and overall maturity level of your group. Inform the learners that children in Mexico receive gifts on the Twelfth Night after Christmas (refer to the first part of the procedure).

Activity II (Making and Breaking a Piñata)

MATERIAL:

A large paper bag and decorations (colored paper, paints, etc.); rope; a stick or plastic bat; candy, nuts, fruit, etc.

PROCEDURE:

The learners can decorate their own piñatas, making them from large grocery bags. Decorations might include colored tissue paper, paste, construction paper, colored chalk, and bright colored tempera or finger paints (red, green, blue, yellow). These piñatas can be hung from the ceiling. Use one decorated piñata for the game, and fill it with oranges, gum, nuts, and paper-wrapped candies. This piñata is strung up and held by a rope. A child is blindfolded, turned around a few times to lose his orientation, and then given a stick or plastic bat with which he tries to crack the piñata. Let many different children have turns trying to whack the piñata. Two adults slyly lower and raise the piñata by its rope, making it more difficult to break the piñata. This game should be planned around snack time when the learners can eat the sweets that spill from the broken piñata.

Activity III (Cardboard
   Box Piñatas)

MATERIAL: Cardboard boxes and tubes; tape; paints.

PROCEDURE: Collect cardboard boxes and cardboard tubes of all sizes and
                              shapes. The learners can make animal or people-shaped piñatas by
                              taping together different boxes and then decorating the shapes
                              with gaily colored finger paints or poster paints.

TERMINAL BEHAVIOR: Learner is more aware of how Christmas is celebrated in Mexico,
                              with its festivities and accompanying traditions (posadas, piña-
                              tas, the Mexican market, etc.).

UNIT:	T 21 / Cultural Sharing — Festivals
EPISODE:	D / Christmas in America
PURPOSE:	In this learning episode the learners share together some of the traditional ways in which American families celebrate Christmas.
ENTRY BEHAVIOR:	None.
PROCEDURE:	Today's Christmas in America represents a collection of customs contributed by colonists from England, Holland, Germany, Sweden, Spain, France, Italy, and others. Christmas customs also differ from family to family. For Christians, Christmas means the birth of the Christ Child. This holiday is particularly exciting for children.

Houses are decorated in early December with wreaths, greens, mistletoe, holly, scarlet poinsettias, and lights. An evergreen tree is set up, sometimes on Christmas Eve and sometimes before this time. The carefully chosen tree is adorned with colored lights, colored balls, tinsel, and treasured ornaments that have been passed on from generation to generation. A symbolic star usually tops the tree and oftentimes a creche is nearby.

Gifts are made or bought for brothers, sisters, parents, relatives and friends, and the air is filled with Christmas secrets. Gifts are wrapped in decorative paper and laid beneath the tree. On Christmas Eve a family might sing carols or read Christmas stories. This is a time when relatives might visit. Children hang their stockings on Christmas Eve, go to bed early, and very likely arouse the family before dawn with their excitement over whether or not Santa filled their stockings. On Christmas Day, after breakfast, the family opens the gifts beneath the tree. Later in the day follows a family Christmas feast, usually including turkey, cranberry sauce, sweet potatoes, pumpkin or mince pie, or plum pudding.

Churches, decorated with evergreens and red or white flowers, offer a Midnight Mass on Christmas Eve, a Christmas pageant, or a special Christmas Day service. A choir sometimes sings carols and the Christmas story is read from the Bible.

Since Christmas is an exciting family event for young children, keep classroom holiday preparations simple and low keyed. If there are learners from poor families in your class, be sensitive to their feelings when discussing gifts. The following activities are merely some ideas which you might want to use individually around this season.

Activity I (Group Discussion about Christmas and Christmas Stories)	
MATERIAL:	Brown, Margaret Wise. 1938. *On Christmas Eve.* Young Scott Books, New York. Lindgren, Astrid, and Wikland, Ilan. 1964. *Christmas in Noisy Village.* Viking Press, New York.

PROCEDURE:

You might ask the learners, "Why do we celebrate Christmas?" This will give you hints as to what this holiday means to different children. Can the learners think of other events we celebrate at winter holiday time (i.e., New Year's)? Have the learners talk about how their families celebrate Christmas (preparations, decorations, Christmas cooking, Christmas tree, Christmas Eve gifts, etc.). Point out the similarities and differences between how each family celebrates this holiday. (In some homes the parents decorate the tree on Christmas Eve and in other homes the children help decorate the tree. In some homes the family attends Midnight Mass, and in other homes the family goes to a Christmas Day service.) The discussion list is endless, but make certain that each family's special way of celebrating Christmas is respected. The learner might paint or draw a story of how he and his family prepare for Christmas.

Now ask the learners if they might share their favorite Christmas storybooks. Perhaps a parent could be invited to tell a Christmas story to the group.

Read *On Christmas Eve* to the group. Why couldn't the four storybook children sleep on Christmas Eve? Have the learners felt the same sort of awe and excitement at this time of year? Encourage the learners to verbalize their ideas as to how the Christmas tree appeared to the four children. What gifts do the learners think are hidden in the stockings and beneath the tree? This book's simple illustrations are in yellow, black, and orange, and allow much room for imaginative speculation.

Read *Christmas in Noisy Village* to the group. This storybook is about an old fashioned Christmas, and certainly its different aspects should be discussed and compared with how the learners celebrate their Christmas. Do the learners help with the Christmas baking? What kinds of special goodies do they make? Does the learner's family chop down or buy their tree? How is their family tree similar to or different from the one in the book? What kind of fun activities are pursued on Christmas Day?

Activity II (Gift Projects for Family Members)

With the learners stress that Christmas time is a time of doing things for others, such as making and giving gifts. Talk about how they might make others happy at Christmas time (gifts do not need to be included here!). With the group, or on an individual basis, discuss the learner's ideas on kinds of gifts he might want to make. Pursue each learner's gift idea, instead of all learners making the same item. Here are some gift ideas for learners — spatter prints of children's hands on burlap tablemats; wall plaque of plaster of Paris handprints — the outer part might be painted blue or red, leaving the handprint white. Then shellac the entire plaque. The following poem might accompany these first two gift suggestions:

> You sometimes get discouraged,
>   Because I am so small,
> And get my fingerprints
>   On furniture and wall.
>
> But here's a Christmas present,
>   So that you will remember,
> Exactly how my fingers looked,
>   In 19____, December.

Macaroni necklace — have the child paint the macaroni pieces in different bright colors. Penholders — cover juice cans or peanut cans with contact paper and decorate. Clay bowls and ashtrays — painted and shellaced. Homemade fudge or Christmas cookies in decorated covered coffee cans or cigar boxes. Homemade greeting cards — have the child mail this to his family.

Activity III (Learning Games Related to Christmas)

A. *What Goes Together?* (classification) Paste magazine pictures of Christmas things that are related to one another. Mount these on separate cardboard cards. Spread pictures out on table, and involve three or four learners at a time. Hold up a card and have the learners take turns in finding another picture that goes with your picture. Here are some examples: reindeer/sleigh, bag of toys/Santa Claus, Christmas tree/ornaments, wrapping paper/boxes, fireplace mantel/stockings.

B. *Classifying Pictures of Christmas Things* Mount all sorts of Christmas and non-Christmas magazine pictures on separate cards. Three to four players can participate at a time. The facilitator retains one duplicate from each of the pictures. The other pictures are spread out on the table. The facilitator holds up a card and has the learners take turns in locating the other picture that matches her picture. Make the game more difficult by substituting silhouette Christmas shapes of the same items.

TERMINAL BEHAVIOR:

Learner is more aware that American families celebrate Christmas in some similar and some different ways, and has verbally shared with the group some favorite Christmas customs practiced in his family. The learner may have planned and made one or more gifts for members of his family.

Game A: The learner can understand and identify the relationship between pictured pairs of Christmas things.

Game B: The learner can visually discriminate and classify those pictures that are associated with Christmas. The learner can visually discriminate and match picture duplicates.

Additional sources of ideas include:

Braun, William. (ed.). 1970. *Kindergarten Curriculum Guide.* Manchester, Conn.

Carmichael, Viola. 1971. *Curriculum Ideas for Young Children.* Southern California Association for Education of Young Children, Los Angeles.

Dobler, LaVinia. 1938. *Customs and Holidays Around the World.* Fleet Publishing Corp., New York.

Millen, Nina. 1964. *Children's Festivals from Many Lands.* Friendship Press, New York.

Rublowsky, Anne. 1968. *Primary Grade Activities.* Field Enterprises Educational Corp., Chicago.

Purdy, Susan. 1969. *Festivals for You to Celebrate.* J. B. Lippincott Co., New York.

Wernecke, Herbert. (ed.). 1967. *Celebrating Christmas Around the World.* Westminster Press, Philadelphia.

Other Christmas stories for children include:

Adams, Adrienne. 1966. *Twelve Dancing Princesses*. Holt, Rinehart & Winston, New York.

Adshead, Gladys. 1955. *Brownies — It's Christmas!* Henry Z. Walck, New York.

Anglund, Joan Walsh. 1961. *Christmas Is a Time of Giving*. Harcourt Brace Jovanovich, New York.

Francoise, Jean. 1953. *Noël for Jeanne-Marie*. Charles Scribner's Sons, New York.

Moore, Clement Clark. 1961. *Night Before Christmas*. Grosset & Dunlap, New York.

Trent, Robbie. 1948. *The First Christmas*. Harper & Row, New York.

Tudor, Tasha. 1950. *The Dolls' Christmas*. Henry Z. Walck, New York.

Zolotow, Charlotte. 1957. *Over and Over*. Harper & Row, New York.

Unit I 22 / READINESS

Many learners who do not have interferences in their development will not be in need of any of the learning episodes in this unit. However, with those who do have deficits, especially those with motor difficulties arising from too stiff or too "floppy" muscles, the facilitator may find these learning episodes invaluable as an aid toward preparation for movement or for good positioning to allow optimal movement capabilities. Since so many of the young learner's expressive abilities, as well as his cognitive awareness and developing understanding, are dependent on movement, positions that foster optimal movement should be used routinely and explicitly with learners who have movement deficits. Physical and occupational therapists should be consulted for advice as to which Readiness Learning Episodes should be applied or developed for learners having various specific motor deficits.

UNIT: I 22 / Readiness

EPISODE: A / Position to Facilitate Head Control

PURPOSE: Learner will maintain head control for looking or listening.

ENTRY BEHAVIOR: None.

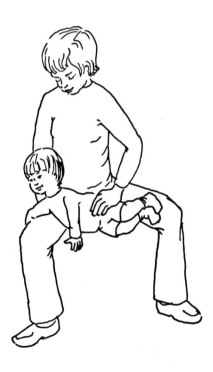

MATERIAL:	Towel over facilitator's legs; Favorite toy, book, or other person.
PROCEDURE:	1. Place the learner on his side, lying across one of the facilitator's legs.
	2. Keep either one or both of the learner's arms over the facilitator's thigh.
	3. The learner may either face toward the facilitator for "talking" or away from the facilitator toward a toy, book, or other person.
	4. Occasionally bounce the learner gently with your leg up and down to relax the learner, but otherwise use constant slow rocking with your legs in this position.
	5. Place your hand over the learner's "upside" hip and apply mild pressure, making sure both of the learner's knees and hips are kept bent, with the "downside" leg in contact with the towel, or for a very small learner, with your thigh.
TERMINAL BEHAVIOR:	Learner lifts head and looks at his toy or someone's face, or listens to the facilitator.

UNIT:	I 22 / Readiness
EPISODE:	B / Positioning on Stomach for a Learner Who Tends to Stay Stiffly Bent
PURPOSE:	Learner will be able to lift his head and maintain both arms in front of him, without stiffness or floppiness interfering, for looking, listening, and/or reaching.
ENTRY BEHAVIOR:	Learner keeps his shoulders back stiffly with arms bent upward. When learner is lying on his stomach, his arms and legs remain stiffly bent. His head tends to turn to either side. There is overall stiffness caused by tight muscles.
MATERIAL:	Favorite toy; one towel roll "A" 2–3 inches thick and 6 inches long; one towel roll "B" 4–5 inches thick and 6 inches long.
PROCEDURE:	The facilitator should have all three items on the mat or rug. He places the towel "A" on the mat and then picks up the learner around the chest. The facilitator positions the learner face down on the mat, carefully repositioning towel roll "A" so it runs across the front part of the learner's hips, as illustrated below.

The facilitator kneels behind the learner and gently places his knees on either side of the learner's legs.

The facilitator uses his two hands to lift the learner's shoulders up. He tucks his right forearm under the learner's armpits in order to maintain the learner's arms in front of his body (toward the mat). The facilitator slowly rocks the learner's body side to side while keeping his left hand on the learner's buttocks in order to maintain the learner's hips over towel "A" and to relax the learner's pelvis, hips, and legs.

When relaxation in arms, trunk, and legs can be felt, the facilitator moves his left hand to the learner's forehead, lifting the learner's head up. The facilitator moves his left hand back and forth between head and buttocks, wherever the learner requires the hand support. After 2 minutes, or after the learner is relaxed, the facilitator places towel roll "B" beneath the learner's forearm. This roll is to replace the facilitator's forearm support under the learner's armpits. The facilitator lifts the learner's head with his left hand and removes his right forearm, drawing it from the armpit to head direction. This should bring the learner's arms near the learner's ears, elbows straight, while lowering the learner onto the towel roll. The facilitator adjusts rolls "A" and "B" to ensure firm contact in armpit and hip areas. The learner is to stay in this position with a toy placed in his hands. After 5–15 minutes, the facilitator removes both rolls and turns the learner to either side in the side-lying position.

TERMINAL BEHAVIOR: Learner is able to lift head and maintain his arms freely in front of him for looking, listening, or playing with a toy.

Variation

PURPOSE: Learner will be able to rest some weight on his forearms and lift his head without stiffening his whole body.

ENTRY BEHAVIOR: There is overall stiffness in learner's body caused by too tight muscles.

MATERIAL: Small foam rubber wedge or small foam roll which allows learner to place his elbows and forearms on the floor.

PROCEDURE: The learner is placed on his stomach. His shoulders are brought forward over the wedge or roll. The facilitator should make sure that the learner's pelvis is in contact with the surface of the mat or floor and that his legs are relaxed. Placing the facilitator's hand gently but firmly over the buttocks of the learner and rocking slowly from side to side can help relax the learner.

TERMINAL BEHAVIOR: Learner is able to maintain position illustrated below.

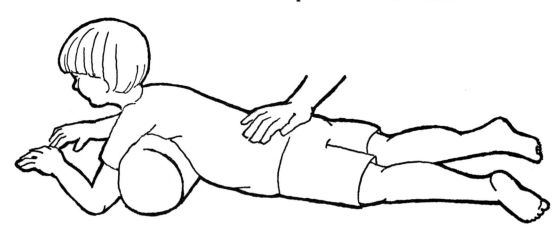

UNIT:	I 22 / Readiness
EPISODE:	C / Positioning on Back for a Learner Who Tends to Stay Stiffly Bent
PURPOSE:	Learner will be able to relax on his back and listen, look around, and/or reach out.
ENTRY BEHAVIOR:	Learner's body tends to be stiff because of tight muscles.
MATERIAL:	Firm pillow; foam roll and/or towels rolled up, favorite toy.
PROCEDURE:	The facilitator places the learner's head and shoulders on a firm pillow so that they are bent slightly forward. The learner's shoulders are kept forward by placing rolled towels under them. A small roll is placed under the learner's knees so that his hips and knees are bent slightly. The two sides of the body should be in balanced alignment. The learner should not remain in this position longer than 15 to 20 minutes without a change.
TERMINAL BEHAVIOR:	Learner will be able to look at and reach out toward a toy.

UNIT:	**I 22 / Readiness**
EPISODE:	**D / Positioning on Side for a Learner Who Tends to Stay Stiffly Bent**
PURPOSE:	Learner will be able to relax and keep both hands in front of him to look at or to reach out.
ENTRY BEHAVIOR:	Learner's body tends to be stiff because of tight muscles.
MATERIAL:	Favorite toy.
PROCEDURE:	The facilitator places the learner on his side with one leg straight and the other leg slightly bent. The learner's head should be slightly bent forward. The facilitator may need to press on the learner's upper chest lightly but firmly to get him to bend his head forward. The facilitator can then encourage the learner to look at his hands or to look at and reach for a toy. The learner may be placed on either side this way, but should not be left for longer than 15 to 20 minutes in any one position.

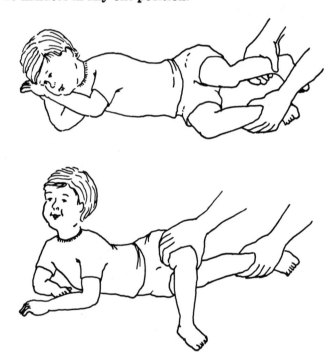

TERMINAL BEHAVIOR:	Learner is able to lie on his side to look at his hands or a toy, or to reach out toward a toy with his hands.

UNIT:	I 22 / Readiness
EPISODE:	E / Towel Rubdown in Preparation for Touching
PURPOSE:	Learner will be able to respond to the feel of textures without avoiding or withdrawing from them.
ENTRY BEHAVIOR:	Learner tends to avoid light touch or touch-pressure to parts of his body. Care should be taken not to use this activity if the surface of the learner's skin is sore, inflamed, or very tender.
MATERIAL:	A rough, terry cloth towel.
PROCEDURE:	Instead of gently patting the learner dry after a bath, the facilitator will rub the learner dry with vigor and pressure, beginning at the shoulders and working down through the trunk to the feet, then down the arms to the hands, ending with a vigorous, prolonged (count slowly to 10) rubbing of the palms of the hands and soles of the feet. The hands should be rubbed from the base of the palms toward the fingers; the feet from the heel toward the toes.
Variation I	The facilitator will rub the learner's palms and soles in the above described manner for about a 10 count, which requires using the hands or bearing body weight on hands or feet as would occur in crawling or standing.
Variation II	
MATERIAL:	Terry cloth, high-pile carpet piece, piece of fur.
PROCEDURE:	The facilitator positions the learner on the floor or a chair so that the learner is relaxed. The learner has his clothes removed, except for shorts or diaper. The facilitator takes terry cloth, carpet, or fur and rubs the learner's chest, pressing firmly. He rubs as long as the learner can tolerate, usually until the learner cries or puts his hands up to his chest and tries to restrict the facilitator's attempts at rubbing. The facilitator should then move the rubbing material to the shoulders and arms and then gradually work toward the hands, again pressing firmly.
TERMINAL BEHAVIOR:	Learner will be aware of and tolerate pressure and other sensations to his hands, feet, and other parts of his body. Learner can play in messy activities without withdrawing.

UNIT:	I 22 / Readiness
EPISODE:	F / Environmental Cues
PURPOSE:	Learner becomes aware of changes in day to day activities.
ENTRY BEHAVIOR:	Learner tends to be unresponsive to changes in his position, routine, or surroundings. The learner has limited sensory awareness.
MATERIAL:	None.
PROCEDURE:	To help a learner become more aware of changes, it is sometimes necessary to give him a consistent cue each time a change is about to occur. Examples of cues include facilitator's hand pressing learner's palm; facilitator stroking learner's face, or facilitator tapping part of the learner's body before turning a light on and off. A consistent vocal cue, such as stating the learner's name, should always accompany the other signals. The cue needs to be used consistently before any changes in the learner's environment or state occurs. For instance, the facilitator may want to alert the learner to feeding, cuddling and playing, or his position being changed.
TERMINAL BEHAVIOR:	Learner shows anticipation of a change in his situation when a cue is given, by a change in his facial expression or body posture.

UNIT:	I 22 / Readiness
EPISODE:	G / No More Yuks!
PURPOSE:	Learner will move away from oral hypersensitivity and tactile defensiveness toward more normal facial and oral sensitivity.
ENTRY BEHAVIOR:	Learner grimaces, pulls away, and/or bites down whenever a spoon or other implement or toy approaches his mouth.
MATERIAL:	Any object, especially one that has a texture that is safe for the learner to put in his mouth and is of an appropriate size and shape for doing so. This could be the learner's own fingers and hands, toys, spoons, keys, washcloths, sponges, etc., as well as different textured foods if these can be eaten without gagging.

PROCEDURE:

Variation I

The learning facilitator will position the learner in such a way as to enable the learner to explore the oral area with his own fingers, i.e., side lying with both hands in the facial area (Learning Episode I 22D).

Variation II

The learning facilitator will begin firm, slow, stroking starting from the learner's ankles and working upward toward his face. If the stroking is tolerated on the face, provide similar stimulation on the outer portion of the mouth. Encourage the learner, through physical manipulation if necessary, to explore the inside of his mouth. The learning facilitator should avoid placing his fingers in the learner's mouth. If the learner's jaw should clamp down in the course of this activity the learning facilitator can best release the learner's jaw by lightly shaking the learner's head and body.

Variation III

The facilitator will place a small object, such as a spoon or a textured object (e.g., a washcloth) in the learner's hand once he has begun to explore his own fingers and will guide the object to the mouth area.

TERMINAL BEHAVIOR:

Learner shows acceptance of the approach and touch of different textured objects and foods in the course of his play or feeding by not grimacing, pulling away, avoiding touch or texture in the oral area, or biting down.

UNIT:	**I 22 / Readiness**
EPISODE:	**H / Frontal Jaw Control for Feeding[1]**
PURPOSE:	Learner will have lip, tongue, and jaw control during chewing, drinking, and swallowing, and have overcome tongue thrust, jaw thrust, and drooling.
ENTRY BEHAVIOR:	Learner tends to lose liquids during cup drinking and/or to lose solid foods during spoon feeding and finger feeding.
MATERIAL:	Food, table, and child-size chair; feeding equipment (i.e., cutout cup, small spoon, commercially available Teflon-coated spoon).
PROCEDURE:	The facilitator positions learner in a relaxed position and faces the learner. The facilitator places his thumb between the learner's chin and lower lip with his index finger on the learner's jaw joint, and his middle finger applied firmly just behind the chin.

Each time the learner chews, the facilitator will encourage closed-mouth chewing by gently moving the learner's chin upward, so that the lips touch. The facilitator will praise the learner verbally to reinforce his efforts. The facilitator will maintain constant pressure with his fingers on the learner's chin, beginning with 5-minute sessions during feeding and gradually increasing the time until a whole meal is eaten.

Variation

While the learner is eating the facilitator will kneel behind the learner. The facilitator will place his index finger across the front of the learner's chin and place his middle finger below the learner's chin. The facilitator will stabilize this position by holding his thumb on the learner's jaw bone near his ear. The facilitator will

[1]From *Handling the Young Cerebral Palsied Child at Home*, by Nancie R. Finnie, F.C.S.P. (2nd Edition). Copyright © 1974 by Nancie R. Finnie, F.C.S.P. By permission of the publisher, E. P. Dutton.

help to keep the learner's head and neck in a straight aligned position throughout the eating period by holding the chin gently without pushing back. The facilitator will then encourage closed-mouth chewing as above.

TERMINAL BEHAVIOR: Learner will chew, drink, and swallow food by himself with his mouth closed.

UNIT:	**I 22 / Readiness**
EPISODE:	**I / Therapeutic Spoon Feeding for Development of Oral-Motor and Prespeech Skills**[1]
PURPOSE:	Learner will have lip closure for removing food from the spoon and be able to inhibit tongue protrusion and thrusting.
ENTRY BEHAVIOR:	None.
MATERIAL:	Foods that are typically spoon fed (e.g., applesauce, pudding), or small pieces of food placed on the spoon (e.g., bits of vegetables, meats, etc.); spoon with a bowl that is small and flat (spoon may also be Teflon coated).
PROCEDURE:	1. Position the learner so that his head, neck and chest are in good alignment (Learning Episode I22H).

2. Use the procedures described in Frontal Jaw Control for Feeding (Learning Episode I22H). If the facilitator provides jaw control, this will assist in keeping the mouth closed and likewise allow a greater chance for active lip movement.
3. Use a small spoon with a fairly flat bowl. It may also be necessary to use a Teflon-coated spoon if the learner has a tendency to bite down on the spoon.
4. The facilitator should be careful not to tip the learner's head back. The spoon should be slipped into the learner's mouth by approaching at mouth level, slipping the spoon through the center, and removing it in a similar manner (i.e., spoon should not approach or be removed from the side of the learner's mouth).
5. The facilitator will slip the spoon into the learner's mouth and wait for a few seconds to allow upper lip movement for removal of the food. Then the facilitator should press down on the midportion of the tongue just before removing the spoon from the mouth. By providing pressure on the tongue, the facilitator is allowing for better action of the upper lip and is reducing tongue protrusion and thrusting. The facilitator should be careful not to bump the learner's teeth with the spoon or scrape the food off the spoon with the teeth.

TERMINAL BEHAVIOR: Learner is able to demonstrate adequate lip closure (particularly of the upper lip) for removal of food from the spoon and does not exhibit tongue protrusion/thrusting before, during, or after the spoon-feeding process (i.e., before entry, during placement, after removal).

---

[1]Adapted from Morris, S. E. 1975. Pre-Speech and Language Programming for the Young Child with Cerebral Palsy (A Workshop Training Manual). Curative Workshops of Milwaukee, July, Milwaukee, Wis.

UNIT:	I 22 / Readiness
EPISODE:	J / Chewing to Develop Oral-Motor and Prespeech Skills[1]
PURPOSE:	Learner will chew with up and down movements of the jaw and rotary movement of the jaw.
ENTRY BEHAVIOR:	Learner can swallow thick and/or semilumpy, textured foods.
MATERIAL:	Chewy, gummy, or crisp foods (e.g., strips of rare-cooked meat, pieces of dried fruit, raisins, bits of dry cereal, potato chips, pretzels). (Save very chewy meats such as beef or pork for later experiences.) Mirror.
PROCEDURE:	1. Jaw control may be necessary with some learners, particularly if the learner has poor jaw control (Learning Episode I22H).
	2. The facilitator places strips of food on the learner's molars (i.e., on the side of his mouth between the biting surface of his teeth). This will stimulate chewing movements and encourage his tongue to move from side to side. Alternate the side of the mouth on which you place the food.
	3. Sometimes it is helpful if the facilitator demonstrates chewing in an exaggerated manner. A mirror is helpful as well.
	4. As the learner improves his chewing skills, the facilitator should increase the chewiness of the food (e.g., beef and pork are chewier foods).
TERMINAL BEHAVIOR:	Learner is able to chew with up and down movements or rotary movement of the jaw.

---

[1]Adapted from Morris, S. E. 1975. Pre-Speech and Language Programming for the Young Child with Cerebral Palsy (A Workshop Training Manual). Curative Workshop of Milwaukee, July, Milwaukee, Wis.

UNIT:	**I 22 / Readiness**
EPISODE:	**K / Relaxing a Fist**
PURPOSE:	Learner whose hand is fisted tightly because of high muscle tone can relax and open his hand.
ENTRY BEHAVIOR:	Learner's hand remains fisted when it should open in the process of reaching and grasping.
MATERIAL:	None.
PROCEDURE:	

1. The facilitator may take the learner's hand in his opposite hand so that the learner's fist lies in the palm of the facilitator's hand. The learning facilitator then grasps the learner's wrist with his fingers underneath and his thumb over the top of the learner's hand. The facilitator gently, then firmly, strokes the top of the learner's hand across the wrist and up the forearm, with the thumb of his hand moving from the knuckles up to the middle of the forearm repeatedly until the learner's hand opens.

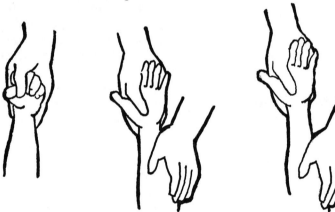

2. The facilitator may press the learner's hand down while holding the forearm up so that the wrist drops, allowing the hand to open. When the hand opens in this position, the facilitator can reach under the learner's palm with his opposite hand, putting his fingers around the top of the learner's hand and his thumb in the learner's palm and pressing against the fleshy part at the base of the learner's thumb. The learning facilitator can then press from the fleshy part of the base of the learner's thumb across the learner's palm toward the base of the little finger, exerting sufficient pressure to enable the fingers to remain open. The facilitator can continue this movement by raising the learner's arm up and stretching it out from the learner's body while at the same time rotating the palm to face toward the learner. This procedure should be repeated until the learner's hand is relaxed.

TERMINAL BEHAVIOR: Learner's hand relaxes and remains open sufficiently to perform reaching and grasping learning episodes.

UNIT:	I 22 / Readiness
EPISODE:	L / Arm Stretch for Reaching
PURPOSE:	Learner will straighten his arms by stretching the muscles that bend the elbows.
ENTRY BEHAVIOR:	Learner's elbows stay in a bent position and will not straighten during voluntary reaching.
MATERIAL:	None.
PROCEDURE:	The facilitator stands in front of learner. The facilitator places his hands around the learner's forearms and raises the learner's arms high above the learner's head, lifting the learner's body weight. The learner's feet should barely come off the floor. The facilitator holds this position for several seconds and then lowers the learner. This can be repeated for several times, especially if included during roughhouse play (Learning Episode I14B).
TERMINAL BEHAVIOR:	Learner's elbows will straighten as he reaches.

UNIT:	I 22 / Readiness
EPISODE:	M / Keeping Both Arms Forward with Wrap to Help with Grasping
PURPOSE:	Learner will be able to maintain his arms and hands in front of him for an activity that involves grasping.
ENTRY BEHAVIOR:	When the learner is in a reclining or upright position he has difficulty keeping his arms in front for an activity because his muscle tone is too high or too low.
MATERIAL:	4–6-inch thick bolster or pillow; wide ace bandage or towel with clips or safety pins; special chair or seat (optional); lap board (optional).
PROCEDURE:	The facilitator places learner on his lap or on a chair fitted to the learner's needs. The facilitator grasps the learner's upper arms and pulls the arms straight out in front of learner at about the learner's shoulder level. The facilitator gently and slowly shakes the learner's arms up and down for 30 seconds to 1 minute. The facilitator inserts the learner's lap board, or places a thick bolster or pillow on the learner's lap so that the learner's arms may rest on top of it in the straight shoulder-level position described above. The facilitator then wraps an ace bandage or towel around the learner's arms, just above the learner's elbows. The wrap should be firm enough, not tight, to maintain the learner's arms in the position mentioned above. The facilitator may use this technique for 20 minutes while doing touching or grasping activities or encouraging the learner to play with a favorite toy. When the facilitator removes the wrap he encourages the learner to continue playing.
TERMINAL BEHAVIOR:	Learner is able to keep both arms in front of himself while engaged in activities or playing with a toy.

UNIT:	I 22 / Readiness
EPISODE:	N / Passive Pressure on Shoulder Joints to Help Learner Reach Out
PURPOSE:	Learner develops shoulder stability, and is able to hold various arm positions and move between these positions without losing control.
ENTRY BEHAVIOR:	Learner has some voluntary movement of arms.
PROCEDURE:	The facilitator will sit the learner in a face-to-face position. The facilitator will rub the learner's palms with firm, brisk pressure. Next, the facilitator will grasp the learner's right hand as though shaking hands, with the learner's hand in a thumbs-up position. The facilitator will support the learner's elbow in the straight position by placing his left hand under the learner's right elbow. In this position the facilitator will exert mild pressure by gently pushing the straight arm into its shoulder joint, working for resistance by the learner's shoulder muscles. The facilitator should push for about 3 seconds and then release, and then switch to the left arm and repeat the procedure. The facilitator should repeat this activity with both arms several times a day.
TERMINAL BEHAVIOR:	Learner will be able to hold various arm positions and move between these positions without losing control.

UNIT:	I 22 / Readiness
EPISODE:	O / Relaxation and Reaching over Ball
PURPOSE:	Learner will be able to hold his head upright and reach forward with relaxed control in other body parts.
ENTRY BEHAVIOR:	Learner can hold up his head and upper trunk when he is placed on his stomach, but stiffens up throughout his body. Learner rolls stiffly (like a log) to his side from stomach lying, rather than rolling in a fluid, relaxed manner with the upper portion of his body completing the roll first.
MATERIAL:	Large beach ball (minimum 24 inches in diameter); towel; favorite toy.
PROCEDURE:	The facilitator places a towel over the beach ball. He then places a favorite toy on a stool or bench, or suspends it from the ceiling, at a height determined by the size of the ball and at a distance determined by the length of the learner's reach.

The facilitator carefully places the learner stomach down on the ball with his arms overhead (Position 1). He slowly rocks the ball from side to side while keeping his hands firmly on learner's pelvis. If the learner's legs stiffen and come together, the facilitator should move his hand to the learner's thighs just above the knees and then turn each leg so that each knee is on the outside with legs spread apart (Position 2). The facilitator continues rocking the ball from side to side. The facilitator then turns the learner's body over on its side either to the right or left. If the learner is over the right side, facilitator should move his own body around the ball and station himself behind the learner while placing his right hand over the left side of learner's chest. The facilitator then gently taps the learner's arms so that both arms are in front of the learner. The facilitator should continue slow rocking (Position 2). The learner should be encouraged to reach out and play with a toy. The facilitator should turn the beach ball and the learner around to face the toy. If needed the ball should be tilted toward the toy so the learner can reach it easily. Slowly the facilitator should roll the learner over onto his stomach, making sure the learner holds his head upright. The facilitator keeps pressure on learner's bottom with his left hand, while making sure the learner's arms are over the ball (Position 3).

Variation

Place the learner on his back on the floor or on a large therapy ball. After a few minutes of gentle rocking back and forth by the facilitator, the facilitator will gently roll the learner's hips toward one side and then the other. Ensure that the learner's shoulder remains in contact with the supporting surface by pressing gently with the other hand. Repeat in a side-to-side, slow rocking motion until the learner relaxes and there is no resistance in the movement of the learner's hips.

TERMINAL BEHAVIOR:

Learner is able to maintain head lift and relaxed body parts while reaching and playing with a toy.

UNIT:	I 22 / Readiness
EPISODE:	P / Lifting a Learner Who Tends to Be Stiff in Order to Relax the Learner
PURPOSE:	Learner will be able to hold his head and shoulders forward and bend his legs in a relaxed manner when being lifted from a lying position.
ENTRY BEHAVIOR:	Learner enjoys being carried. His body is straight and stiff in most lying positions.
MATERIAL:	None.

PROCEDURE:

1. The learner is lying on a flat surface such as a couch.
2. The facilitator rolls the learner slightly to one side.
3. With one arm the facilitator brings the learner's head and shoulders forward.
4. With the other arm the facilitator bends the learner's legs, especially at the learner's hips.
5. From this point the learner can be lifted completely up to a carrying position, or he can be shifted to sitting and other positions.
6. As the learner develops ability to spontaneously lift his head forward on his own, the facilitator can release head control with his arm as mentioned in #3 above. The facilitator should continue arm control at shoulders and legs.

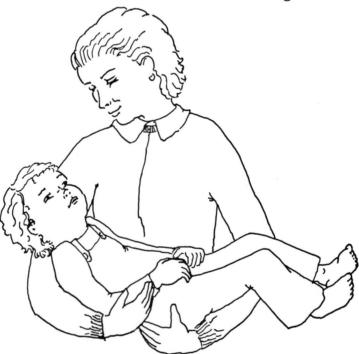

TERMINAL BEHAVIOR: Learner cooperates in the process of being lifted from a lying position without stiffening up.

UNIT:	**I 22 / Readiness**
EPISODE:	**Q / Carrying a Learner Who Tends to Be Stiff in Order to Relax the Learner**
PURPOSE:	Learner will be able to hold his head and trunk up without stiffening up in other body parts when carried.
ENTRY BEHAVIOR:	Learner tends to stiffen up with straight legs and head back. Learner enjoys being picked up and carried.
MATERIAL:	None.
PROCEDURE:	1. The facilitator brings the learner up into a sitting position by controlling the learner's shoulders and holding him under the top of his arms, which should be lifted and turned out. This will help to bring the learner's head and arms forward and enable the learner's hips and knees to bend. The facilitator's forearms should keep the learner's knees apart.
	2. To lift the learner from the sitting position the facilitator places the learner's arms over his shoulders. The facilitator then parts the learner's legs and puts them around the facilitator's waist.
	3. As the learner learns to balance and hold his trunk erect, the facilitator gradually reduces his support.

TERMINAL BEHAVIOR:	Learner holds up his head and trunk without stiffening up when he is carried.

UNIT:	I 22 / Readiness
EPISODE:	R / Trunk Rotation for Relaxation and Facilitation of Movement
PURPOSE:	Learner will increase rotation in his trunk to relax his muscles.
ENTRY BEHAVIOR:	Learner cannot turn his shoulders without turning his whole body.
MATERIAL:	Large beach ball (optional).
PROCEDURE:	The learner is lying on his back on the floor or on a large therapy ball. After a few minutes of rocking the learner gently from side to side, the facilitator places one hand on the learner's shoulder. With the other hand the facilitator gently rolls both of the learner's hips to the opposite side, while the learner's shoulder remains in contact with the supporting surface. The facilitator then rocks the learner's hips to the other side. This gentle rocking of the learner's hips should continue until the learner's legs begin to relax and feel more limp and there is little or no resistance in the trunk when the hips are rocked.
TERMINAL BEHAVIOR:	Learner is able to turn his shoulders while his hips remain stationary.

Variation

PROCEDURE:	Place the learner on his back on the floor or on a large therapy ball. After a few minutes of gentle rocking back and forth by the facilitator, the facilitator will gently roll the learner's hips toward one side. Ensure that the learner's shoulder remains in contact with the supporting surface by pressing gently with the other hand. Repeat in a side-to-side, slow, rocking motion until the learner relaxes and there is no resistance in the movement of the learner's hips.
TERMINAL BEHAVIOR:	Learner achieves active rotation of hips against his trunk and is able to roll over without stiffness.

UNIT:	**I 22 / Readiness**
EPISODE:	**S / Deep Pressure for Preparing the Learner to Sit, Crawl, or Stand**
PURPOSE:	Learner will begin to relate the feeling of pressure to the position of his body.
ENTRY BEHAVIOR:	None.
MATERIAL:	None.
PROCEDURE:	Place the learner on the floor or on a mat on his back. Lift one of the learner's arms at a right angle to his body (Position 1). Open the learner's hand. Keeping the learner's elbow straight, push into the learner's palm, pressing toward the floor. Repeat with the learner's other arm. Repeat procedure with both legs, keeping knees straight (Position 2 or 3). Press gently on the sole of the foot, exerting pressure from the sole of the foot into the hip joint.

1

2

3

Follow with weight-bearing activities for arms and legs (Learning Episodes I22X and I22Y). Some positions are illustrated below.

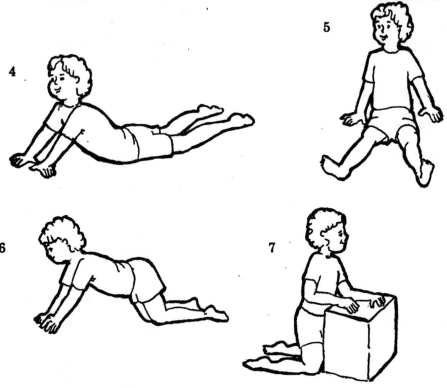

TERMINAL BEHAVIOR: Learner will be able to bear weight through his arms and legs without withdrawing from a surface.

UNIT:	I 22 / Readiness
EPISODE:	T / Trunk Rotation for Rolling and Reaching
PURPOSE:	Learner will be able to move into and out of the side-lying position, without stiffening up, in preparation for turning motion in erect postures.
ENTRY BEHAVIOR:	Learner stiffens up frequently in all positions. He can barely lift his head up when lying on his stomach. He supports himself on his forearms, but his arms tend to stiffen and to be pulled close to his chest. Learner can reach forward with both hands and, with some difficulty, can use a gross grasp.
MATERIAL:	Small, soft rubber, squeeze toy.
PROCEDURE:	The facilitator places the learner on carpeted floor or on mat and rolls him over to his left side. The facilitator positions himself at the learner's backside. The learning facilitator places his right hand over the learner's right hip and pulls it backward, moving it over toward the left hip. (The learner's body weight will then be over his left hip.) The facilitator then moves his right hand away from the learner's hip to the right shoulder of the learner. The facilitator places his left hand under learner's left shoulder and lifts the learner's head and upper trunk up. He then tucks learner's left elbow directly below learner's left shoulder and places the learner down. The learner's left forearm and elbow should be supporting his body weight while the learner's head is lifted up by his position. The facilitator maintains his left hand hold, but shifts his right hand back to learner's right hip and stabilizes the learner's body.

Holding this position the facilitator rocks the learner back and forth slowly until any stiffness lessens. The facilitator removes his right hand again to reach for a toy. He places the toy within

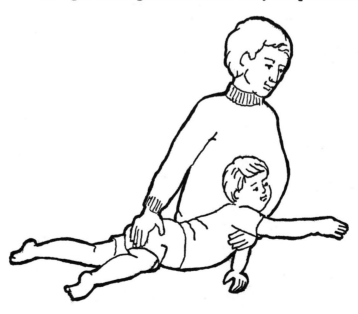

easy reach of learner's right hand. The facilitator works with learner in this position until the learner is able to reach and balance without stiffening up.

After the learner plays in this position for a few minutes the facilitator should roll the learner over to the other side and switch all hand placements, continuing to encourage play by the learner on this other side.

TERMINAL BEHAVIOR: Learner will move onto one side and then the other without stiffening up.

UNIT:	**I 22 / Readiness**
EPISODE:	**U / Stretching Tight Hamstrings in Preparation for Standing**
PURPOSE:	Learner will be able to straighten his knees by stretching the muscles that bend the knees.
ENTRY BEHAVIOR:	Learner's knees bend when he is lying on his back and the facilitator raises his leg upward (toward 12 o'clock). The learner cannot straighten his leg out.
MATERIAL:	None.
PROCEDURE:	The facilitator places the learner on his back. The facilitator holds one of the learner's legs flat on the ground and raises the other leg toward the 12 o'clock position, attempting to keep the learner's knees straight. The leg should be raised first to the point at which the knee begins to bend and should be held there for at least 10 seconds. This exercise should be performed several times with one leg and then repeated with the other leg.
TERMINAL BEHAVIOR:	Learner is able to raise his leg to the 12 o'clock position from the floor without his leg bending.

UNIT:	**I 22 / Readiness**
EPISODE:	**V / Bending Over with Support to Help with Standing**
PURPOSE:	Learner will be able to bend over with support to pick up an object, stretching his heel cords naturally.
ENTRY BEHAVIOR:	Learner has shortened or tight heel cords, so that his foot tends to stay pointed down.
MATERIAL:	A piece of clothing or an attractive toy that can be grasped easily.
PROCEDURE:	The facilitator will kneel with the learner standing in front of him facing away. With one hand the facilitator will hold the learner's knees in so that they are straight. The facilitator will hold the learner with his other arm by wrapping his arm around the learner at waist level. The facilitator will direct the learner to lean over and pick up an article placed on the floor in front of learner. The facilitator will repeat this activity several times a day or include it in the learner's daily routine.
TERMINAL BEHAVIOR:	Learner's heel cords will be stretched and his feet will remain relaxed, with heels down, while he is standing.

UNIT:	I 22 / Readiness
EPISODE:	W / Active Stretch to Heel Cords for Standing
PURPOSE:	Learner will actively stretch his heel cords.
ENTRY BEHAVIOR:	Learner has muscle tightness in his legs and tends to walk on his toes.
MATERIAL:	Toys placed on floor or on a low table.
PROCEDURE:	The facilitator places a toy on a table or other surface so that the learner needs to reach down to retrieve it. The learner stands in front of the facilitator, who helps him keep his legs turned out and his heels on the floor. The facilitator grasps the knees of the learner to keep the learner's knees apart. He gently rocks the learner from side to side to relax the muscles of his legs. Then the facilitator encourages the learner to lean over to pick up toys. It is important that the facilitator not require the learner to lean over so far as to make his knees bend. Gradually the learner should be able to reach lower and lower.
TERMINAL BEHAVIOR:	Learner is able to stand or walk without going up on his toes.

UNIT:	I 22 / Readiness
EPISODE:	X / Balance Activities to Increase Trunk Rotation in Preparation for Erect Postures
PURPOSE:	Learner will increase his trunk rotation to get ready for standing, cruising, and walking.
ENTRY BEHAVIOR:	Learner has muscle stiffness in his legs and decreased mobility in his hips. Learner has floppy muscles in his legs and excessive mobility in his hips.
MATERIAL:	None.
PROCEDURE:	The learner stands with his legs turned out in front of the facilitator. The facilitator places both hands on the hips of the learner and gently rotates the hips of the learner while shifting the learner's weight from one of his feet to the other.
TERMINAL BEHAVIOR:	Learner has just enough mobility in his hips to be able to shift weight from one foot to the other and to turn his body when cruising or walking.

UNIT:	I 22 / Readiness
EPISODE:	Y / Standing Balance Activities to Increase Trunk Rotation for Standing
PURPOSE:	Learner will increase his trunk rotation when standing to increase stability in his legs.
ENTRY BEHAVIOR:	Learner has floppy muscles in his legs and excessive mobility in his hips.
MATERIAL:	None.
PROCEDURE:	The learner stands with his legs turned out in front of the facilitator. The facilitator places both hands on the hips of the learner and gently rotates the hips of the learner while shifting the learner's weight from one of his feet to the other.
TERMINAL BEHAVIOR:	Learner has stability in his hips and is able to shift weight from one foot to the other without losing stability in his legs.

UNIT:	**I 22 / Readiness**
EPISODE:	**Z / Regularization of Bowel Movements**[1]
PURPOSE:	This episode will tone up the abdominal walls and help to regulate bowel movements of the learner (helpful for constipation).
ENTRY BEHAVIOR:	None.
MATERIAL:	None.
PROCEDURE:	Place the learner in a relaxed position on his back. With your fingernail, lightly trace a series of precise straight lines on the child's stomach, cross-hatching around the naval. Watch and feel for the abdomen tightening.

Place your whole hand over the learner's abdomen delicately, but firmly. As you feel the learner pulling in his tummy, take your hand away immediately.

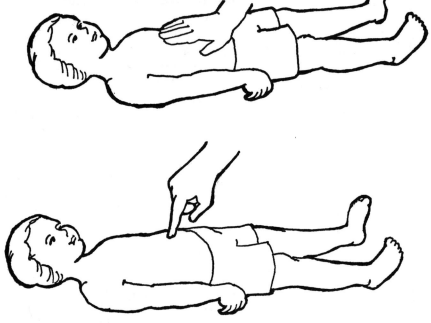

Repeat this activity 4–5 times at bathtime. If the learner is constipated, also repeat 5–10 times at each diaper change.

Encourage the learner's participation with your voice and movements.

TERMINAL BEHAVIOR:	The muscles of the abdomen become firmer and bowel movements will become more regular.

[1]From Levy, Janine, 1976. *The Baby Exercise Book: For the First Fifteen Months.* (Updated and expanded edition). By permission of the publisher, Pantheon Books, New York.

UNIT:	I 22 / Readiness
EPISODE:	AA / Therapeutic Toothbrushing and Mouth Cleaning[1]
PURPOSE:	Learner will reduce oral hypersensitivity and biting reflex. Good oral hygiene will be promoted.
ENTRY BEHAVIOR:	Learner grimaces, pulls away, and bites down whenever toothbrush is inserted in his mouth or even brought to his lips.
MATERIAL:	Bicarbonate of soda or salt solution; toothpaste; water; absorbent cotton; small infant-size toothbrush; equipment for positioning if needed.

PROCEDURE:

1. The learning facilitator positions learner in a sitting position that allows the learner to be upright and maintain good head control. Positioning techniques suggested for other activities, particularly those in sitting, should be utilized for toothbrushing (Learning Episode I14J).

2. If the learner has difficulty maintaining a closed mouth or appears hypersensitive in the mouth area, jaw control should be used (Learning Episode I22H). Care should be taken to inhibit as much as possible any pushing back of the learner's head, shoulders, or trunk. This can best be alleviated by bending the head slightly forward and bending the legs at the hips.

3. For those learners who are especially hypersensitive around the face and mouth, begin the toothbrushing activity with Learning Episode I22G, gradually working toward the learner's face and mouth.

4. For learners who do not have teeth or who are only beginning to get teeth, use an absorbent cotton swab and bicarbonate of soda, salt solution, or plain water. The learning facilitator massages the learner's gums in a circular manner keeping the learner's jaw closed as much as possible throughout the entire procedure and his head bent slightly forward by correct positioning and use of jaw control. To massage the inside of the learner's gums, allow jaw opening only as much as needed to place the cotton swab in the learner's mouth. Saliva, bicarbonate of soda, saline solution, or the water will most likely accumulate in the learner's mouth. Therefore, it is important that the facilitator keep the learner's head bent slightly forward to prevent choking or gagging. As the learner gains more jaw, lip, and tongue control and becomes less sensitive in the mouth area, less drooling will occur and improved ability in spitting the residue out will develop.

5. As teeth begin to emerge, the learning facilitator should introduce an infant-sized toothbrush that has soft bristles. The facilitator may continue to use the salt solution or bicarbonate of soda on the brush, or may introduce a mild toothpaste. However, the most important aspect of toothbrushing

[1]From *Handling the Young Cerebral Palsied Child at Home*, by Nancie R. Finnie, F.C.S.P. (2nd Edition). Copyright © 1974 by Nancie R. Finnie, F.C.S.P. By permission of the publisher, E. P. Dutton.

is the actual massaging or brushing of the gums and/or teeth on a regular basis rather than the using of the toothpaste.

6. For learners who have teeth provide the massaging and brushing in a similar manner as described in #3. Always massage the gums toward the roots of the teeth and in a circular manner, maintaining a forward bend to the learner's head and a closed jaw. To brush the inside of the learner's teeth and gums, the facilitator encourages the learner to open his jaw only as much as needed to place the cotton swab or toothbrush in the learner's mouth.

7. The facilitator should clean the learner's teeth daily after every meal and try, as much as possible, to avoid snacks between meals.

8. If an electric toothbrush is available, the facilitator can provide the massaging and brushing with it, because the electric toothbrush tends to provide more massaging and brushing action. It is suggested, however, that for those learners who are especially hypersensitive the electric toothbrush be introduced very slowly and perhaps not until the learner has successfully accepted the cotton swab or manual toothbrush.

9. Foods to avoid that cause tooth decay are sugary foods, sweets and confectionery, and soft drinks containing sugar. The learner should be encouraged to eat snack foods such as apples and carrots instead of sugary foods and drinks.

10. Visits to the dentist may begin as soon as teeth begin to emerge and should continue at 6-month intervals. It is suggested that the learner go to the dentist at the same time as other family members go until he becomes comfortable with the visits before actually having to go through the dental examination.

TERMINAL BEHAVIOR: Learner's oral hypersensitivity and biting reflex are reduced, as demonstrated by his receptivity to toothbrushing. Learner is enabled to perform good oral hygiene practices.

Unit T 22 / READINESS

UNIT:

T 22 / Readiness

EPISODE:

A / Touching Textures Artistically

PURPOSE:

Learner overcomes tactile defensiveness or ceases to avoid touching textured surfaces.

ENTRY BEHAVIOR:

Learner tends to avoid placing his hands in contact with different kinds of textures.

MATERIAL:

Sand, pieces of fur, high-pile rugs, mirrors with baby powder on them, etc.

PROCEDURE:

The facilitator will draw a design in the medium with his fingers. The facilitator will encourage the learner to copy his design or "draw" a design of his own. If the learner refuses, the facilitator can offer a peg or other stylus-type of instrument, and encourage the learner to use that. Gradually the learner should be encouraged to put his whole hand in contact with the material. It is generally best to start with whatever material the learner does not completely avoid. Do not push the learner to overcome his hesitancy immediately, and especially do not plunge the learner's hands onto the texture. Rather, encourage him through your own actions or by reinforcement to touch the material of his own accord. At first the learner may only briefly touch the texture with a fingertip. Gradually try to increase the time engaged and to widen the area of the learner's hand that comes into contact with the texture.

When the learner accepts the first texture (the one that he had least avoided) you can repeat the procedure with another somewhat similar, yet more tactilely stimulating, texture to scribble on and erase.

Generally learners will tend to scribble with their fingers and then erase the pattern with the whole hand. However, they should be encouraged to imitate a variety of motions and hand surfaces. For example the learner could scribble with his palm and use his forearm to erase, scribble with the side of his hand and use the back of his hand to erase, etc.

TERMINAL BEHAVIOR:

Learner will accept contact with the palmar and finger surfaces of his hand of any textured material.

UNIT:	T 22 / Readiness
EPISODE:	B / Straightening an Outward Pointing Foot While Cruising or Walking
PURPOSE:	Learner will have a normal sensorimotor experience of cruising or walking with both feet in good alignment with the legs.
ENTRY BEHAVIOR:	Learner is able to stand and cruise holding onto a low table, or walk holding onto a rollalator or carriage. While the learner is cruising or walking, one foot, or the other, or both, is turned outward or away from the body, but it can be passively pushed back into alignment so that it is in the same position as the other foot or in line with the leg.
MATERIAL:	Table, rollalator, or heavy-weight carriage (wooden or weighted down and handle about chest level in height); favorite toy or cookie.
PROCEDURE:	The learner is standing and holding onto a table, carriage, or rollalator with feet 4 inches apart. The facilitator places his third finger along the outer portion and thumb along the inner portion of the foot that is pointing out. The facilitator gently pushes the learner's foot inward (toward the midline of the body) without pressing the foot downward or in any other direction. The facilitator should use his third finger to press inward and use the thumb as a counterpressure to push outward. Once the foot is in straight alignment, check the alignment of the other foot. Repeat the procedure if necessary. Encourage the learner to cruise or walk. Maintain the gentle inward turning pressure with the third finger and thumb on the foot. Try not to limit any other movement initiated by the learner — your purpose is only to straighten the foot. After several trials of walking across the room, gradually lessen the pressure and see if the learner can help straighten his foot by himself.

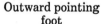

Outward pointing
foot

Corrected foot
position

TERMINAL BEHAVIOR:	Learner can cruise or walk with both feet in good alignment with the legs.

UNIT:	T 22 / Readiness
EPISODE:	C / Play in Stimulus-Free Environment
PURPOSE:	Learner can complete a task without being distracted by irrelevant sounds and objects in the environment. Learner will increase attention span and prepare for group setting.
ENTRY BEHAVIOR:	Learner is easily distracted by noise, people, and objects in a room when he is playing.
MATERIAL:	Toy or activity in which the learner has previously shown interest, for example, Busy Box, puzzles, or building blocks may be appropriate.
PROCEDURE:	To help the learner complete a task without being distracted, he must first be able to complete a task in an environment that is as free of noise and visual distractions as possible. Therefore, a quiet room with as few things as possible around the area is necessary. The facilitator may have to prepare the room by having only one toy available at a time for the learner to play with, having a cleared table, and removing attractive objects or covering those that cannot be removed. The facilitator can then present the activity to the learner. However, the facilitator may still have to help the learner redirect his attention to the task by verbal cues, manual guidance, visual redirection, etc. The facilitator should praise the learner when he does any related appropriate action correctly as well as when he completes the task.
TERMINAL BEHAVIOR:	Learner can complete a developmentally appropriate task in a quiet environment without prompting during the task.

UNIT:	**T 22 / Readiness**
EPISODE:	**D / Play in Environment with Some Distractions**
PURPOSE:	Learner can complete a task without being distracted by irrelevant sounds and objects in the environment. The learner will increase attention span and prepare for group setting.
ENTRY BEHAVIOR:	Learner can complete a task in a stimulus-free environment without prompts during the task.
MATERIAL:	Toy or activity in which the learner is interested, for example, a Busy Box, puzzle, or building blocks may be developmentally appropriate.
PROCEDURE:	Set up a stimulus-free room as described in Learning Episode T 22C. Add one stimulus before the learner begins the task. For instance, a radio could be left on in another room, or the door to the room might be left partially open. As the learner is able to adapt to the extra stimulus and not be distracted during a task, the facilitator can gradually increase the stimulus. For instance, the radio could be turned up a little louder, the door may be opened wider, or a visually attractive object in the room might be uncovered. Judging by the learner's response to the added stimulus, the facilitator may add or take away different sound and visual attractions. Eventually the learner will be able to concentrate on an activity without being distracted by visual and auditory stimuli. Other people should be introduced last as a type of distractions because people are the most compelling stimuli for most learners and thus would be the most difficult to ignore.
TERMINAL BEHAVIOR:	Learner can complete a task in an environment with visual and auditory distractions.